METHODS FOR TEACHING ELEMENTARY SCHOOL SCIENCE

METHODS FOR TEACHING ELEMENTARY SCHOOL SCIENCE

Fifth Edition

Joseph M. Peters
The University of West Florida

David L. Stout
The University of West Florida

PEARSON

Merrill
Prentice Hall

Upper Saddle River, New Jersey
Columbus, Ohio

Library of Congress Cataloging in Publication Data

Peters, Joseph M.

    Methods for teaching elementary school science / Joseph M. Peters, David L. Stout.—5th ed.
       p. cm.
    Rev. ed. of: How to teach elementary school science / Joseph M. Peters, Peter C. Gega.
  4th ed. c2002

    Includes bibliographical references and index.
    ISBN 0-13-171599-2
     1. Science—Study and teaching (Elementary) I. Stout, David L. II. Peters, Joseph M.
How to teach elementary school science. III. Title.

LB1585.G39 2006
372.3'5044—dc22

2005040827

Vice President and Executive Publisher: Jeffery W. Johnston
Senior Editor: Linda Ashe Montgomery
Senior Editorial Assistant: Laura J. Weaver
Senior Development Editor: Hope Madden
Production Coordination: Jolynn Feller, Carlisle Publishers Services
Senior Production Editor: Linda Hillis Bayma
Design Coordinator: Diane C. Lorenzo
Photo Coordinator: Monica Merkel
Cover and Text Designer: Kristina Holmes
Cover photos: Nature Picture Library
Production Manager: Pamela D. Bennett
Director of Marketing: Ann Castel Davis
Marketing Manager: Darcy Betts Prybella
Marketing Coordinator: Brian Mounts

This book was set in Goudy by Carlisle Communications, Ltd. It was printed and bound by Courier Kendallville, Inc. The cover was printed by Phoenix Color Corp.

Photo Credits: Courtesy of Uncle Milton Industries: 2; Silver Burdett Ginn Needham: 8; Israel Office of Information: 13; Ken Karp/PH College: 20; Jet Propulsion Laboratory/NASA Headquarters: 30; Anne Vega/Merrill: 42; Michael Newman/PhotoEdit: 46; Cary I. Sneider/Great Explorations in Math and Science: 72; James Kudlack and Barb Eldridge/Onekama Elementary School: 80; Tim Daniel/ODNR/Division of Wildlife: 91; Kenneth P. Davis/PH College: 100; Scott Cunningham/Merrill: 110, 183; Richard Hoyt/Great Explorations in Math and Science: 116; Anthony Magnacca/Merrill: 126, 160, 173; Barbara Schwartz/Merrill: 138; Joseph M. Peters: 142; T. Hubbard/Merrill: 152; LWA–JDC/Corbis/Stock Market: 164; Diasuke Morita/Getty Images, Inc.–Photodisc: 177; KS Studios/Merrill: 192; Alan and Sandy Carey/Getty Images, Inc.–Photodisc: 201; David J. Sams/Getty Images, Inc.–Stone Allstock: 206.

Pearson Education Ltd.
Pearson Education Singapore Pte. Ltd.
Pearson Education Canada, Ltd.
Pearson Education—Japan

Pearson Education Australia Pty. Limited
Pearson Education North Asia Ltd.
Pearson Educación de Mexico, S.A. de C.V.
Pearson Education Malaysia Pte. Ltd.

PEARSON
Merrill
Prentice Hall

10 9 8 7 6 5 4
ISBN 0-13-171599-2

This book is dedicated to Darlene, Joseph B., and
Brenda Peters and Patty, Danny, and Kelly Stout
for their inspiration and support throughout this project.

PREFACE

Elementary and middle school teaching is a rewarding and exciting career. Your future as a professional educator includes the responsibility to help your students meet the demands and challenges of society, and the elementary and middle school classroom is where it all begins. It is your job to build the skills, content knowledge, and desire for inquiry that will allow your students to function in a society that will be highly scientific and technologically developed. This new edition of *Methods for Teaching Elementary School Science* has been crafted to help you do just that.

Focusing on the methods of teaching elementary and middle school science, the text centers on why science education is basic to children's schooling and explains the foundations that give it form and substance. Each of the eight chapters develops a broad concept or a cluster of related teaching skills through descriptions and the use of many real-life examples.

The chapters and special features should enable you to do the following:

- Decide what areas of science are basic, useful, and curious to children.

- Recognize and assess differences in children's thinking.

- Use open-ended and closed-ended teaching activities in planning and implementing lessons and units.

- Improve children's scientific skills.

- Develop technological applications.

- Locate and use a variety of resources to teach science.

- Arrange and manage learning centers, computer centers, and projects.

- Assess science teaching.

Each chapter focuses on an overall concept such as learning, assessment, or technology. Practical teaching tips are highlighted and sprinkled throughout each chapter, and teaching concepts are aligned to the National Research Council's *National Science Education Standards*. In addition, learning objectives are linked to the American Association for the Advancement of Science (AAAS) *Benchmarks for Science Literacy*, which are cited throughout the text when applicable. To help summarize and extend the content, each chapter includes a summary, reflection, and additional readings.

A Closer Look at the Text's Features

Modeling Inquiry Teaching

By taking you into successful inquiry-based classrooms, we contextualize the concepts being covered and help you envision your own constructivist science classroom:

- *Focus on Inquiry* vignettes beginning every chapter and peppered throughout provide you with a glimpse of meaningful science lessons.

- *Free CD-ROM Science in Elementary Education: Visit an Inquiry Classroom,* containing footage of master teacher Glenn McKnight, models constructivist teaching and successful inquiry-based science classroom management.

- *Visit an Inquiry Classroom* features throughout chapters integrate the chapter content, CD footage, and the text's Companion Website.

- Portfolio questions relating to the CD are found at the end of each chapter.

- More CD-related activities are available on the text's Companion Website.

Addressing Today's Science Teaching Realities

Today's science teachers must be accountable to state and national standards as they ensure their teaching meets the needs of every learner in their classroom:

- *Benchmarks and Standards* features throughout chapters help you see how to integrate the *National Science Education Standards* in your own teaching.

- *Teaching Tips* throughout chapters provide starting points, suggest activities, and consider safety to help you master constructivist science teaching.

Supplements ————

CD-ROM Science in Elementary Education: Visit an Inquiry Classroom   By modeling a constructivist, inquiry approach to teaching science, master teacher Glenn McKnight and his lively fourth graders illustrate science teaching and learning at its best and most effective.

CD Features

The CD footage helps you envision all aspects of inquiry science teaching by exploring the following:

- Model inquiry unit

- Nature of science

- Constructivist pedagogy

- Lesson planning and classroom management

Each topic illustrates its component parts through nine video clips. To help you truly understand the construction and implementation of a model inquiry, for example, we provide you with footage of the following:

- Instructional planning

- Preparing resources

- Invitation to explore

- Team formation

- Inquiry exploration

- Concept invention

- Concept application

- Ongoing assessment

- Putting it all together—4 days of science

Accompanying every piece of footage are the perspectives of text author Joseph Peters, teacher Glenn McKnight, a teaching colleague, and fourth-grade students. Each voice interprets what he or she sees in each clip, helping you notice the details of teaching and learning. Quotes from the professional literature identify research that supports McKnight's teaching discussions, stimulating further thinking about the video contents.

Additional Features

- Bonus lessons on the CD provide you with meaningful lessons you can use right in your own classroom.

- Links to the Internet allow you to move back and forth between the CD and the Companion Website, where more questions and lessons connect the footage to the text material and to your own classroom.

- Look for CD icons throughout the text to point you toward features, reflection questions, and applications that will help you make the most of this meaningful media.

- *Visit an Inquiry Classroom* features in the text lead you to reflect on specific clips in terms of their relation to the chapter concepts. Answer questions about these clips on the Companion Website.

- Chapter-ending questions help you make connections between the material you learned in the chapter and the footage you find on the CD.

Electronic Instructor's Manual

This useful tool for instructors, available online at **www.prenhall.com** with an instructor's access code, provides the following rich instructional support:

- Test bank, including multiple choice and essay tests

- PowerPoints® specifically designed for each chapter

- Chapter-by-chapter materials, including chapter objectives, suggested readings, discussion questions, and online integration

Additional Titles of Interest ———————

- *Science in Elementary Education: Methods, Concepts, and Inquiries,* Tenth Edition, 0-13-171601-8

- *Concepts and Inquiries for Teaching Elementary School Science,* Fifth Edition, 0-13-171598-4

Acknowledgments ———————

We thank the many people who helped with the fifth edition of *Methods for Teaching Elementary School Science,* especially editors Linda Montgomery and Hope Madden of Merrill/Prentice Hall for their extensive editorial support, insight, encouragement, continued assistance, and constructive comments.

This edition of *Methods for Teaching Elementary School Science* includes many *Focus on Inquiry* vignettes. We extend our sincere thanks to Norman Lederman, Ken Tobin, Jerry Mayernik, George O'Brien, Angela Alexander, Christine Peters, Kata McCarville, Pam Northrup, Charlotte Boling, and Sue Dale Tunnicliffe for sharing their experiences with us.

We also acknowledge the external reviewers of this text: Mary Margaret Capraro, Texas A&M; Huabin Chen, Saint Martin's College; Raymond W. Francis, Central Michigan University; Karen Ivers, California State University, Fullerton; Robbie V. McCarty, Southwestern Oklahoma State University; James T. McDonald, Central Michigan University; Leah M. Melber, California State University, Los Angeles; Michael Odell, University of Idaho; John Shimkanin, California University of Pennsylvania; Lori-Anne Stelmark, Teachers College Columbia University; and Rita K. Voltmer, Miami University, Oxford, Ohio.

References

Barman, C. R. (1989). A procedure for helping prospective elementary teachers integrate the learning cycle into science textbooks. *Journal of Science Teacher Education, 1*(2), 21–26.
Yager, R. (1991). The constructivist learning model. *The Science Teacher, 58*(6), 52–57.

DISCOVER THE COMPANION WEBSITE ACCOMPANYING THIS BOOK

The Prentice Hall Companion Website: A Virtual Learning Environment

Technology is a constantly growing and changing aspect of our field that is creating a need for content and resources. To address this emerging need, Prentice Hall has developed an online learning environment for students and professors alike—Companion Websites—to support our textbooks.

In creating a Companion Website, our goal is to build on and enhance what the textbook already offers. For this reason, the content for each user-friendly website is organized by chapter and provides the professor and student with a variety of meaningful resources.

For the Professor

Every Companion Website integrates **Syllabus Manager**™, an online syllabus creation and management utility.

- **Syllabus Manager**™ provides you, the instructor, with an easy, step-by-step process to create and revise syllabi, with direct links into Companion Website and other online content without having to learn HTML.

- Students may logon to your syllabus during any study session. All they need to know is the web address for the Companion Website and the password you've assigned to your syllabus.

- After you have created a syllabus using **Syllabus Manager**™, students may enter the syllabus for their course section from any point in the Companion Website.

- Clicking on a date, the student is shown the list of activities for the assignment. The activities for each assignment are linked directly to actual content, saving time for students.

- Adding assignments consists of clicking on the desired due date, then filling in the details of the assignment—name of the assignment, instructions, and whether it is a one-time or repeating assignment.

- In addition, links to other activities can be created easily. If the activity is online, a URL can be entered in the space provided, and it will be linked automatically in the final syllabus.

- Your completed syllabus is hosted on our servers, allowing convenient updates from any computer on the Internet. Changes you make to your syllabus are immediately available to your students at their next logon.

For the Student

- **Meeting the Standards**—provides *National Science Education Standards* integration, delivered through adaptable lessons that can be saved to your hard drive or disk. This module provides you with lessons to take right into your own classroom that align with both national and state standards.

- **Praxis Practice quizzes**—help prepare pre-service teachers for the Praxis 2 exam.

- **Additional CD ROM Activities**—help you continue to deepen your understanding of inquiry science teaching.

- **Focus Questions**—provide a useful advanced organizer for each chapter's online companion.

- **Self-Assessments**—help you gauge your understanding of text concepts.

- **Web Links**—provide useful connections to all standards and many other invaluable online science sources.

- **Learning Network**—the Pearson Learning Network offers a wealth of additional resources to aid in your understanding and application of content.

- **Message Board**—serves as a virtual bulletin board to post—or respond to—questions or comments to/from a national audience.

This robust online support system offers many rich and meaningful ways to deepen and expand the information presented to you in the text. To take advantage of the many available resources, visit the online supplement at

www.prenhall.com/peters

EDUCATOR LEARNING CENTER: AN INVALUABLE ONLINE RESOURCE

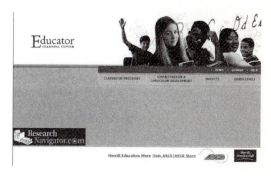

Merrill Education and the Association for Supervision and Curriculum Development (ASCD) invite you to take advantage of a new online resource, one that provides access to the top research and proven strategies associated with ASCD and Merrill—the Educator Learning Center. At **www.educatorlearningcenter.com,** you will find resources that will enhance your students' understanding of course topics and of current educational issues, in addition to being invaluable for further research.

How the Educator Learning Center Will Help Your Students Become Better Teachers

With the combined resources of Merrill Education and ASCD, you and your students will find a wealth of tools and materials to better prepare them for the classroom.

Research

- More than 600 articles from the ASCD journal *Educational Leadership* discuss everyday issues faced by practicing teachers.
- A direct link on the site to Research Navigator™ gives students access to many of the leading education journals, as well as extensive content detailing the research process.
- Excerpts from Merrill Education texts give your students insights on important topics of instructional method diverse populations, assessment, classroom management, technology, and refining classroom practice.

Classroom Practice

- Hundreds of lesson plans and teaching strategies are categorized by content area and age range.
- Case studies and classroom video footage provide virtual field experience for student reflection.
- Computer simulations and other electronic tools keep your students abreast of today's classrooms and current technologies.

Look into the Value of Educator Learning Center Yourself

A four-month subscription to Educator Learning Center is $25 but is **FREE** when packaged with any Merrill Education text. In order for your students to have access to this site, you must use this special value-pack ISBN number **WHEN** placing your textbook order with the bookstore: 0-13-172887-3. Your students will then receive a copy of the text packaged with a free ASCD pincode. To preview the value of this website to you and your students, please go to **www.educatorlearningcenter.com** and click on "Demo."

CONTENTS

NOTE: Every effort has been made to provide accurate and current Internet information in this book. However, the Internet and information posted on it are constantly changing, and it is inevitable that some of the Internet addresses listed in this textbook will change.

METHODS FOR TEACHING ELEMENTARY SCHOOL SCIENCE

CHAPTER 1

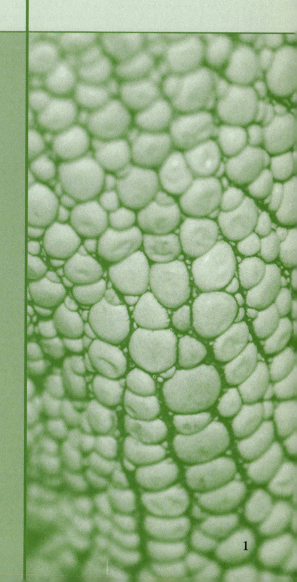

SCIENCE INQUIRY AND THE NATURE OF SCIENCE

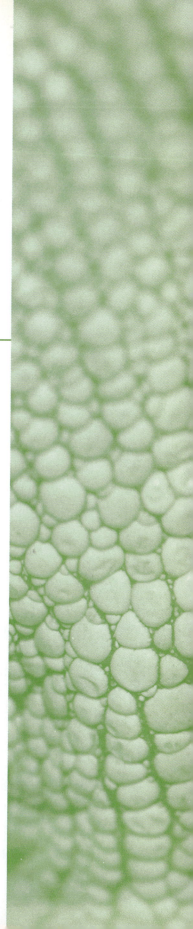

- What is the "nature of science"?
- Can you use an inquiry approach to demonstrate the nature of science with your students?
- What guiding documents and other societal concerns will you incorporate into your teaching of children?

Focus on Inquiry

Teaching the Nature of Science

Dr. Norman Lederman,
Illinois Institute of Technology

The year is 1971, and Peter is a typically self-conscious high school sophomore. Like several of his friends, Peter has a slight acne problem. After trying several creams and ointments available at the local drugstore, he convinces his parents that the problem requires the help of the family physician. The physician tells Peter and his parents that the cause of his problem is an abundance of oil production by the glands on his face and that this extra oil provides a good nutritional source for common bacteria. She also tells Peter that eating less chocolate, among other things, might solve the problem but that there is a more reliable approach. Naturally, Peter and his parents are anxious to listen further. The physician recommends that Peter's parents purchase a sunlamp. The U.V. rays emitted by the sunlamp do an excellent job of "drying" the skin and eliminating acne problems. In fact, the physician adds, sunlamps are generally good for most people's skin regardless of whether they have an acne problem. Peter would only have to use the sunlamp about 10 minutes per day and, in addition to relieving his acne problems, he can have a desirable tanned look year-round. So, Peter, with his parents' permission, did what thousands of Americans did in the 1970s.

Thirty years later, the medical profession has recognized the possible carcinogenic effects of ultraviolet radiation. Acne patients are no longer advised to use sunlamp therapy. Indeed, the current advice regarding U.V. rays is to avoid them as much as possible. Consequently, the availability of sunscreen lotions and sunglasses designed to protect both the skin and the eyes from harmful light rays has increased significantly. The physician's advice to Peter and his parents in the 2000s would be much different from what it was in 1971.

How does the general public react to this "change of heart" by the scientific community? Although we have seen a proliferation of ointments and creams designed to block the harmful rays of the sun, tanning is as popular as ever in the United States and, indeed, around the world. A significant number of individuals have decided to ignore the advice of the scientific community. It is not uncommon to hear people say, "Why can't scientists make up their minds? One day something is good for you, and next day you hear that it causes cancer. It seems that everything causes cancer. I'm not going to do anything different until they decide once and for all."

See the Chapter 1 Web Destinations on the Companion Website (*http://www.prenhall.com/peters*) for links to documents such as *Inquiry and the National Science Education Standards* (National Research Council, 2000) that contain information to further illustrate the nature of science as it applies to science teaching.

The case of U.V. rays is not unique. "Flip-flops" in the opinions of scientists and physicians have occurred with respect to aspirin, alcohol, cold fusion, and vitamin C, and many foods. Indeed, such changes have become the object of jokes.

THE NATURE OF SCIENCE

What does the idea of scientific flip-flops have to do with teaching elementary and middle-level students about the nature of science? These flip-flops we so often see are really not weaknesses of science. They are not reasons for the general public to disregard scientific knowledge or to lose faith in the scientific way of thinking. These flip-flops constitute one of the most important strengths of science—in fact, they *are* science. That is, scientific knowledge is self-correcting on the basis of new empirical evidence or new ways of interpreting data. The knowledge, though tentative, is based on volumes of data and should not be disregarded. Disregarding scientific knowledge severely limits the quality of decisions that we each make about our lives.

See the Web Destinations for Chapter 1 of the Companion Website for a link to *Teaching About Evolution and the Nature of Science* (National Academy of Sciences, 1998).

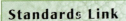

What is the nature of science? There are as many answers to this question as there are books; however, at the level of generality that will be useful to you as an elementary or middle school teacher there is a strong consensus. Strictly speaking, *science* can be defined as a body of knowledge, a process, and a way of knowing or constructing reality. The *nature of science* refers to six characteristics of scientific knowledge that derive directly from how the knowledge is developed. Of importance to you as an elementary or middle school science teacher are the following characteristics.

1. There is no single set or sequence of steps that always directs a scientific investigation. There is no such thing as "the scientific method."
2. Scientific knowledge, both theories and laws, is subject to change. All scientific knowledge is tentative.
3. Scientific knowledge must be at least partially supported by empirical evidence. Scientific knowledge must involve the collection of data, be consistent with what we "know" about the world, and be testable.
4. Scientific knowledge is partially the product of the creative imagination of the scientist. All scientific knowledge combines both empirical evidence and the creative interpretation of data by scientists.
5. Given the importance of scientists' individual creativity, scientific knowledge is necessarily subjective to some degree. Scientific knowledge is not totally objective as is commonly believed.
6. Scientific knowledge is a product of both observation and inference.

In your future classroom, you will need to carefully address the characteristics of scientific knowledge as you teach. You will also need to consider the developmental level of your students. Then, you will be able to help your students develop the understandings that will guide them in making decisions for the rest of their lives. In particular, your students will begin to develop a more balanced view of the truth of scientific knowledge. They will take the so-called truth of science with an informed "grain of salt." This means your students will heed the notion that the sun's rays can cause cancer. It also means they will not disregard all future knowledge about the effects of the sun's rays if the scientific community alters its current position.

As you begin to explore your own teaching of the nature of science, keep your learners in mind. Developing content knowledge and inquiry skills with your students is helped by their inherent natural curiosity. Children enjoy observing the world around them. Picture a group of students on a playground during lunch, as they watch ants move about on the pavement. Looking at the ants, the students begin to ask the following questions.

Why do ants follow each other?
Why do the ants live in the ground and not above the ground?
How can the ants carry things twice their size?

How thoughtfully did *your* teachers handle questions that you asked in school? Were you able to explore some of your own interests in the classroom, or was learning more restricted? Were you guided to think through some problems for yourself, or were standard answers always given? How your teachers worked with you and your classmates reflected their notions about science and science teaching. We hope that what you learn through this methods course will affect how you will teach science. Take time to question your beliefs and your understandings as you explore science and science teaching in this course.

Find the complete text of the *National Science Education Standards*, as well as your own state's standards, in the Web Destinations for Chapter 1 of the Companion Website (*http://www.prenhall. com/ peters*).

Visit an Inquiry Classroom
The Child as a Scientist

As you view *The Child as a Scientist* video in the "Nature of Science" section of the Companion CD, notice how Mr. McKnight involves the students in thinking about the activity. One of the goals of science teaching is for every child to experience inquiry in the classroom similar to the way a scientist experiences inquiry in the field. You see evidence of this in how the children identify questions or hypotheses to explore and then carry out their investigations.

Review the video and ask yourself the following:
- How would your beliefs about the nature of science affect how you would teach this lesson?
- How would you modify this lesson if you were to teach it to elementary or middle school students?

Do a web search and find a sample science lesson plan. Compare the approach in that plan to how Mr. McKnight teaches. Record your ideas and the answers to the previous questions in your portfolio or use the Companion Website to share your ideas.

Visit an Inquiry Classroom
Science as Inquiry

View the *Science as Inquiry* video in the "Nature of Science" section of the Companion CD. We see Glenn promoting inquiry by working with children to identify problems to solve.

Review the video and ask yourself the following:

- How does Mr. McKnight interact with the students when they are developing questions to explore?
- Why doesn't Mr. McKnight just tell the students what to do with their experiments?
- We talk about promoting "process over product" in the narrative of this video. What does this mean and what example do you see in the video?

Think about a science lesson you will teach in your field placement. What are some ways you will promote process over product? Record your ideas and the answers to the previous questions in your portfolio or use the Companion Website to share your ideas.

The nature of science means those characteristics of scientific knowledge that derive directly from how the knowledge is developed.

Scientific concepts relate to the knowledge of science, or what scientists have found out as a result of their work.

Scientific processes are the skills that students develop, such as observation, classification, inference, and measurement.

See the Web Destinations for Chapter 1 at *http://www.prenhall. com/peters* for links to supporting documents on the nature of science, inquiry, educating teachers, and instructional materials as they relate to the *National Science Education Standards*.

Your school or district office will probably give you some instructional materials for teaching science, but your own concepts and values about science teaching will strongly affect what children actually learn in your science classroom. If you desire to understand **the nature of science, scientific concepts,** and **scientific processes,** this desire to learn more about the world around you will be transferred to your students.

How you and your students learn science will be related to your desire for inquiry and the nature of science. You will need to "[i]mplement approaches to teaching science that cause students to question and explore and to use those experiences to raise and answer questions about the natural world" (National Science Teachers Association [NSTA], 2004). In the following sections, we use contrasting teaching approaches to show how your teaching can affect students' curiosity about the nature of science. As you read, think about the National Research Council (NRC) History and Nature of Science Standard in the Standards Link box.

THE NATURE OF INQUIRY

Imagine that you are sitting in on two teachers as they use a teachable moment to engage students in the topic of "ants." Students from Martin Luther King Jr. Elementary School have just come back from their noon recess. While walking back from the playground, students from the classes discussed what they had witnessed: fire ants attacking a baby bird that could not fly. They are now wondering why ants behave the way they do, why they eat what they eat, and what their underground homes may look like.

Grade 3 Examples

Two teachers draw off of the students' natural curiosity, and introduce a lesson on ants. Compare each of the two approaches.

Mr. Bryant's Class

In his classroom, Mr. Bryant captures an opportunity to follow up the ant discussion with the classic story *A Bug's Life* (Steiner, 1998). Over the next few days, he substitutes reciting from the reading series for *Ant Cities* (Dorros, 1987) and *It's an Ant's Life* (Parker, 1999). They discuss the anthills and tunnels and the worker ants, males, and queens. Later, they make a homemade Ant Farm® as suggested in *Ant Cities*. Mr. Bryant introduces ants to the farm, and the children periodically feed them. During free time for the next few weeks, the students intermittently observe the ants to see what they are doing.

Ms. Davis's Class

Ms. Davis begins asking her students what they observed outside. She has students take turns recording this information on a flip chart. She also includes questions about what the students would like to know about ants. Later, she reads the fable *The Little Red Ant and the Great Big Crumb* (Climo, 1995) to begin a discussion on which foods ants eat. She then reads *The Magic School Bus Gets Ants in Its Pants* (Cole, 1996) and *Hey Little Ant* (Hoose, Tilley, & Hoose, 1998) to initiate conversation on ant behaviors and habitats. Her class discusses the anthills and tunnels and the worker ants, males, and queens. Next, the students set up an Ant Farm® as outlined in *The Practical Entomologist* (Imes, 1992). After students build the farm, Ms. Davis asks them to predict what will happen as the ants are introduced to the ant habitat and what will occur over the next few weeks. Students hypothesize that the ants will develop small sections of the farm into colonies.

Ms. Davis's students write these predictions and the accompanying observations on the flip chart. They also record brief daily observations and compare these against their predictions. Ms. Davis's students infer what kinds of food ants like. They place different containers of food near the ant mound outside the classroom to see what will happen (see Cole, 1996). They predict which food will be found first and infer which food the ants will appear to like best. They periodically have class discussions to communicate the facts they find out about ants. Ms. Davis ends the lessons by returning to the students' questions to see if they were all answered. She also follows up to be sure the students have no **misconceptions** about ants.

Misconceptions are mistaken ideas that students have about how something works or how it is otherwise unlike what the scientific community has found to be true.

Classroom Comparisons

In the previous two situations, the teachers discuss ants. Mr. Bryant and Ms. Davis both expand on the opportunity presented to them by the students. They answer questions about ants and integrate children's natural wonder with their literature, activities such as building Ant Farms®[1], and opportunities for observation. Mr. Bryant uses this activity as a fun way to see ants in their habitat and to learn about ants in general. Ms. Davis, however,

1. Ant Farm® is a registered trademark of Uncle Milton Industries, Inc. Used with permission

Visit an Inquiry Classroom
Approaches to Teaching

Watch the *Learning to Think* video in the "Constructivist Pedagogy" section of the Companion CD. Mr. McKnight interacts with students as they explore earthworms.

Review the video and ask yourself the following:
- How will you use questioning to promote ideas in your own science teaching?
- How does Mr. McKnight's approach to teaching about earthworms compare to Ms. Davis's approach?
- Based on Mr. McKnight's lesson, what suggestions would you make to Mr. Bryant?

 Think about the advantages to Ms. Davis's approach to science as compared to Mr. Bryant's approach. Based on the video, what suggestions could you make to Mr. Bryant? Record your ideas and the answers to the previous questions in your portfolio or use the Companion Website to share your ideas.

sees this as not only a fun learning activity but also an opportunity for her students to make systematic observations of ants and to develop other related scientific skills. She wants her students to infer, predict, communicate, experiment, and form tentative theories as scientists would in similar situations. Ms. Davis also wants her students to understand that scientific knowledge is based on observation and inference as with their ant studies—all part of learning the nature of science.

Grade 5 Examples

Students in two fifth-grade classrooms at Martin Luther King Jr. Elementary School have also witnessed the ants. Their teachers are preparing ant lessons, too.

Mrs. Brown's Class

Mrs. Brown begins with reading to the class *Life Story: Ant* (Chinery, 1991). They discuss anthills, ant life cycles, and ant food behaviors. She has Tanezia read *Those Amazing Ants* (Demuth, 1994). This book offers interesting information, such as the mating dance, cleaning habits, and the way ants use secretions to mark food trails. The students discuss this information. Guided by the activity "A Special Plot" from the **AIMS** book *Field Detectives: Investigating Playground Habitats* (Gazlay, 1998), Mrs. Brown completes a skill-development activity with her students. They observe and sketch several ant mounds near the school and develop **Venn diagrams** of the commonalties and differences in the habitats. The students then discuss what they found out from their diagrams.

Mrs. Malloy's Class

Mrs. Malloy's fifth-grade class decides on ants as a study theme for the next few days. Karolyn reads aloud the story *The 512 Ants on Sullivan Street* (Losi, 1997); Taylor reads *A*

AIMS (Activities for the Integration of Mathematics and Science) are hands-on/minds-on integrated activities found in a series of books available from the AIMS Foundation. (See http://www.prenhall.com/peters for links and further information.)

Venn diagrams, named after John Venn, use circles inside of a rectangle to represent sets of objects, to show relationships between the objects.

Children discuss animals that live underground as part of their research related to the study of ants.

Remainder of One (Pinczes, 1995); and Rochelle reads *One Hundred Hungry Ants* (Pinczes, 1993). These stories incorporate number sense and division to lay the foundation for related mathematics activities. Casen then reads aloud the story *Antics!* (Hepworth, 1992), and Hoa reads *There's an Ant in Anthony* (Most, 1980). These alphabetical anthologies lend themselves to language activities during which Mrs. Malloy's students try to find as many words as possible with *ant* in them. Finally, they explore "Ants Around the World" from the book *Ants* (Teacher Created Materials, 1997).

Continuing the ant theme, Mrs. Malloy asks the students what they have already found out about ants and what else they would like to know about ants. They generate a list of topics such as the following, to copy into their science journals.

> *How do ants tunnel? Are all tunnels alike?*
> *What is the ant's body structure? Is it different for males, females, and queens?*
> *How do ants reproduce and grow?*
> *What is a scent trail, and how is it made?*

Mrs. Malloy makes available for her students resource materials, including *AIMS Field Detectives* (Gazlay, 1998), *Ant Homes Under the Ground* (Lawrence Hall of Science, 1996), and *Project WILD* (Council for Environmental Education, 1992). She also arranges a table with several other activity and field identification books and materials for making an Ant Farm®. Her students use these in small groups to plan science activities. She also bookmarks an Internet ant cam (online video camera) and movie site for her class to use in their studies.

> **Teaching Tips** Project WILD, Project Aquatic WILD, Project Learning Tree, and Project WET are national programs that enhance environmental education. (See http://www.prenhall.com/peters for links to these and related programs.)

Mrs. Malloy loads *SimAnt* (Broderbund/Maxis) onto the classroom computer. Students take on roles of ants with this program. They learn ant behaviors, including how to communicate with one another and how to avoid being "done in" by fierce red ants, ravenous spiders, and heavy human feet. Students use scientific information to develop strategies to survive, increase the size of their colony, and finally reach the ultimate reward—a safe home with a food supply.

> See *http://www.prenhall.com/peters* for ant cam and related links.

Mrs. Malloy facilitates and provides other resources as her class works in small groups to plan and participate in numerous activities related to ants. Later, they share what they have discovered about ants. They conclude when they have answered the questions in their science journals.

Classroom Examination

Mrs. Malloy generates interest in ants through mathematics and language activities. She uses the ant theme as a starting point to help her students generate ideas for experiments and other hands-on activities. These activities will help her initiate student discussion, seek answers to their related questions, and develop scientific skills. In this less teacher-directed approach, the children act like scientists as they explore and experiment with ants—constructing understandings and answers to their questions. They find that there is no one correct way to explore ants. They also see that their theories related to ants often change with new observations and inferences that better explain things. In short, they not only are learning about ants but also are experiencing the nature of science through inquiry, a connection with other school subjects as suggested in the NRC's *Science Program of Study Standard*.

Questions as an Invitation to Learn

In exemplary classrooms, teachers carefully use questioning techniques to engage the students. Let's look at two more classrooms building on their students' interest in ants. Compare the examples to see how each teacher began his or her lesson.

Teacher 1

- A queen ant is usually bigger than the other ants, and new queens and males have wings.
- Ants may eat honeydew from aphids or juices from insects and plants.
- An ant develops from an egg, to a larva, to a pupa, to an adult that will emerge from a cocoon.

Teacher 2

- Why did some ants look different from others in the ant nest we observed?
- I wonder if the ants we observed today and last week all eat the same food.
- Why did we find eggs, grubs, and cocoons in the ant nests?

The first teacher simply states what will be taught. For example, in her first lesson, children will learn that queen ants are bigger than worker ants and new queens and males have wings. Once the initial teaching is accomplished, the lesson is completed.

The second teacher always begins his lessons with a question referring to children's everyday experiences. This teacher agrees with current reform efforts that ask teachers to base science on students' everyday lives. This method supports the notion that science is

Visit an Inquiry Classroom
Questioning

Watch the *Questioning* video in the "Planning and Management" section of the Companion CD. Mr. McKnight uses questioning in this video as he often does with his class. Did you notice that many of his questions are open, meaning they have no one right or predetermined answer?

Review the video and ask yourself the following:
- Why does Mr. McKnight ask so many questions?
- What would make you think that Mr. McKnight's questions were not predetermined (i.e., written down in a lesson plan)?
- How do Mr. McKnight's questions indicate children's concept development and concept attainment?

The authors of the *National Science Education Standards* (1996) suggest teachers "ask a question about objects, organisms, and events in the environment" in order to promote inquiry. What are some specific examples of Mr. McKnight doing this? Record your answers in your portfolio or use the Companion Website to share your ideas.

a human endeavor. Science principles, or concepts, typically have many real-life applications. They are a result of the creative imagination of the scientist. Beginning and ending lessons with applications enable children to reflect on their own experiences, to interpret their observations creatively, and to construct new knowledge. The second approach also takes the pressure off the teacher to know everything about the topic under study. The teacher can explore the subject *with* his or her students.

You probably see by now that the second way of teaching is likely to be more interesting and productive to you and your students. Yet, if you're like most college students who select elementary or middle school teaching as a profession, science is probably not your strongest subject. You may not feel confident about teaching science. Do not worry about this; you and your class will learn together. What's important is to develop an awareness of the nature of science and how you can develop scientific skills and understandings with the students. Let's look at how you would teach the nature of science.

How Can You Demonstrate the Nature of Science?

Although the current reforms in science education place a strong emphasis on students' understandings of the nature of science, there are not abundant resources to help you share that concept. The following idea has been found to be successful for teaching students about each of the six characteristics of scientific knowledge. This activity requires virtually no scientific background on the part of the students. Consequently, it is relatively risk free.

Creating the Tube

1. Re-create the tube pictured in Figure 1–1. I suggest that you obtain a mailing tube from the post office, the map room at a local library, or a store that sells posters. You may also use a meter-long piece of PVC pipe or an empty oatmeal container. Clothesline, twine, or rope from a local hardware store will do for the rope. The ring holding the ropes together is plastic; you can buy one at a craft store. If a ring is not available, the lower rope can simply be looped over the upper rope. The ends of the tube can be sealed with rubber stoppers or be taped.
2. Make an overhead (and class set of handouts) of what is pictured in Figure 1–2.

Teaching the Concept

3. Have the students carefully observe several sequential pulls of the various rope ends. It makes no difference which rope ends you choose to pull.
4. Have individual students, pairs, or groups speculate about what is inside the tube in an effort to explain what they have seen. After several minutes, allow students to manipulate the ropes. At this point, they will be testing their hypotheses about the contents of the tube.
5. Allow the students several more minutes to revise their speculations on the basis of the additional data that they have just collected.
6. Allow several volunteers the opportunity to share their hypotheses with the rest of the class on the overhead diagram. There are a variety of workable explanations; allow the sharing of ideas until at least two alternatives are

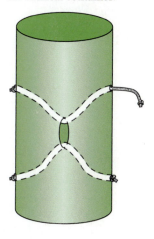

Figure 1–1   Inside view of the oatmeal container.

Figure 1–2   Outside view of the oatmeal container.

presented. If the students seem to be fixed on only one approach, be prepared to offer other possibilities. Be sure not to imply that any one of the explanations is correct or better than the others.

7. You and the students can discuss the ideas presented. Restrict the focus of the discussion to the relationship between the inferred ideas and the data collected through your demonstration.

8. Have the students construct models of the tube they developed, using a toilet paper or paper towel roll. Provide string, scissors, and paper tubes, or direct students to bring these from home.

9. After construction of the models, have the students follow along as you pull various ropes on your model. This gives the students a chance to see how consistent their models are with the actions of your model.

10. Some students' tubes will not "behave" the same way as yours, but most probably will. Stress two ideas at this point: First, lead the class to the idea that there are several ways to construct the tube so that it functions like yours. Second, ask the students if they can now know for sure what is in your tube, just because their model "behaved" the same as yours. The primary point is that we are never certain whether the proposed explanation is correct unless the tube can be opened.

Depending on the grade level of your students, the following ideas should be discussed.

- The tube is analogous to the universe; what your students did is analogous to what scientists do. But we have no way of actually opening the universe to see how it really works.
- Students collected empirical data and developed inferences to explain the data. These activities are similar to the way scientists collect data and develop inferences

Visit an Inquiry Classroom
Collecting and Using Data

Watch the *Collecting and Using Data* video in the "Nature of Science" section of the Companion CD for examples of students collecting data. They are engaged in both data collection and inference based on the data.

After looking at the video, read Mr. McKnight's perspective on collecting and using data. Can you answer the following questions?

- What is Mr. McKnight's primary reason for having the children collect data?
- How does Mr. McKnight want the children to use the data?
- It would be much easier if all of the students did the exact same experiment and collected the same data which could be compared for accuracy. Why doesn't Mr. McKnight use these "cookbook" type activities instead of allowing students to explore their own questions and collect and interpret their own data?

 Think about an elementary or middle school teacher you had who taught science. What was this person's questioning technique? How does it compare to Mr. McKnight's technique? Record your ideas and the answers to the previous questions in your portfolio or use the Companion Website to share your ideas.

to explain the data. In essence, the speculations about the contents of your tube are theoretical models used to explain necessarily limited data. What your students have done is analogous to what a scientist does all the time. What your students have done is not very different from what the scientists of the 1970s did when they observed acne and inferred possible explanations and solutions for the problem.

- Finally, explicitly discuss with your students how each of the six characteristics of scientific knowledge is evident in the activity.

Take a moment to see if you can identify the six characteristics of science in this activity.

The pulling of the rope in the container clearly points out some tenets of the nature of science. In *Benchmarks for Science Literacy* (American Association for the Advancement of Science [AAAS], 1993), the authors make the following point about the study of science.

> When people know how scientists go about their work and reach scientific conclusions, and what the limitations of such conclusions are, they are more likely to react thoughtfully to scientific claims and less likely to reject them out of hand or accept them uncritically. Once people gain a good sense of how science operates—along with a basic inventory of key science concepts as a basis for learning more later— they can follow the science adventure story as it plays out during their lifetimes. (p. 3)

Visit the standards module on the Companion Website at *http://www. prenhall. com/peters* for a link to *Benchmarks for Science Literacy.*

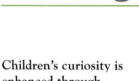

Children's curiosity is enhanced through science experiences such as the exploration of ant environments.

This passage means that it is critical for students to understand how the scientific process works in order to be good science consumers and lifelong learners. Students must see science as a human enterprise, not as a body of knowledge to be memorized. When they read and appraise an item in the newspaper or have a problem to solve, the students' past scientific experiences will assist them.

Like the examples in the rope and container activity, you may also wonder about some scientific "changes of heart," or new theories. Your knowledge of the nature of science will assist you in understanding the scientific information as presented. Remember that the products of science are constantly changing with new experimentation. Lederman (1992) asserts that "the nature of science is as tentative, if not more so, than scientific knowledge itself" (p. 352), meaning that the nature of science itself develops over time. What remains constant is that good science education originates with your understanding of the nature of science and your ability to teach science to children. How will you teach children about science?

> Visit the Companion Website for an overview of the concepts and process of science that are in the *National Science Education Standards and Benchmarks for Science Literacy*, which will be at the core of your science teaching. Scientific processes are also discussed in Chapter 4 of this textbook, and concepts are found in the inquiry chapters.

TEACHING CHILDREN

Applying concepts and processes of science to society's problems is the reason why science education is such an important subject in school. Because we are dealing with elementary and middle-level students, however, we need to match what is taught with the students' interests and developmental levels.

You may have heard the expression, "To a child who's discovered the hammer, the entire world is a nail." This idea illustrates children's broad curiosity and inner need to try things for themselves. Science education encourages and rewards this natural curiosity; but science educators need to guide the learning, keeping the instruction developmentally appropriate.

> **Generalizations** can be seen as principles or statements that have a general application to a specific body of knowledge.

For example, broad **generalizations** and skills are useful in science study. As a generalization or process approaches the most advanced scientific model, however, it is less likely that children can learn it or will even want to try. To persist is simply to have them bite off more than they can chew. So, teaching generalizations about molecules in the primary years, for example, or insisting that all variables be controlled in experiments, is likely to be self-defeating. Our elementary students will understand that ants may bite and are male and female. They may have trouble understanding the hymenopteran's specialized mouthparts or the concept of how males originate from unfertilized eggs and females from fertilized eggs.

> **Teaching Tips**
>
> It is unlikely that any publisher or curriculum office can develop a program that suits every child or class. It will be your responsibility to create a suitable match between students and the curriculum. This task will require understanding how children learn science, children's developmental levels, and what is required of your science education program.

It is important for children to understand and see the purpose of what they are doing. Children also need to reach short-range goals as they progress toward goals that are farther away. Children usually learn best when working with concrete or semiconcrete materials and limited generalizations. Keep this key factor in mind when working with young students.

Guiding Documents for Science Education

How can you tell what is appropriate for your students to learn? One way to see the types of processes and concepts with which students at a particular grade level should be familiar is to look at two of the guiding documents in science education. We have already referred to *National Science Education Standards* (NRC, 1996) and *Benchmarks for Science Literacy* (AAAS, 1993). The benchmarks were developed as part of Project 2061 (AAAS, 1989), which was an undertaking of the American Association for the Advancement of Science to help reform science, mathematics, and technology education. They focus on the science that should be learned by all Americans. The standards were a national collaborative headed by the National Research Council, again with the focus on scientific literacy for all. There is a high level of correlation between the two projects. Many states have adopted the benchmarks, the standards, or a state-specific variation of one of the projects as their own statewide standards for which you will be accountable in your classroom. We refer to the benchmarks and the standards throughout the text.

Are there other considerations besides process and content? The authors of Project 2061 and the standards both discuss societal perspectives as they relate to science education.

Refer to the Companion Website (*http://www.prenhall.com/peters*) for links to the online versions of the standards, benchmarks, and other documents.

Societal Considerations

We began this chapter with a discussion of the nature of science and how students observed ant mounds in the schoolyard. These observations provided the basis for deeper exploration into ants—allowing students to further construct concepts of ants and their behaviors, as well as scientific process skills. A well-planned and flexible curriculum usually contains many of these everyday applications.

It is important to educate people and thus change attitudes in order to cope with today's challenges. Naturally, the education system plays a major role in this process. For example, the focus of science education centers on such topics as AIDS, endangered species, wetlands, energy exploration and conservation, environmentally safe food, uncontaminated drinking water, multicultural career opportunities, and gender equity in science-related careers.

Every society wants its contributing members to be literate, that is, to have enough background knowledge and ability to make informed decisions, communicate, produce, and improve the general welfare. In a society as advanced and dynamic as ours is today, the amount of information increases at an accelerating rate. Under such conditions, people need a common core of knowledge. A common ground allows us to communicate more efficiently with one another and facilitates public policy.

Literacy serves as the common ground for discussing and understanding diverse and complex issues. Issues such as toxic waste dumps, in vitro fertilization, AIDS, nuclear accidents, the hole in the ozone layer, the greenhouse effect, genetically altered foods, and artificial body parts are examined in our everyday encounters with the media. Knowledge of specific technical information may be considered when making purchases. For example, when buying a car, it is helpful to have some knowledge of horsepower, fuel economy, and antilock brakes. To secure a job, we are expected to know something about the nature of the position we are seeking. The ability to function and survive in our society is linked to literacy.

Science literacy is imperative in a society that leans heavily on science and technology. The AAAS (1993) views literacy in the following way.

See Chapter 1 Web Destinations on the Companion Website (*http://www. prenhall.com/peters*) for links to Nova Science in the News and the National Academies Science in the Headlines.

> Project 2061 promotes literacy in science, mathematics, and technology in order to help people live interesting, responsible, and productive lives. In a culture increasingly pervaded by science, mathematics, and technology, science literacy requires understandings and habits of mind that enable citizens to grasp what those enterprises are up to, to make some sense of how the natural and designed worlds work, to think critically and independently, to recognize and weigh alternative explanations of events and design trade offs, and to deal sensibly with problems that involve evidence, numbers, patterns, logical arguments, and uncertainties. (p. XI)

All children need a rich array of firsthand experiences to grow toward a full measure of science literacy. Quality science programs make it possible for advanced study, which can lead to many occupational choices and benefits for all society. An important area related to societal considerations is equity as suggested by the NRC Program Equity Standard.

Equity

Think for a moment about what the world would be like if women cultivated half of the technological developments. What advances would be made? What current problems would be minimized? What if minorities developed an equivalent proportion of scientific discoveries? How might the world be different? Some estimates indicate that 85% or more of the workforce is composed of minorities, persons with disabilities, and women (e.g., Florence, 1992). How is this new workforce affecting science?

Current science education reforms promote scientific literacy for all students—or equity—as their central theme (AAAS, 1998). The belief is that science should be comprehensible, accessible, and exciting for all students from kindergarten through grade 12. In reality, these goals are rarely achieved, especially for underrepresented populations. The National Science Foundation (NSF, 1996) reports the typical pattern indicates that males score higher than females and white students score higher than black or Hispanic students on national assessments.

Science has long been studied in the traditions of the white, Anglo-Saxon male. This focus makes it difficult for females or minorities to place science in an understandable social context. Think about a living scientist. Is this person male or female? Is this a person of color or white? What does this person look like? Stop for a moment and consider your image of a scientist. Is your image stereotypical?

Children often view a scientist as a white male with a lab coat, a pocket protector full of pencils, and unkempt hair—a nerd with glasses. This view furthers the problem of equity. Not only do most boys not want to be this "scientist," but also what woman or minority would want to be perceived as this image? As a teacher, you will probably pass your views of a scientist on to your students. Make sure that your view is consistent with the diverse group represented in the scientific community. View your children as scientists, too. This further ensures equity since your curriculum is based on your children's experiences as "scientists." Equity can even become a function of the diversity of the children that you teach, because your classroom will have children of mixed gender and cultural backgrounds.

Teaching Tips
You can begin to remediate stereotypical images by bringing local minority and female scientists into the classroom.

The Language of Science

Another way to help correct the imbalance of science achievement is to think about how science is taught at the elementary level. If science is just rote learning of disjointed facts, it becomes an especially difficult enterprise for minorities who do not have a strong command of the language. It is no wonder that these students do not elect to take more than the required minimum of science courses as they go on to high school. It's surprising that every student is not eventually turned off by this language-intensive, fact-only approach.

In an attempt to help students understand the "language" of the scientist, the National Science Teachers Association published *The Language of Science* (Mandell, 1974, p. 1). The author of this book equates the language of science to a foreign language and stresses the importance of knowing the language in order to be a participant in the science classroom. Along these lines, Gallas (1995) discusses why "science talk" is so important for children and why teachers need to help them develop the language of science. Lemke (1990) states:

> It is not surprising that those who succeed in science tend to be like those who define the "appropriate" way to talk science: male rather than female, white rather than black, middle- and upper-middle-class, native English speakers, standard dialect speakers, committed to the values of Northern European middle-class culture. (p. 138)

What Mandell, Gallas, Lemke, and many other authors are saying is that teachers need to understand that the language of science is often a barrier to equity in the classroom.

Another major consideration in the development of a quality elementary or middle school science program is the matter of gender equity. As an educator, it will be your responsibility to select science textbooks, teaching materials, and methodologies that present realistic role models for men and women in all walks of life. In addition to arranging for female role models to visit your classroom, you may want to try assigning student biographies of famous female scientists. The importance of this issue cannot be understated as we go into an era where we will need a growing number of science and technology professionals who are women.

The current science literacy problem that exists in many minority populations may be a forewarning of an increasing science literacy problem with all students. Your contribution in the classroom will have a major impact on the types of career decisions your students make.

One way to become a better teacher is to investigate your own teaching. See the "Teacher as Researcher" Links on the Companion Website for more information.

Summary

- The nature of science suggests that (1) there is no single set or sequence of steps in a scientific investigation; (2) scientific knowledge is subject to change; (3) scientific knowledge must be at least partially supported by empirical evidence; (4) scientific knowledge is partially the product of the creative imagination of the scientist; (5) given the importance of scientists' individual creativity, scientific knowledge is necessarily subjective to some degree; and (6) scientific knowledge is a product of both observation and inference.
- Scientists use tools and organized ways to search for patterns in objects and events. They generalize the data they collect and form explanations in the form of principles, theories, and laws. Elementary and middle school students can construct and refine their own concepts by using similar methods.
- Children need to experience the processes of science by making observations, interacting with objects, testing hypotheses, working with data, and experimenting.
- An interrelationship exists between science and society. It is important to understand the roles of women and minorities in the scientific enterprise as you plan and facilitate science lessons.

Reflection

Companion CD

1. Based on your understanding of the nature of science, what changes would you make to the "Importance of Food and Nutrients" lesson linked to the *Child as Scientist* video on the Companion CD?

2. Look at the "Earthworm's Cousin—Espinal" lesson linked to the *Questioning* video on the Companion CD. Identify any misconceptions you may have had about worms based on this lesson. Would your students have similar misconceptions?

3. Look at the "What Is Anatomy" lesson linked to the *Science as Inquiry* video on the Companion CD. What generalizations can be made about

earthworms, humans, or other animals with respect to the digestive, reproductive, circulatory, respiratory, muscular, and skeletal systems?

Portfolio Ideas

1. One way to begin exploring how you will teach elementary or middle school science is to investigate your attitudes toward science. Do you feel science is exciting, rewarding, and fun or monotonous, boring, and discouraging? Is it important or trivial? Were your science experiences inclusive or exclusive of certain populations? If you have time, compare your attitudes with those of your parents, friends, or study partner and record these in your portfolio.

2. In your portfolio, record your memories of elementary science experiences. Which of these experiences are hands-on activities that promote the nature of science and scientific understanding? Which are entertainment, show-and-tell, or memorization activities? Be ready to share with others the implications of why you would remember one experience more than another, or which have helped more with later science experiences.

3. Observe an elementary or middle school science class at your practicum site and note how the teacher provides equity in terms of gender. Does the teacher call on boys more than girls? Are the boys dominating the experiments? Are the girls afraid to answer questions or provide explanations? Think of

ways to promote equity in your classroom, and share these ideas in your portfolio.

4. Use the resource *Multicultural Women of Science: Three Centuries of Contributions* (Harris-Stewart, 1996) to enhance your own understanding of the contributions of multicultural women to the field of science. This book contains many hands-on activities. An increasing number of other related resources are available for use with your students. The books *From Sorceress to Scientist: Biographies of Women Physical Scientists* (Nies, 1990) and *From Priestess to Physician: Biographies of Women Life Scientists* (Nies, 1996) include biographies, demonstrations, and lab activities. Use aids from these two books to help promote positive female role models with your practicum class and future elementary or middle school students. Record ideas in your portfolio.

5. *Teaching About Evolution and the Nature of Science* (National Academy of Sciences, 1998) is available online (*http://books.nap.edu/html/evolution98/*) and includes activities that relate to the nature of science. Try some of these activities and share them through your portfolio.

References

American Association for the Advancement of Science (AAAS). (1989). *Science for all Americans*. Washington, DC: Author.

American Association for the Advancement of Science (AAAS). (1993). *Benchmarks for science literacy*. New York: Oxford University Press.

American Association for the Advancement of Science (AAAS). (1998). *Blueprints for reform*. New York: Oxford University Press.

Chinery, M. (1991). *Life story: Ant*. New York: Troll Associates.

Climo, S. (1995). *The little red ant and the great big crumb: A Mexican fable*. New York: Clarion Books.

Cole, J. (1996). *The magic school bus gets ants in its pants*. New York: Scholastic.

Council for Environmental Education. (1992). *Project WILD*. Bethesda, MD: Author.

Demuth, P. D. (1994). *Those amazing ants*. New York: Simon & Schuster.

Dorros, A. (1987). *Ant cities*. New York: HarperCollins.

Florence, P. (1992). *Northwest women in science: Women making a difference—a role model guide*. Richland, WA: Northwest College and University Association for Science, Northwest Women in Science.

Gallas, K. (1995). *Talking their way into science: Hearing children's questions and theories, responding with curricula*. New York: Teachers College Press.

Gazlay, S. (1998). *Field detectives: Investigating playground habitats*. Fresno, CA: AIMS Education Foundation.

Harris-Stewart, C. (Ed.). (1996). *Multicultural Women of Science*. Maywood, NJ: The Peoples Publishing Press.

Hepworth, C. (1992). *Antics!* Los Angeles: Putnam & Grosset.

Hoose, P. M., Tilley, D., & Hoose, H. (1998). *Hey little ant*. Berkeley, CA: Tricycle Press.

Imes, R. (1992). *The practical entomologist*. New York: Simon & Schuster.

Lawrence Hall of Science. (1996). *Ant homes under the ground*. Berkeley, CA: Author.

Lederman, N. G. (1992). Students' and teachers' conceptions of the nature of science: A review of research. *Journal of Research in Science Teaching, 29*, 331–359.

Lemke, J. L. (1990). *Talking science: Language learning and values*. Norwood, NJ: Ablex.

Losi, C. A. (1997). *The 512 ants on Sullivan Street*. New York: Scholastic.

Mandell, A. (1974). *The language of science*. Arlington, VA: National Science Teachers Association.

Most, B. (1980). *There's an ant in Anthony*. New York: Mulberry Books.

National Academy of Sciences. (1998). *Teaching about evolution and the nature of science*. Washington, DC: National Academy Press.

National Research Council (NRC). (1996). *National science education standards*. Washington, DC: National Academy Press.

National Science Foundation (NSF). (1996). *The learning curve*. Washington, DC: Author.

National Science Teachers Association (NSTA). (2004). *Scientific inquiry. A position statement*. Washington, DC: Author. Retrieved October 1, 2004, from www.nsta.org/positionstatement&psid=43

Nies, K. A., (1990). *From Sorceress to Scientist and Biographies of Women Physical Scientists*. Tarzana, CA: California Video Institute.

Nies, K. A. (1996). From *Priestess to Physician: Biographics of Woman Life Scientists*. Tarzana, CA: California Video Institute.

Parker, S. (1999). *It's an ant's life*. Pleasantville, NY: Reader's Digest.

Pinczes, E. (1993). *One hundred hungry ants*. Boston: Houghton Mifflin.

Pinczes, E. (1995). *A remainder of one*. Boston: Houghton Mifflin.

Steiner, T. J. (1998). *A bug's life*. Burbank, CA: Mouse Works.

Teacher Created Materials. (1997). *Thematic unit: Ants*. Huntington, CA: Author.

Suggested Readings

Alcoze, T., Bradley, C., Hernandez, J., Kashima, T., Kane, I. M., & Madrazo, G. (1993). *Multi-culturalism in mathematics, science, and technology: Readings and activities*. Menlo Park, CA: Addison-Wesley. (a teacher resource for exploring many cultures and global perspectives)

American Association for the Advancement of Science (AAAS). (1993). The nature of science. In *Benchmarks for science literacy* (pp. 3–21). New York: Oxford University Press. (explores the nature of science in the context of various grade levels)

Barr, B. B. (1994). Research on problem solving: Elementary school. In D. L. Gable (Ed.), *Handbook of research on science teaching and learning* (pp. 237–247). New York: Macmillan. (problem-solving research to apply to future teaching)

Dunbar, R. (1995). *The trouble with science*. Cambridge, MA: Harvard University Press. (a history of science and the nature of science)

Hatton, J., & Plouffe, P. B. (1997). *Science and its ways of knowing*. Upper Saddle River, NJ: Prentice Hall. (a collection of essays showing the relationships between fact and theory and the nature of science)

National Research Council (NRC). (1998). *Every child a scientist: Achieving scientific literacy for all*. Washington, DC: National Academy Press.

National Research Council (NRC). (1999). *Selecting instructional materials: A guide for K–12 science*. Washington, DC: National Academy Press.

National Research Council (NRC). (2000). *Inquiry and the national science education standards*. Washington, DC: National Academy Press.

National Science Resources Center, National Academy of Sciences, Smithsonian Institution. (1997). *Science for all children: A guide to improving science education in your school district*. Washington, DC: National Academy Press. (a comprehensive book on how science education can be changed at the elementary and middle school level)

Chapter 2

CONSTRUCTING SCIENCE EXPERIENCES

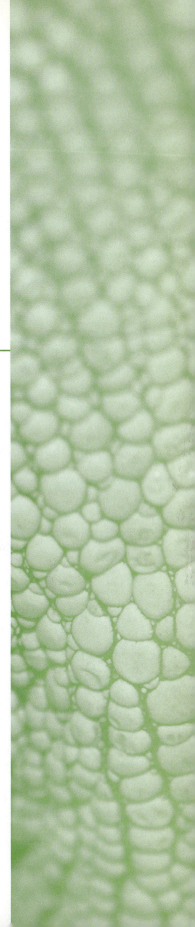

Focus on Inquiry ─────────────

How Do Children Learn?

Dr. Ken Tobin,
The Graduate Center of City University of New York

"Hold it! Hold it! Oh, no! Ana, you've got to hold it while I connect the roof on." Michael is agitated with Ana. They have been working on building a castle for 3 days now, and still the walls will not stay up. They planned to build a castle that had strong walls and two stories. Their drawings looked good but the materials Ms. Roberts had given them to build their castle with were not working.

Losing confidence in their ability to succeed, Ana is feeling grumpy about this whole activity. The walls will not stay up. Every time she holds them up, the sewing pins connecting the straws come loose. Why can't they use glue anyway? "Castles are not made out of pins and straws!" she asserts.

Ana and Michael's teacher, Ms. Roberts, is pleased with the castle-building activity. The students are busy and they are doing science. The activities she has planned for students engage them in the use of manipulatives, problem solving, an opportunity to exchange ideas, and the ability to integrate writing, social studies, and literature. The idea of building castles arose from the class's study of Germany. Most importantly, students are engaged in problem solving. Ms. Roberts perceives her role to be that of a facilitator: closely observing her students, listening to their ideas, and offering support to help them meet their goal of building castles.

Teachers like Ms. Roberts have long accepted that a hands-on approach is an appropriate way to teach science. Recently the term *hands-on/minds-on* has become a popular way to describe school science. Ms. Roberts's grade 3 science lesson is typical of what can be observed in many elementary classrooms. The activity is consistent with a hands-on/minds-on metaphor and the teacher's role as facilitator. Problematic, however, is that even though Ms. Roberts's students are involved in an extensive hands-on activity that promotes communication and problem solving, the development of scientific ideas is absent.

Problem solving as a way to engage students in constructing their own understanding of science concepts must be connected to specific science learning goals. Scientific knowledge does not reside in the materials students use. Rather, scientific knowledge needs to be co-constructed in interactions in which students and teacher converse verbally, using a shared language during the activity. For example, the realization that a structure can be made rigid through the use of triangular braces is a reasonable goal for the activity described. In this castle activity, however, it is unlikely that Ms. Roberts's students will construct that understanding. Even if some students include triangular braces in their structures, it is unlikely that they will associate that inclusion with increased rigidity of the structures they are trying to build. Manipulation of materials is a context for rich conversations in which those who know science can facilitate the learning of those who do not know. It is essential to student understanding and quality science instruction that the teacher mediate the language of the child and the language of science. This does not imply a return to the days when teachers transmitted facts in lectures with prescribed language, but it does require engagement in problem-solving experiences that promote conversation. Student understanding is facilitated when students talk science in ways that connect their experiences with other subject areas. It is at this point that students will begin to see the relevance science plays in their lives both in and outside of school.

SCIENCE LEARNING

Teaching is seen as the actions or methods used by an educator to create an environment that will promote learning by students.

Learning is a process by which students' knowledge, attitudes, behaviors, and beliefs are formulated or modified.

Think back to your elementary school experiences. Was **teaching** viewed as a class reading of the textbook, a daily student worksheet, a predetermined outcome type of activity, or a lecture where the teacher handed down the "body of knowledge"? Was your **learning** about scientific ideas and concepts the focus of your classes? Or, consistent with the science inquiry standard, did your teacher actively engage you in seeking new knowledge, team you up with others to help one another learn, and guide you by emphasizing scientific understanding and inquiry? Were your scientific understandings useful in other situations, both in school and outside school? Answering these questions provides you an indication of a teaching perspective and a perspective of how children can learn science more effectively.

Effective science learning is crucial for your future elementary and middle school students. Today's global society is experiencing explosive changes in scientific knowledge and the application of scientific knowledge in the form of technology (National Science Teachers Association [NSTA], 2003). Predictions once indicated that the total amount of knowledge doubles every 18 months or less and that 80% of the scientists who have ever lived are alive right now (Petersen, 1994, 1997). Current studies show that stored information grows so rapidly that in 2002 alone, print, film, magnetic, and optical storage media produced about 5 exabytes of new information (School of Information Management and Systems University of California at Berkeley, 2003). In perspective, 5 exabytes is equivalent to the information contained in 37,000 new libraries the size of the Library of Congress

Standards Link

Science Inquiry Standard

As a result of activities in grades K–8, all students should develop

- **Abilities necessary to do scientific inquiry**

- **Understandings about scientific inquiry**

(Content Standard A, National Research Council, 1996, pp. 121, 143.)

book collections. We are in the information age and to be able to utilize this ever-growing pool of information, our students will need to know how to access and apply this information in meaningful ways.

The science experiences you provide will develop the foundation your students need to continue meaningful learning experiences throughout their lives. Thus, a first step to successful science teaching is to consider your own views of science and science learning.

Paradigms

Teachers should be aware that science is not just a body of knowledge but a paradigm through which to see the world. (American Association for the Advancement of Science [AAAS], 1998, p. 202)

Take a moment to think about how you currently view the nature of science and science learning. Is it different now from when you were in elementary school? If so, what changed your viewpoint? Maybe you are science phobic because of past experiences. If you are, then what could have been done differently to dispel your fear of science? What influences how science is currently taught and how you will teach science? The current paradigm for teaching and learning science is seen as integral to helping students better realize the nature of science and the value of understanding science concepts. This new paradigm is leading educational reform.

Understanding Paradigms

Where did the idea of paradigms begin? Thomas Kuhn (1962) first defined a **paradigm** as a commonly accepted viewpoint. He defined a *paradigm shift* as a radical change in this viewpoint. For example, the paradigm of a sun-centered solar system replaced the paradigm of the earth-centered solar system. Paradigm shifts occur because scientists use experimentation and new technologies to better explain observed scientific phenomena.

> **Paradigm** is a typical viewpoint or ideal example that provides a model for all related processes or systems.

Scientific discussion, experimentation, and publication generally center on current paradigms. Deviating from the paradigm is apt to place a scientist's research funding and acceptance of publications in jeopardy. Ideas that are inconsistent with current paradigms are generally dismissed. Occasionally, however, because of advances in technology or new research, a paradigm shift and an accompanying revolution in the scientific community occur. Old ideas are discarded as a new theory emerges and becomes the dominant paradigm. An example is the presentation of the plate tectonics theory in 1956. Scientists explaining this theory discussed how continental land masses were resting on a small number of "plates" or semirigid sections of the earth's crust. Earthquakes and volcanoes occur primarily at the margins of these sections as the plates drift together, apart, or alongside each other. The plate tectonics theory changed how scientists viewed the movement of continents and seafloor spreading. Even as paradigms in science change our perspectives and understanding of how the world works, they also transcend science education and our understanding of how to better teach science.

> **Constructivism** is an approach to teaching based on research about how people learn. Many researchers say that each individual constructs knowledge rather than receiving it from others. Constructive teaching is based on the belief that students learn best when they gain knowledge through exploration and active learning. Hands-on materials are used instead of textbooks, and students are encouraged to think and explain their reasoning instead of memorizing and reciting facts. Education is centered on themes and concepts and the connections between them, rather than isolated information. (McBrien & Brandt, 1997)

Paradigms of Science Education

Looking at the research related to the National Science Education Standards of the National Research Council (NRC, 1996) and Project 2061 of the American Association for the Advancement of Science (AAAS, 1993), we find that **constructivism** is the current

Science Teaching and Learning Standard

Teachers of science guide and facilitate learning. In doing this, teachers

- Focus and support inquiries while interacting with students.

- Orchestrate discourse among students about scientific ideas.

- Challenge students to accept and share responsibility for their own learning.

- Recognize and respond to student diversity and encourage all students to participate fully in science learning.

- Encourage and model the skills of scientific inquiry, as well as the curiosity, openness to new ideas and data, and skepticism that characterize science.

(Teaching Standard B, National Research Council, 1996, p. 3.)

Inquiry is a term used to describe the activities that students engage in to help them construct knowledge and understanding of scientific ideas.

paradigm in science education. This paradigm supports inquiry teaching and is reflected in the Science Teaching and Learning Standard in the Standards Link.

The authors of the Science Teaching and Learning Standard provide a research-based explanation of how children engage in inquiry to construct personal knowledge and learn science. They underscore the need for teachers to guide and facilitate learning in science and to provide inquiry experiences for their students. They also emphasize the importance of student discourse.

You will notice that **inquiry** is a strand throughout the Science Teaching and Learning Standard, as it is throughout the standards document. Figure 2–1 contains characteristics of classroom inquiry.

As you read about different perspectives of teaching and learning science in this chapter, consider the ability of each perspective to support scientific inquiry as outlined in Figure 2–1.

Children's Learning and Your Classroom

Pause for a moment and contemplate yourself teaching science in an elementary or middle school classroom. What methods will you employ to be consistent with the standards? Will the continuous need to infuse science and technology in your curriculum make it impossible for you to teach science as you learned it in school? Will you be able to engage students effectively in understanding science?

Thinking about and sharing your viewpoints related to the questions and statements presented here may bring about many new questions. As you continue to read and reflect on this chapter, you will come to understand constructivism and inquiry. You will see why constructivism has emerged as the paradigm for the construction of knowledge in science education.

Figure 2–1   Essential features of classroom inquiry.

- Learners are engaged by scientifically oriented questions.
- Learners give priority to evidence, which allows them to develop and evaluate explanations that address scientifically oriented questions.
- Learners formulate explanations from evidence to address scientifically oriented questions.
- Learners evaluate their explanations in light of alternative explanations, particularly those reflecting scientific understanding.
- Learners communicate and justify their proposed explanations.

Source: From *Inquiry and the National Science Education Standards: A Guide for Teaching and Learning* (p. 25). Copyright © 2000 by the National Academy of Sciences. Courtesy of the National Academy Press, Washington, DC.

CONSTRUCTIVISM

What does it mean to know?
What does it mean to be a knower?
Is there a relationship between the knower and the known?

These questions may be too philosophical for you at first glance. They are, however, at the heart of the constructivist-learning paradigm. The knower–known relationship is also the basis for the current reform movement in education. This movement emphasizes *the active role of the learner* as constructing her own knowledge. It also places the teacher in a more facilitative role in the learning process.

Those who adhere to the constructivist paradigm hold the belief that all knowledge is constructed by an individual, not passed on from the teacher to the student (Driver, 1995; McBrien & Brandt, 1997; Tobin & Tippins, 1993). Using constructivism as a referent for science teaching maximizes student learning, because the teacher's role is to *facilitate* the learning process, as opposed to transferring knowledge. The teacher's purpose is to provide the best materials and learning situations to make learning individually meaningful for each student. Students change in some way as a result of the learning. They may replace a prior belief about a science concept, add to their existing knowledge, or modify something they already know. The learning, or construction, takes place in a context of what learners already have in their own mental store.

Cobern (1993) likens the constructivist approach to a construction site where existing structures are the foundation upon which to build new knowledge. To get a better idea of constructivism in general, study the following teaching example. As you think about the

Visit an Inquiry Classroom
Inquiry Learning

View the *Four Days of Science* video in the "Model Inquiry Unit" section of the Companion CD. Note the constructivist approach to teaching and learning, and that the inquiry seen in the video involves a *learner-centered* process. The once popular listen-to-learn paradigm of the classroom has been replaced with an inquiry approach. You will see a process of exploring the world that leads to asking children questions and their making discoveries in the search for new understandings.

Review the video and ask yourself the following:
- Are the children passive or active in the video?
- What specific indicators are they learning?
- What evidence is there that Mr. McKnight is probing the students' understandings of earthworms?
- What evidence is there that the children are learning?

    Go to the Companion Website's Web Destinations for Chapter 2 and look at the *Field Guide to Earthworms* from NatureWatch at the *http://www.naturewatch.ca/ english/ wormwatch/about/guide/intro.html* link. Students could also learn about earthworms through this medium. Compare and contrast Mr. McKnight's and NatureWatch's approaches to learning about earthworms. Would Nature-Watch's approach also be considered a constructivist approach to teaching and learning? Record your ideas and the answers to these questions in your portfolio or use the Companion Website to share your ideas.

example, ask yourself, "Will this activity provide a meaningful learning experience for the students?" or "How will the children learn?"

A General Constructivist Approach to Teaching

Ms. Terrell, a fourth-grade teacher, refers to the K–4 Earth and Space Content Standard D (see Standards Link), to develop this lesson objective: "The students will discover the observable changes in the moon as it travels across the sky over the coming months." As she prepares for the phases of the moon activity, she asks the students what they have observed in relation to the moon as it appears in the sky.

Ms. Terrell then asks the students to assemble a science journal with blank pages. Today there is a new moon, and she instructs students to look at the moon each day or night, as it becomes visible. Students should date each journal page and draw and describe the moon as they observe it in the sky. Each day, they will compare their pictures with one another and with the predictions they find on the Internet and in the newspaper. They will also explore children's books such as *The Moon Seems to Change* (Branley, 1987) and *Day Light, Night Light* (Branley, 1975). At the end of this exploration period, Ms. Terrell will have the students discuss what they found out and generate ideas about this phenomenon.

To test students' ideas, Ms. Terrell brings in a homemade **astronomy dome.** Her instruction with the class about this subject takes place from inside the dome. There, she has one student hold up a spotlight to indicate the sun. Other students hold up a model earth (basketball) and moon (tennis ball). Together, they replicate the motions of the earth, the sun, and the moon. They demonstrate what happened throughout the month as the moon circled the earth. Ms. Terrell asks the students to explain what is going on and whether this matches their moon drawings. As an informal assessment, students shade in a series of blank circles that represent moon images as the sun would light them. Finally, the class discusses the vocabulary associated with the phases of the moon.

As you may infer from this constructivist-based lesson, students learn the material in a context that they can understand. They will readily recall the information in the future and apply the processes they learned in this and other situations.

Students have observed the process of the **waxing** and **waning** of the moon and recorded it in illustrations. (See Inquiry Unit 12, "Moon Phases," for an activity and related concepts.) The terms, such as *new, full, crescent, quarter,* and *gibbous,* as well as processes such as observation of the earth–moon–sun interactions, make sense because this relevant context is provided. The learners engage in activities that relate to their own previous experiences. To better understand constructivism, let us look at early influences on research that led us to a constructivist approach to teaching and learning.

Standards Link

K–4 Earth and Space Content Standard D

As a result of their activities in grades K–4, all students should develop an understanding of

- **Properties of earth materials**
- **Objects in the sky**
- **Changes in the earth and sky**

(K–4 Earth and Space Content Standard D, National Research Council, 1996, p. 130.)

An **astronomy dome** is made from black painter's plastic taped on the side with box tape to form a "dome." The 20-foot by 100-foot sheet can be cut to fit the available classroom space. A box fan is taped to one end to inflate the dome, and the other end is sealed shut. A class of 25 students can sit inside the dark dome. Other versions use cardboard and binder clips (see *http://www.cccoe.net/stars/*). Also see the Companion Website for teaching ideas in the dome.

Waxing   refers to increasing in size.

Waning   refers to decreasing in size.

THEORETICAL FOUNDATIONS FOR CONSTRUCTIVIST TEACHING

The 18th-century work of the Neapolitan philosopher Giambattista Vico was an early form of constructivism, in that he believed humans can clearly understand only what they have themselves constructed. Contemporary constructivism has its origins with John Dewey, who theorized that education depends on action. Dewey believed that knowledge and ideas emerge from a situation in which learners draw them out of experiences of meaning and importance (see Dewey, 1966). Dewey saw learning as occurring in a social context where students manipulate materials, thus creating a community of learners building their knowledge together. Today, constructivism is a broad-based theory about learning that includes such areas as the *cognitive* constructivism associated with Jean Piaget and the *sociocultural* constructivism linked with Lev Vygotsky.

Piaget and Cognition

Often viewed as an early constructivist, Jean Piaget focused his research on children's construction of knowledge through **equilibration** (Bettencourt, 1993; Bybee & Sund, 1990). Piaget's theory involves mediating mental processes for mental cognition (Labinowicz, 1980). To understand these processes, it is important to understand the notion of a schema.

> **Equilibration** is a process by which a learner compensates for a mental dilemma and constructs new knowledge.

Schemata

A **schema** is viewed as a concept, pattern of action, theory, model, or idea that is part of our cognitive repertoire. Schemata (the plural of *schema*) are "meaningful units" that are used repeatedly (Henriques, 1990, p. 143). Schemata can be specific, sequential, or elaborate and often involve an entire network of context-specific bodies of knowledge that learners apply to specific situations. For example, we may have a "hammering" schemata. At the novice level, this involves identification of the tool (e.g., scheme of a hammer) and how to use it to pound a nail (e.g., schemata of striking the nail). At an expert level, it may involve knowledge of explicit types of hammers for specific uses (e.g., claw, roofing, ball-peen, finishing, tack, brick, drywall), understanding of the numerous types of nails (e.g., common, box, finishing, flooring, concrete, wallboard, roofing), and advanced techniques for driving in the nails (e.g., using more wrist than elbow and more elbow than shoulder for good rhythm, toenailing to join studs, spacing of reroof nailing to prevent wind damage).

> **Schema** is a cognitive framework used to store and organize information such as knowledge and experiences.

Schemata become relevant as we need them. They help us function on a daily basis and deal with new experiences. For schemata to be effective, they need the capability to be modified to fit new experiences through the processes of **assimilation** and **accommodation.** We assimilate when we adjust our schemata to include new details; we try to transform incoming information so that it fits with our existing way of thinking (Siegler, 1986). Accommodation means restructuring our schemata so that we can make sense of situations.

> **Assimilation** can be seen as the way we adapt new information into existing mental structures so that our minds can seek equilibration.

An example of assimilation is when a child has a schema that involves birds such as robins, sparrows, and pigeons. When the child sees a new type of bird, like an osprey or hawk, she may need to adjust the schema to assimilate the new information of a much larger bird that is flying overhead. Later, if the child sees a penguin or an ostrich at the zoo, assimilation may not be as useful. This new information includes birds that do not fly. The child may not be able to simply assimilate the new information. Now the child must adapt her way of thinking to new experiences (Siegler, 1986). This process is called accommodation, because the schema can now accommodate the new information.

> **Accommodation** is a circumstance where no preexisting mental structures are available for assimilation and children must adapt their own mental structures to accommodate new information.

The result of the accommodation is that the child's schema can now accept birds that fly and birds that do not fly. Equilibration is primary to children's construction of reality, as it involves both assimilation and accommodation. It is the overall interaction between existing ways of thinking and a new experience (Siegler, 1986). For example, with the phases of the moon activity, the students may not have known that the moon reflects light. Their schema may have been that all objects in the night sky give off light. Certainly assimilation and accommodation are useful in resolving this **disequilibrium.**

In general, Piaget sees cognitive development as resolving the disequilibrium that may exist in the child's mind. In his theory of development, equilibration, through assimilation and accommodation, is the foundation for significant developmental changes in the child. What does this say to us as future teachers? We can assist children in building their neural connections. To better understand how, it is helpful to take into consideration Piaget's stages of children's cognitive development.

Piaget's Stages of Development

Piaget developed his theory based on his observations and studies regarding scientific conceptions of children. With this, Piaget proposed stages in the development of thought at different ages. The three stages that elementary teachers are most concerned with are the preoperational stage, from about 2 to 7 years old; concrete operational stage, from about 7 to 12 years old; and the formal operational stage, from about 12 years old and beyond (see Appendix E).

Children who are preoperational are not yet able to do the kind of thinking Piaget calls **operations,** or mental tasks. The latter part of the stage, which lasts from about ages 4 to 7, is known as the *intuitive thought substage.* Because this is the time when most children begin school, we start our study of children's thinking at the intuitive period of their mental development.

"Intuitive thought" describes how 4- to 7-year-olds think. They typically use their sense impressions or intuition rather than logic in forming judgments. They also tend to remember only one thing at a time. A common activity to demonstrate intuitive thought is to have a child roll out a ball of clay and then to ask the child about what happened. Children at this stage will suggest that there is "more clay" because it is rolled out and appears longer.

Children who are concrete operational, in contrast, are logical thinkers, but the ideas they consider must be tied to concrete materials they can manipulate. They must have some firsthand experience with the materials to think about them. Specific examples, models, and detailed explanations are needed with concrete operational children.

In the stage of formal operations, older children are able to think much more abstractly. They have far less need to refer to concrete objects. This stage generally occurs after elementary or middle school. It is considered the summit of cognitive development because students can handle formal logic and abstract reasoning.

A Piagetian Approach to Teaching

Returning to Ms. Terrell's students, they are not yet at the formal operations stage. Their teacher is engaging them in concrete activities during which they are actually manipulating materials versus thinking about them abstractly as they will later do in the formal operations stage. In class, the children are building a "moon phaser" with a paper dial, downloaded from the Internet. They will use the moon phaser to predict when the next full and new moons will occur and to study related terms. Ms. Terrell's objectives for the students are as follows:

1. Locate the horizon and zenith with their moon phaser.
2. Determine the current moon phase.

Disequilibrium is when a child's conception of a thing or event is no longer adequate and the child seeks to establish a balance through assimilation and accommodation.

Operation, as described in this textbook, is a mental action such as adding numbers or classifying objects.

To better understand the preoperations and concrete operations stages, see the related activities for Chapter 2 at the *http://www.prenhall. com/peters* website.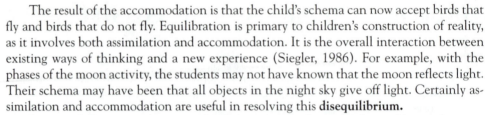

3. Find the moon's approximate position in the sky for a given date and time.
4. Determine the approximate time of moonrise and moonset for eight moon phases.

This activity meets all of these objectives and appears to be at an appropriate developmental level for her students. Because her students have never used a device like the moon phaser, Ms. Terrell anticipates that they will be very active assimilating and accommodating new information. Later, her students will apply the information from this activity as they work with balls and flashlights to re-create the phases of the moon in a different way.

Throughout the stages of development, concrete activities play an important role in the process of cognitive growth. Assimilation, accommodation, and equilibration all require thought processes. As teachers, we must facilitate learning that keeps the mind active, as we see done with the moon activity (particularly when students are unable to manipulate "real" space objects such as in space science activities). We also need to keep in mind that reality is something children construct from their own actions. It is not something waiting to be found or discovered (Piaget, 1954; Piaget & Inhelder, 1969).

But is it solely a teacher's activities that cause children's development and construction of meaning? What other factors or influences may come into play in children's development, such as social or cultural influences? Some theorists believe that culture and social exchange are important in the knowledge development process.

Go to *http://www.prenhal.com/peters* for links related to resources for a lesson on moon phases and earth and space science sites.

Vygotsky and Social Constructivism

Is the role of others important to our learning? Lev Vygotsky's sociocultural constructivist theory involves the role of culture and society. Vygotsky believed that behavior must be studied in a social and historical context, giving rise to the term *sociohistorical*. Vygotsky theorized that children do not simply reproduce what is said or shown to them, rather they undergo socially mediated cognitive constructions.

Vygotsky was born in the same year as Piaget. Although he died at the age of 38 and was not well known in the United States, English translations of his more than 180 writ-

See *http://www.prenhall.com/peters* for additional information on Vygotsky.

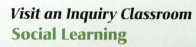
Visit an Inquiry Classroom
Social Learning

View the *Social Learning* video in the "Constructivist Pedagogy" section of the Companion CD. The video shows a group of students huddled around computers viewing content and online movies about earthworms. The students are exchanging ideas and information.

Review the video and ask yourself the following:
- Many educators believe that children learn from other children at least as well or better than they learn from the teacher. What evidence is there on the video segment to support or refute this claim?
- What is the teacher's role in social learning?

Recall a lesson that you have observed in your field placement. Was there an exchange between students? Was it similar to what was seen with Mr. McKnight's class? Did this social interaction promote learning? Explain your answer in terms of Vygotsky's sociocultural constructivist theory. Record your ideas and the answers to these questions in your portfolio or use the Companion Website to share your ideas.

Children look at the moon as it appears in space to help construct understandings of the phases of the moon.

ten works indicate that Vygotsky understood an important facet of cognitive development. For Vygotsky, cognitive development is a matter of an individual's social interaction within the environment (Vygotsky, 1978).

Vygotsky Versus Piaget

How does Vygotsky compare to Piaget? Although both theorists believed that learners construct their own knowledge, the two theories held a major difference. Piaget was a developmental constructivist and saw development as leading learning, which he described in his stages of development. Piaget emphasized the child's internal thinking processes. Vygotsky, however, saw learning as leading development. Students who are engaged in learning **spontaneous concepts** with their peers later restructure these same concepts into **scientific concepts** within their own cognitive structures. In other words, a concept such as "light" begins in an informal social setting as children talk about light and darkness (e.g., a child telling her peers that she thinks she needs a nightlight because her bedroom is too dark). Later, through time and repeated use, this concept and related spontaneous concepts become better organized in the child's cognitive structure as a more systematic "scientific concept." The child will better understand the nature of light and be able to apply this concept as needed to make sense of her world (e.g., light sources penetrate the dark because of the movement of electromagnetic waves).

Spontaneous concepts are acquired informally from everyday life experiences.

Scientific concepts are represented by a systematically organized body of knowledge and are usually learned through formal instruction.

Social Construction of Scientific Concepts

According to Vygotsky (1986), as a child grows, words begin to take on meaning and communication begins to develop. The child finds names for objects; and informal, spontaneous concepts begin to develop as a result of verbal exchange with others. These concepts are often vague and tend to be illogical and unsystematic, but they are further developed through the use of **psychological tools** or signs.

Using Psychological Tools and Semantic Mediation

Psychological tools are used like the tools that any craftsperson uses to perform tasks better. Psychological tools, as mental tools, allow us to improve our communication and to adapt to our environment. They can be either external or internal. Writing notes in a notebook is an example of an external psychological tool; these notes help to augment the mind's capacity. Internal psychological tools, such as the formulas and rhymes we call mnemonic devices, also assist in mental development.

> **Psychological tools** are the culturally developed signs used in mental and social activities; examples are letters, words, numbers, speech, and pictures.

Signs, as a kind of mental tool, assist in regulating our thinking and are part of Vygotsky's theory. For instance, if we write a note and stick it to the refrigerator or if we place a name in an appointment book, we are creating a sign. These activities help us remember important dates or information. Vygotsky's term **semantic mediation** refers to how we, as humans, use tools and signs to assist us in remembering. Mental tools, such as signs, are representative of our culture and are unique to humans. All animals share mental behaviors such as attention and perception (lower or biological forms); however, semantic mediation provides a level of understanding that separates human thoughts from those of other animals. This higher order thought process is known as *cultural mental behavior,* as opposed to the *natural mental behavior* common to all animals (Vygotsky, 1981).

> **Semantic mediation** is the transformation of lower forms of mental behavior to higher forms of mental behavior through the use of signs.

Social Collaboration

The main difference between lower biological forms and higher social forms is the shift that occurs from outside control (teacher and peer-supported activity) to self-directed (autonomous) control. Social collaboration is gradually lessened as a child takes on more responsibility for her own learning. To put it another way, the development of higher forms of mental processes occurs through a child's enculturation into society as a result of the educational process. Instruction is a principle source of the child's concepts. For Vygotsky, as for Piaget, the stages of concept development reflect a maturation process. Figure 2–2 illustrates the stages of concept development from simple labeling of objects to abstract and systemized knowledge of scientific concepts (Dixon-Krauss, 1996).

Figure 2–2   **Vygotsky's stages of concept development.**

Heaps	Child groups objects into random categories.
Complexes	Traits of objects are analyzed and concrete factual relationships among diverse objects are established.
Potential Concepts	Transition from the concrete and spontaneous to the abstract and scientific concept.
Genuine Concepts	Abstract and systematic concepts that are common to a culture.

Source: From Table 1.1, p. 12, *Vygotsky in the Classroom* by Lisbeth Dixon-Krauss. Copyright © 1996 by Longman Publishers USA. Reprinted by permission of Addison-Wesley Educational Publishers Inc.

Note the similarities and differences between the stages proposed by Vygotsky and those proposed by Piaget. You can see that Piaget focused on children's mental development as they pass through the stages of development that lead to higher learning. For Piaget, moving into higher development levels also leads to the ability for more advanced learning. Vygotsky, conversely, emphasized learning as leading development. He saw learning on a continuum of simply naming things, to developing spontaneous concepts, to refining the spontaneous concepts as scientific concepts. For Vygotsky, opportunities for learning lead to higher developmental levels.

Teachers as Mediators

Can we, as elementary or middle school science teachers, maximize learning by taking advantage of social collaboration? Is group work important in the classroom?

Vygotsky (1978) noted that when children were placed in groups that were under the guidance of an adult or when they collaborated with a more experienced peer, they could perform at levels higher than were possible when working on their own. Furthermore, what was possible in the group situation now would be possible on an individual basis later. For instance, if a child was able to complete a classification of leaves based on common properties with the assistance of a more knowledgeable classmate, this same child could later complete this classification task independently.

Teaching Tips

The importance of working with others supports the use of cooperative learning in the classroom.

Social constructivists would argue that the only good kind of instruction is that which marches ahead of and leads development. Vygotsky (1962) saw instruction not as the *ripe*, finished product, but as the *ripening* product in development. So with group or teacher assistance, a child's instruction should always be slightly ahead of what was possible for that child on her own level. If the student can already complete a classification based on two properties but not on three, instruction should be directed at classifying with three properties under the guidance of the teacher or learning group. For example, a student may be able to perform a dichotomous classification of objects that are either animals or plants. This same child may not be able to classify objects that are plants, animals, or monerans.

Zone of Proximal Development

Zone of proximal development is the gap between a child's current level of development and potential level of development when supported by collaboration with a more capable peer.

The term **zone of proximal development** indicates the difference between what a child can do with the help of a more knowledgeable person and what the child can do independently. The goal of instruction is to actively engage the student in solving problems within the zone of proximal development. The teacher's role is that of a facilitator or mediator. The teacher provides an environment where learning in the zone of proximal development is maximized. The teacher, through **scaffolding,** provides just the right amount of support to accomplish the developmental goal. Alternatively, the teacher can arrange a cooperative learning group in which another student will be the knowledgeable other.

Scaffolding is when an adult first structures a learning task and then provides the dialogue needed to guide a child's successful participation in that task.

Scaffolding and Teacher Support

The scaffolding support that a teacher provides is analogous to the scaffolding that painters use. Painters may reach many areas independently, but when they cannot reach an area on their own, painters require a scaffold to assist them in performing the task. Correspondingly, painters would not use high scaffolding to paint a baseboard or normal wall. The implication here is that the teacher should not provide more guidance than is needed for developmental support; too much support will not promote the development of independent thought in children.

Visit an Inquiry Classroom
Zone of Proximal Development

View the *Zone of Proximal Development* video in the "Constructivist Pedagogy" section of the Companion CD. Robert receives assistance from Ashley and Josh with the earthworm activity. With the help of these "more knowledgeable people," Robert is able to complete an activity that he would not otherwise be able to complete independently.

Review the video and ask yourself the following:
- What are other examples of students working within the zone of proximal development?
- What is the function of communication in this lesson?
- What role does Mr. McKnight play in this lesson?

> Some educators argue that computer software works as the "knowledgeable other," allowing children to work in their zone of proximal development. Look at the Virtual Worm lesson at the *http://www.naturewatch.ca/english/wormwatch/virtual_worm/Introduction.html* link. Do you agree or disagree that this medium can work as a knowledgeable other, much like his peers assisted Robert in the *Zone of Proximal Development* video on the Companion CD? Record your ideas and the answers to these questions in your portfolio or use the Companion Website to share your ideas.

A Vygotskian Approach to Teaching

As an extension to their moon activities, Joshua's class discusses the principles of light, mirrors, and reflection. As Joshua shares his newfound knowledge with his sister, Melanie, she becomes curious about light, how it travels, and its everyday effects. She decides to aim their new laser pointer near the cat and see if the cat will chase the light beam. Joshua instructs Melanie not to look at the light beam directly and not to let the cat see her pointing the laser. He also describes for her how light travels in a straight line and how light is reflected by a mirror.

Melanie tries out many different ideas but is now using a large mirror in the hallway and some hand mirrors borrowed from her parents' bathroom. She got the idea to try the mirrors from her brother talking about reflections. She also saw how the light reflected from her own vanity mirror as she tried different ways to make the light shine into another room.

Melanie is involved in experimentation here. She is looking at the relationship among mirrors, reflections, and pathways of light. She is also engaged in dialog with her older brother. She asks questions and tries out some new ways of doing things to answer her question about the light beam and the cat. She is absorbed with the activity and motivated to figure out how the light beam can be redirected to reach her goal. Together, the children are engaged in an interactive learning situation.

Application of the Vygotskian Approach

Think about how scientists, engineers, physicians, computer technicians, and other professionals carry on activities within the workplace. Do they work independently or as a team? Do physicians imply that, to be effective, they must know the answer to every question and not rely on others? It is the same with the laser activity. For example, a child's concept of a mirror tends to be that of an object used to see themselves and not that of an instrument to reflect light. Melanie relies on her brother for guidance. He leads her into thinking about mirrors in new ways.

Has Melanie changed in her knowledge of mirrors? As Melanie communicates, she begins to have a more logical and systematically structured verbal definition for the mirror. She uses psychological tools and signs to assist her in controlling her mental behavior. It is now more in keeping with culture's accepted body of knowledge related to mirrors. Melanie now has the beginning of a scientific concept. Her previous spontaneous concept becomes a part of this new scientific concept, making the new concept more meaningful. Melanie is eventually able to complete the task with the laser pointer because she received some assistance from her older brother. Her brother became the scaffold for her learning in this situation.

Our role as teachers is to assist students in developing tools and signs, as well as in maximizing the integration of spontaneous concepts and their related concrete experiences into scientific concepts. When this happens, spontaneous concepts can be logically defined, retrieved, and used by the child.

Collaborative learning and thinking, as seen with the laser activity, is the foundation of Vygotsky's theory. It is the very means by which a child learns the fundamentals of society. It is the method of moving from lower learning to higher learning and is the system by which activities within a child's zone of proximal development are successful. Scientific experimentation and problem-centered activities, or those that have multiple-solution paths, provide the framework for successful science experiences. Much like scientists and engineers engaged in collaborative research, your interactions with students will promote learning.

Your role as a teacher will be to facilitate this type of activity and to adapt the curriculum to meet your students' needs. Like the physician who must consult on many cases, you will not be an expert in all areas and will rely on others, including students, to assist you in knowledge acquisition. Just as the physician cannot be available at all times for every patient and needs to employ the help of nurses, technicians, and others, you cannot be available at all times for every student, and will need to employ the help of others, including students. These knowledgeable others will assist in the scaffolding process, communicating the terminology and processes to their peers.

Visit an Inquiry Classroom
Scaffolding

View the *Scaffolding* video in the "Constructivist Pedagogy" section of the Companion CD. Mr. McKnight ensures that students have the things they need to be successful with the activity. He also provides verbal prompts to guide the students in the activity.

Review the video and ask yourself the following:
- Patricia Mason Spigarelli's perspective of this video clip includes the statement, "We don't want to give them all the information, we just give them enough help so that they can do it for themselves and I think that's what scaffolding is and how it works in science." Do you agree or disagree with this statement? Explain your viewpoint.
- What might happen with this activity if Mr. McKnight was not there to provide verbal guidance? Discuss specific statements made by Mr. McKnight and the effect on the students.

 How have you provided scaffolding to another student in your field placement or in your methods class? Was it successful? Explain your activity and its effect on the other individual's learning. Record your ideas and the answers to these questions in your portfolio or use the Companion Website to share your ideas.

The Role of Language

Because language is central to Vygotsky's theory, it is important that students understand and use the language of science (Gallas, 1995; Lemke, 1993). Science is a foreign language for them—one with comparatively more new terms than found in a foreign language text. Social constructivist theory suggests that a child constructs an understanding of language from the whole to its parts. If this is the case, then the classroom should surround children with information on science topics so that the children are exposed to the content of science through a whole language or integrated approach to learning. Vocabulary should remain in the context of what is read, not be encountered as a separate, out-of-context, memorization drill. Science instruction should be a model of how science is performed by scientists. Figure 2–3 presents further suggestions for teaching within a social constructivist framework.

 Teaching Tips Peer tutoring, when a high-achieving student tutors a lower-achieving student, is an excellent application of Vygotsky's theory.

Figure 2–3   Social constructivist teaching suggestions.

Planning the Curriculum	• Plan to assess student's preconceptions through class and individual discussions, drawings, writing activities, and other assessment procedures. • Plan to build on student's prior knowledge to take advantage of spontaneous concepts. • Plan to keep students involved in the lesson through the use of challenging and open-ended activities.
Opportunities to Develop Scientific Concepts	• Provide as many chances as possible for students to explore phenomena and communicate with each other. • Use concrete examples whenever possible. • Organize many opportunities for oral and written language so that students share meanings and construct concepts.
Time and Classroom Management	• Provide ample time for small-group activities. • Leave plenty of time after instruction for reflection and questions by the students. • Arrange the classroom to maximize peer interaction and small-group activities. • Use reading, writing, and science centers effectively and not just as a management tool for those who get their work done early.
Listening and Questioning Skills	• Ask questions before the lesson to evaluate student's prior knowledge and to assist students in recalling the information. • Listen carefully to students as they are talking to you and others so that you can adjust their lessons to fit their zone of proximal development. • Ask open-ended questions and encourage elaboration of student's answers.
Planning and Facilitating Classroom Activities	• Develop lessons that offer multiple pathways to learning, such as reading, writing, listening, and small-group activities. • Plan activities that connect in-school learning to out-of-school learning. • Construct lessons that are culturally diverse. • Use creative writing and subject-specific journals. • Use assessment procedures that can show where a student is on the continuum of learning. • Vary assessment procedures to check for student understanding.

Driver, Asoko, Leach, Mortimer, and Scott (1994) sum up the learning of science as follows:

> [Science learning] involves being initiated into scientific ways of knowing. Science entities and ideas, which are constructed, validated, and communicated through cultural institutions of science, are unlikely to be discovered by their own empirical enquiry; learning science thus involves being initiated into the ideas and practices of the scientific community and making these ideas and practices meaningful at the individual level. The role of the science educator is to mediate scientific knowledge for learners, to help them to make personal sense of the ways in which knowledge claims are generalized and validated. (p. 6)

> **Teaching Tips**
> Activities in the classroom should promote the use of language, which is central to a child's development.

As you can see, social constructivism has important implications for the teacher. Students construct new knowledge within a sociohistorical framework, where language is an important component.

A CONSTRUCTIVIST APPROACH TO TEACHING

A constructivist model describes the learning process in terms of the student, not the teacher. We cannot prescribe a curriculum for everyone. Notwithstanding, when students are actively engaged, they are constructing knowledge. Learning is taking place, not as a result of the transference of knowledge from teacher to student via text or a personal knowledge base, but as students interpret and make sense of their surroundings.

> **Teaching Tips**
> A constructivist approach implies that the use of a variety of activities in the classroom promotes a child's making sense of the world and developing scientific concepts.

Similar to the social constructivist theories, as the students interpret their surroundings, the new interpretation is influenced by their prior knowledge. It is therefore the teacher's role to facilitate activities that will guide the learner into developing meaningful concepts. Constructivists generally agree that discourse is especially important in negotiating meaning and developing socially agreeable constructs. Therefore, open-ended questioning is important before, during, and after activity periods.

Constructivist Teaching Promotes Active Learning

If knowledge is the result of constructive activity, then it cannot be transferred effectively to a passive receiver. The construction of knowledge must be an active process by the individual learner. The role of the teacher is to orient the learner in a general direction and then attempt to prevent the learner from going in directions that would be inappropriate. This is exactly what we find with the following luneometer activity.

As they continue their moon studies, Ms. Terrell's class looks at the question, "What kind of information can we collect in order to predict when the moon will appear tomorrow evening?" From a page in the *Out of This World* activity guide (shown on page 37), students document the angle of elevation of the moon every 30 minutes for a total of 5 hours. They build luneometers with rulers and protractors to measure the moon's angle as it rises. They also graph the results of their observations and actively engage in making sense of the data.

How can we make today's science classrooms better than those in the past? One way is to change our perception of teaching from promoting rote learning proposed by behav-

Children determine the angle of elevation of the moon as part of their exploration of the phases of the moon.

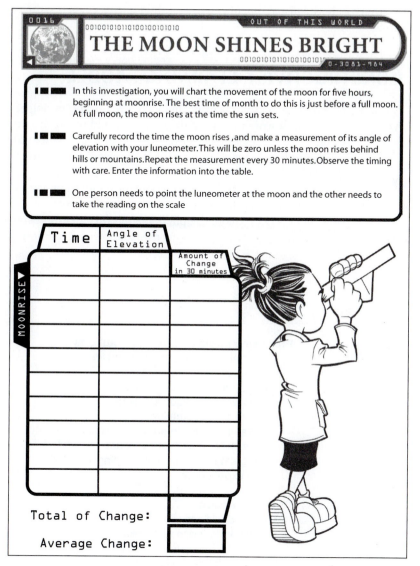

THE MOON SHINES BRIGHT

OUT OF THIS WORLD

In this investigation, you will chart the movement of the moon for five hours, beginning at moonrise. The best time of month to do this is just before a full moon. At full moon, the moon rises at the time the sun sets.

Carefully record the time the moon rises, and make a measurement of its angle of elevation with your luneometer. This will be zero unless the moon rises behind hills or mountains. Repeat the measurement every 30 minutes. Observe the timing with care. Enter the information into the table.

One person needs to point the luneometer at the moon and the other needs to take the reading on the scale

Time	Angle of Elevation	Amount of Change in 30 minutes

Total of Change:

Average Change:

iorists to engaging students in a series of well-thought-out logical steps. Teachers should scaffold a child's growth in building conceptual knowledge from the child's prior knowledge to that which is the cultural development of society.

The teacher's role as a facilitator of the curriculum is to provide the resources for learning, to engage students actively, and to refocus students' activity when appropriate so that they remain productive in the learning process. For example, Ms. Terrell provided the luneometer template and then guided students in making sense of the data as they were collected. Her role in the activity was to pose a problem to solve and invite students to make observations that accomplish the task. She then steps aside and allows the students to interact with the environment and each other. Ms. Terrell intervenes only when necessary. Intervention is used to refocus student discussion in a more productive way, initiate a new pattern of activity, or begin an assessment activity for the students to express their personal understanding.

THE CONSTRUCTIVIST LEARNING MODEL

Yager (1991) described the constructivist learning model (CLM) as a promising new model in learning. It focuses on the learner instead of the teacher. Building on the work of researchers at the National Center for Improving Science Education, Yager introduced a set of constructivist strategies for teaching, which are provided in Figure 2–4.

 Teaching Tips | Try using the constructivist learning model in planning your next lesson.

As you can see, the CLM is an ongoing four-part process. First, you get the students to think about a phenomenon in a new way (invitation part). Then, they explore the phenomenon (exploration part) and develop explanations or solutions (constructs; proposing explanations and solutions part). Fi-

Figure 2–4   **Constructivist strategies for teaching.**

Invitation
- Observe surroundings for points of curiosity
- Ask questions
- Consider possible responses to questions
- Note unexpected phenomena
- Identify situations where student perceptions vary

Exploration
- Engage in focused play
- Brainstorm possible alternatives
- Look for information
- Experiment with materials
- Observe specific phenomena
- Design a model
- Collect and organize data
- Employ problem-solving strategies
- Select appropriate resources
- Discuss solutions with others
- Design and conduct experiments
- Evaluate choices
- Engage in debate
- Identify risks and consequences
- Develop parameters of an investigation
- Analyze data

Proposing Explanations and Solutions
- Communicate information and ideas
- Construct and explain a model
- Construct a new explanation
- Review and critique solutions
- Utilize peer evaluation
- Assemble multiple answers/solutions
- Determine appropriate closure
- Integrate a solution with existing knowledge and experiences

Taking Action
- Make decisions
- Apply knowledge and skills
- Transfer knowledge and skills
- Share information and ideas
- Ask new questions
- Develop products and promote ideas
- Use models and ideas to elicit discussions and acceptance by others

Source: R. Yager, "The Constructivist Learning Model." Reprinted with permission from NSTA Publications, September 1991, from *The Science Teacher,* National Science Teachers Association, 1840 Wilson Blvd., Arlington, VA 22201-3000.

Visit an Inquiry Classroom
Invitations to Learn

View the *Invitation* video within the "Model Inquiry Unit" section of the Companion CD. Mr. McKnight asks the children questions to stimulate their curiosity of earthworms and set the stage for future activities. This is in keeping with the first stage of the constructivist learning model, invitation.

Review the video and ask yourself the following:
- What specific questions could be used to cause students to want to engage in the exploration stage of the constructivist learning model?
- How can Mr. McKnight best transition into the exploration stage of the constructivist learning model?

 "The search for meaning is innate" is the third brain/mind learning principle (*http://cainelearning.com/pwheel/*). The authors suggest that "we are born to function as scientists, discovering what our world is about." How does the constructivist learning model support this brain/mind learning principle? Record your ideas and the answers to these questions in your portfolio or use the Companion Website to share your ideas.

nally, they share their new ideas with others or reexplore the phenomenon in a new way (taking action part).

When constructivist theories such as the CLM are used, the focus is on the learner and the learning environment. This makes your job as a teacher–facilitator different from what you may have experienced from your teachers in elementary or middle school. As you read through the remaining chapters of this text, think about how you can use the tenets of constructivism to enhance the learning environment for your students.

Summary

- Piaget's work helps provide insight into how children grow intellectually. He defined the stages that children go through as they develop and the characteristics of these stages. Piaget also explained the learning process as a dynamic balance between assimilation and accommodation and a result of seeking equilibrium because of new experiences. Piaget was a developmental constructivist who viewed development as leading learning.

- Vygotsky's constructivism is a sociohistorical theory in which behavior is studied in a social and historical context. In this theory, children undergo socially mediated cognitive constructions. Psychological tools and signs assist us in semantic mediation and the development of scientific concepts. The zone of proximal development allows a child's instruction to be slightly ahead of her development. Later, what she could do with the assistance of another, she can now do on her own. Vygotsky was a sociohistorical constructivist who saw learning as leading development.

- In either constructivist theory, the curriculum is not a set of right answers and truths to be taught, rather a set of culturally accepted ideals used to guide learning. Elementary and middle school science teachers must understand the goals of the curriculum guided by science standards, the individual children in their classrooms, and how to structure the learning environment to meet these individual needs in the elementary and middle school science classroom.

Reflection

Companion CD

1. Look at the "Living Versus Nonliving Things" lesson linked to the *Planning* video on the Companion CD. Does this lesson support an inquiry approach to science teaching and learning? Support your answer with references to the science standards.
2. Look at "The Reproductive System" lesson linked to the *Moral Dimensions* video on the Companion CD. Why might the fact that earthworms are both male and female cause disequilibrium with elementary students? How could you use assimilation or accommodation to resolve this disequilibrium?
3. Look at the "Classification of Living Things" lesson linked to the *Preparing Resources* video on the Companion CD. Apply the constructivist learning model to this lesson. What changes would you make with this lesson based on the CLM?

Portfolio Ideas

1. Discuss with your classmates the following common ideas related to scientific knowledge, teaching, and learning.
   - Elementary students already have conceptions of science when they arrive at the elementary classroom.
   - Every child is a scientist.
   - Teachers and students can learn science together.
   Record your findings in your portfolio.
2. Try some Piagetian tests on children at your practicum site (see the Companion Website). What observations can you make? Record your observations and compare these with others made by students in your methods class. What do you note?
3. Discuss constructivism with a teacher at your practicum site. What is her or his viewpoint? Discuss it with your educational psychology professor. What is her or his viewpoint? The current science education research trend, or paradigm, is toward a constructivist perspective. Why do you think this is so? Mathematics educators also operate under a constructivist paradigm. What does your mathematics methods instructor have to say about constructivism? What are some views of your other methods instructors? Record your ideas in your portfolio.
4. Observe students in a classroom working together to solve a problem. Does it become clear that some students could not have completed the problem on their own? What is the teacher's role as students engage in the collaborative activity? How can you, as an outside observer, tell whether the students are learning? How will the teacher know whether learning has occurred? Share your findings with classmates and in your portfolio.

References

American Association for the Advancement of Science (AAAS). (1993). *Benchmarks for science literacy.* New York: Oxford University Press.

American Association for the Advancement of Science (AAAS). (1998). *Blueprints for reform.* New York: Oxford University Press.

Bettencourt, A. (1993). The construction of knowledge: A radical constructivist view. In K. Tobin (Ed.), *The practice of constructivism in science education* (pp. 39–50). Washington, DC: AAAS Press.

Branley, F. (1975). *Day light, night light.* New York: HarperCollins.

Branley, F. (1987). *The moon seems to change.* New York: HarperCollins.

Bybee, R. W., & Sund, R. B. (1990). *Piaget for educators* (2nd ed.). Prospect Heights, IL: Wavelend Press.

Cobern, W. W. (1993). Contextual constructivism: The impact of culture on the learning and teaching of science. In K. Tobin (Ed.), *The practice of constructivism in science education* (pp. 51–69). Washington, DC: AAAS Press.

Dewey, J. (1966). *Democracy and education.* New York: Free Press.

Dixon-Krauss, L. (1996). Vygotsky's sociohistorical perspective on learning and its application to Western literacy instruction. In L. Dixon-Krauss (Ed.), *Vygotsky in the classroom: Mediated literacy instruction and assessment* (pp. 7–24). White Plains, NY: Longman.

Driver, R. (1995). Constructivist approaches in science teaching. In L. P. Steffe & J. Gale (Eds.), *Constructivism in education* (pp. 385–400). Hillsdale, NJ: Lawrence Erlbaum Associates.

Driver, R., Asoko, H., Leach, J., Mortimer, E., & Scott, P. (1994). Constructing scientific knowledge in the classroom. *Educational Researcher, 23*(7), 5–12.

Gallas, K. (1995). *Talking their way into science: Hearing children's questions and theories, responding with curricula.* New York: Teachers College Press.

Henriques, A. (1990). Experiments in teaching. In E. Duckworth, J. Easley, D. Hawkins, & A. Henriques (Eds.), *Science education: A minds-on approach for the elementary years.* Mahwah, NJ: Lawrence Erlbaum.

Kuhn, T. (1962). *The structure of scientific revolutions* (2nd ed.). Chicago: University of Chicago Press.

Labinowicz, E. (1980). *The Piaget primer: Thinking. Learning. Teaching.* Menlo Park, CA: Addison-Wesley.

Lemke, J. L. (1993). *Talking science: Language, learning, and values.* Norwood, NJ: Ablex.

McBrien, J. L., & Brandt, R. S. (1997). *The language of learning: A guide to education terms.* Alexandria, VA: Association for Supervision and Curriculum Development.

National Research Council (NRC). (1996). *National science education standards.* Washington, DC: National Academy Press.

National Research Council (NRC). (2000). *Inquiry in the national science education standards.* Washington, DC: National Academy Press.

National Science Teachers Association (NSTA). (2003). *Beyond 2000—Teachers of science speak out. A position statement.* Washington, DC: Author. Retrieved October 1, 2004, from www.nsta.org/positionstatement&psid=17

Petersen, J. (1994). *The road to 2015.* Corte Madera, CA: Waite Group Press.

Petersen, J. (1997). *Out of the blue: Wild cards and other big future surprises—How to anticipate and respond to profound change.* Arlington, VA: Arlington Institute.

Piaget, J. (1954). *The construction of reality in the child.* New York: Basic Books.

Piaget, J., & Inhelder, B. (1969). *The psychology of the child.* New York: Basic Books.

School of Information Management and Systems University of California at Berkeley. (2003). *How much information 2003.* Berkeley, CA: Regents of the University of California. Retrieved October 1, 2004, from www.sims.berkeley.edu/research/projects/how-much-info-2003/execsum.htm#summary

Siegler, R. S. (1986). *Children's thinking.* Upper Saddle River, NJ: Prentice Hall.

Tobin, K., & Tippins, D. (1993). Constructivism as a referent for teaching and learning. In K. Tobin (Ed.), *The practice of constructivism in science education* (pp. 3–21). Washington, DC: AAAS Press.

Vygotsky, L. (1962). *Thought and language* (E. Hanfmann & G. Vakar, Eds.). Cambridge: MIT Press.

Vygotsky, L. (1978). *Mind in society: The development of higher psychological processes* (M. Cole, V. John-Steiner, S. Scribner, & E. Souberman, Eds.). Cambridge, MA: Harvard University Press.

Vygotsky, L. (1981). The genesis of higher mental functions. In J. V. Wertsch (Ed.), *The concept of activity in Soviet psychology* (pp. 144–188). Armonk, NY: Sharpe.

Vygotsky, L. S. (1986). *Thought and language* (A. Kuzulin, Ed.). Cambridge: MIT Press.

Yager, R. (1991). The constructivist learning model. *The Science Teacher, 58*(6), 52–57.

Suggested Readings

Bodrova, E., & Leong, D. J. (1996). *Tools of the mind: The Vygotskian approach to early childhood education.* Upper Saddle River, NJ: Merrill/Prentice Hall. (a guide to incorporating Vygotsky's ideas into teaching)

Brooks, J. G., & Brooks, M. G. (1993). *In search of understanding: The case for constructivist classrooms.* Alexandria, VA: Association for Supervision and Curriculum Development. (a guide to developing classrooms that encourage understanding of concepts)

Chaille, C., & Britain, L. (1991). *The young child as scientist: A constructivist approach to early childhood education.* New York: HarperCollins. (an overview of how children construct knowledge)

Dixon-Krauss, L. (Ed.). (1996). *Vygotsky in the classroom: Mediated literacy instruction and assessment.* White Plains, NY: Longman. (an overview of Vygotsky's theory, including the zone of proximal development and scaffolding)

Duckworth, E. (1987). *"The having of wonderful ideas" and other essays on teaching and learning.* New York: Teachers College Press. (a Piagetian view of education)

Tobin, K. (Ed.). (1993). *The practice of constructivism in science education.* Washington, DC: AAAS Press. (an edited compilation of the nature of constructivism and what it means for teachers)

von Glasersfeld, E. (1995). *Radical constructivism: A way of knowing and learning.* Washington, DC: Falmer Press. (a comprehensive work on radical constructivism)

CHAPTER 3

PLANNING
FOR INQUIRY

- How can you use the national standards in science program, unit, and lesson planning?
- What is involved in unit planning?
- How do you plan for inquiry-based teaching?
- What is involved in lesson planning?
- What are some planning models that support scientific inquiry?

Focus on Inquiry

Divergent Thinking Activity

Jerry Mayernik,
Northway Elementary School, North Hills School District, Pennsylvania

A thin stripe of yellow tape in the school hallway marks the starting line for the test track. In a few minutes, colorful cans of many sizes will clink, clank, and thump their way down the long, narrow test course, with students whispering encouragement to their carefully constructed devices as the cans slow down, wiggle, and begin the trip back to the starting line. At no time is science terminology, textbook pages, or vocabulary words referred to as the children test, refine, and retest their "comeback cans."

In my science class, the school year begins with a demonstration of "Herbie, the Wonder Can," a 3-pound coffee can rigged with a rubber band and a large fishing sinker inside.

 Teaching Tips Before the "comeback can" activity, you may want to use the "rolling cans" activity: Try rolling a full can of sand, an empty can, and a half-full can of sand down a ramp.

When Herbie is carefully rolled across the classroom, it magically slows, stops, and returns to its starting point. After students are shown how to construct a similar device, they are challenged to build their own comeback cans and test them against the best efforts of Herbie.

The next day, cans of all sizes and construction litter the windowsill, ready to challenge Herbie in a test of endurance.

Which can will roll the longest distance and return to the yellow stripe? After several cans traverse the track, students begin to realize that variations exist in their methods of construction. Some cans have thicker rubber bands, some thinner. Some devices are larger, some fatter, some longer. The masses inside are small, huge, and everywhere in between. Which of these variables are critical to can performance? What are the optimal can size, rubber band width, and mass? Students are encouraged to study the construction of the leading cans and to modify or refine their cans, as they like. Finally, after weeks of testing and retesting, trial and error, and elation and frustration, the top cans compete in the

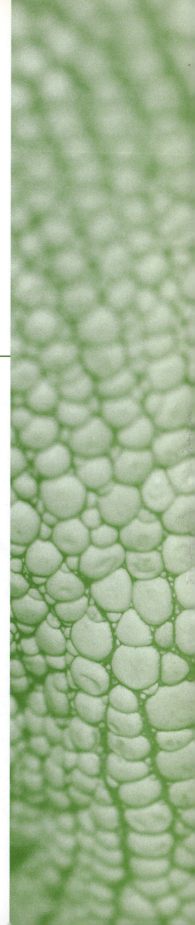

See *http://www.prenhall. com/peters* for links to the comeback can and similar activities.

Comeback Can Derby. The five winning can-builders are awarded small trophies in honor of their efforts.

This activity promotes divergent thinking. Although the comeback cans have a common construction, the task encourages a wide variety of responses. The winning cans have never been constructed in quite the same way. This activity allows students to explore, analyze, and adapt. It encourages children to attempt a novel approach (like a "Bigfoot" can, with Plexiglas "wheels" twice the diameter of other competitors'). The experience provides the "mental hooks" upon which learners will hang physics concepts in high school.

NATIONAL STANDARDS AND PLANNING

In the "Focus on Inquiry: Divergent Thinking Activity," Mr. Mayernik's class is involved in a challenging inquiry activity. How will you plan for inquiry activities in your own classroom? What considerations did Mr. Mayernik make as he prepared for this activity?

To help you think about planning and your classroom activities in a different way, envision yourself working in a manufacturing company that makes sport utility vehicles (SUVs). Your job is to assist in developing a new SUV. As you think about your new job, consider that you cannot talk with any other employees throughout the day. More experienced employees do not help you in any way. You also have to separate the workday into time periods. First, you will complete all the scientific undertakings, then the mathematical duties, some people-related responsibilities, and finally the language-type assignments. You spend the same amount of time each day on the four categories of tasks, regardless of how successful you are with any one type of task. You never spend very much time on reflection. You do not consider why the new vehicle needs to be built, whom it is being built for, or how it can be made differently. Nor do you spend any time trying to make the process or product better. You just want to meet a minimal standard for the construction of a new vehicle.

How successful will you be in your job with these constraints? Now, think how successful elementary or middle-level students will be with similar constraints. As a teacher, you assist children in constructing new knowledge. A big part of this process is planning. Good planning will produce a better automotive product just as it worked to promote inquiry with the students in Mr. Mayernik's class.

The authors of the *National Science Education Standards* (National Research Council [NRC], 1996) provide specific guidelines for how you can plan a science program. These are illustrated in the Inquiry Planning Standard shown in the Standards Link box.

As you may have determined from reading the Inquiry Planning Standard, the National Science Education Standards, like most state and district standards, provide a flexible framework for the "yearlong and short-term goals" to be taught. They recommend a general sequencing of topics from the early elementary through high school levels. As we begin to think about and apply the standards to our own planning, first we discuss the big picture of a unit plan, and then we can talk about individual lesson plans.

See *http://www.prenhall.com/peters* for links to all National Science Education Standards.

PLANNING UNITS

When you begin a unit, keep the following questions in mind.

- Is the unit based on a small number of concepts?
- Do the lessons relate to students' experiences, provide feedback about their current knowledge, and move smoothly into the first activity of each sequence?
- Are open activities included?
- Can a variety of science processes be used in the activities?
- Are the activities appropriate for the students' abilities?
- Are useful activities from other subject areas integrated into learning sequences?
- Do students apply their knowledge in assessments, or simply recall it?
- Does the unit plan allow enough time for students to learn what is proposed?

See *http://www.prenhall.com/peters* for a link to the document *Inquiry and the National Science Education Standards: A Guide for Teaching and Learning.*

In deciding how to make your units, you must know the following three things.

1. How to determine which generalizations to use
2. How to gather more activities, if needed, to teach each generalization
3. How to introduce, or bridge into, each generalization's sequence of activities

Determining Generalizations

The chapters or units of most textbooks are organized around up to 10 main generalizations or concepts. Make a tentative list of such generalizations. Then, go through the chapter to see whether your list reflects the main parts of the chapter. Change your list of generalizations as needed to match what you find in the chapter if you want to stick closely to the textbook's contents. Alternatively, you may want to supplement the chapter's concepts with other generalizations found in ancillary materials. You may also want to look for science generalizations in thematic resources. In any event, your task is to wind up with as few big ideas as possible without combining unrelated ideas. When making a unit, you need to know the generalizations in order to compile extra activities.

Whether you use text chapters or a main integrated theme as a base for a unit, it is important to think through the basic organization. This sort of analysis boosts your confidence by providing a sense of direction. It leads to the feeling that, if needed, you can make a few changes and add some ideas. It helps you decide what is important and what is not.

Finding Activities

Activities can come from a wide variety of sources, including trade books and the teacher's guide to the student science text. Many other activity books are available from the National Science Teachers Association (1840 Wilson Blvd., Arlington, VA 22201, *http://www.nsta.org/*). A series of activity books are also available from the Activities Integrating Math and Science (AIMS) Education Foundation (P.O. Box 8120, Fresno, CA

See *http://www. prenhall.com/peters* for other activity source links.

93747-8120, *http://www.aimsedu.org/*) and the Great Explorations in Math and Science (GEMS) group (Lawrence Hall of Science, University of California, Berkeley, CA 94720, *http://www.lhs.berkeley.edu/GEMS*).

How many open investigations should you plan for? The number depends greatly on the diversity of your class. Cultural diversity and disadvantaged populations in the classroom may require more experiences to make connections.

After you have researched the topic and grouped good learning activities under each generalization, arrange them in a logical teaching order. The sequence of content in the class textbook can provide the overall direction here. Remember to cluster concrete activities ahead of reading and other secondhand activities when possible.

Determining Bridges or Introductions

Now that you have located some activities for each generalization, you will need a way to introduce each of these main parts of the unit to students and move smoothly into each accompanying set of activities. Teachers call this phase "bridging" because it takes the children from where they are now to the beginning of where they need to go next.

Children use an earthquake activity as a supplement to a textbook unit on the earth's changing surface.

A useful introduction, or bridge, relates to students' experiences and current under-standings. It stimulates them to use their current constructions as you interact with them. Students' responses and questions give you insight into what the students already know about the generalization or topic to be studied, including their misconceptions. The last part of the bridge also leads into the first activity in each sequence.

You may want to introduce your students to the entire unit at one time by asking questions based on all the generalizations. Many teachers believe, however, that it is easier and more meaningful to the children to introduce only one section at a time. Of course, a brief statement about the overall unit topic should be made in any case.

Ideas for bridging into each set of activities usually can be found in the textbook, a text's teacher's edition, or an activity book. Most programs reflect the constructivist view. They are likely to begin a unit or lesson with an opportunity for the teacher to find out what children already know and relate this to what they will learn.

When supplementing a textbook unit, consider the following suggestions.

1. Thoroughly read the unit to grasp what it is about.
2. Look for places where you can use local resources.
3. Look for opportunities to integrate reading, mathematics, language, and other subjects into lessons.
4. Look for chances to use concrete activities.
5. Estimate the total time needed to teach the unit and then fit the text's lessons into the block of available time.

Some teachers feel restricted by the book format. Without the publisher's full array of multimedia resources as aids, teachers see mostly closed activities that illustrate ideas in the book rather than broad chances for real inquiry. They see relatively short, tightly controlled lessons when they want students to ask more questions and pursue strong interests over longer periods of time. These teachers are aware of some ways to augment the book unit, but for them these measures do not go far enough. They want the book to be one tool among several, rather than the main event. What they really want is a practical way to design their own multimedia unit and a format that allows them to work flexibly with their students.

See *http://www.prenhall.com/peters* for links to the *Atlas of Science Literacy* (AAAS). This document is a collection of strand maps that show how students' understanding of the ideas and skills that lead to scientific literacy grow over time.

CW

A Sample Unit

For a sample unit developed in this way, see Figure 3–1. The unit is written on index cards, which is a convenient way to keep track of generalizations, activities, and bridges. Suggestions for using the format follow.

Write one broad generalization at the top of each 5-inch by 8-inch card. This is for your reference only, not for teaching to the children. Sections of the book may be headed by problems, topics, or themes. If one seems useful, you might prefer to first write this heading, then the generalization. Next, write your sequentially arranged activities under each generalization, leaving a space for the bridge. Then write the bridge. Be sure to relate the last part of the bridge to the first activity so that you can move smoothly into it.

The use of cards has advantages. Cards can be shuffled in any desired sequence. It is easy to add and take away generalizations and activities. Special sections can be added: bulletin board ideas, news clippings, notes, whatever else is desired to make the unit complete and easier to teach.

Notice the marginal notes for science processes written next to some activities. These can remind you of what to stress in such activities. Several "open" notes serve the same function. Open activities are often the easiest and best way to meet students' individual differences in unit teaching.

Figure 3–1   Sample unit: Volcanoes.

Earth's Changing Surface

This is a fourth-grade unit on the forces that tear down and build up the earth's surface. Children also learn how rocks are formed and several ways soil is conserved. Fifteen periods of about 50 minutes each are planned for the unit. (See block plan on back of this card.)

(Front of card)

	April 6–10	April 13–17	April 20–24
Monday	Generalization I, Activity 1 (Ask class for materials for Act. 2.)	Gen. II, Act. 1	III, Act. 3 (Ask for rocks and jars Gen. IV, Act. 2, 4.)
Tuesday	I, Act. 2 (See custodian for materials for Act. 3.)	II, Act. 2	III, Act. 6, assess. (Ask for rocks and jars, IV, Act. 2, 4.)
Wednesday	I, Act. 3 (Ask class for materials for Act. 6.)	II, Act. 3 or 5	Gen. IV, Act. 1, 2
Thursday	I, Act. 4 or 5	II, Act. 4, assess.	IV, Act. 2, 3
Friday	I, Act. 5 or 6, assess. (Ask for materials for Gen. II, Act. 1, and milk cartons from cafeteria.)	Gen. III, Act. 1, 2 (Ask volunteers to bring materials for Act. 3.)	IV, Act 4, 5 assess. (Follow up on crystal growth next week.)

Order library books. Also AV materials by March 6 for I (4), II (3), III (1, 2). Phone II (5), III (4).

Gen. I. Weathering and erosion constantly wear down the earth's surface. (Class text pages 61–68.)

Bridge

How far down do you think the soil goes? What is beneath the soil? What are some ways rock may get broken up? How might broken up rocks and soil be removed? What does *weathering* mean? What is *erosion?*

Activities

(obs.)	1.	Define weathering and erosion. Tour school grounds for examples. (Open-ended.)
(exp.)	2.	Plants break rocks experiment, text p. 63. (Open-ended.)
(infer.)	3.	Dirt mountain erosion demonstration, Schmidt p. 56.
	4.	Films: Face of Earth (15 min.), Work of Rivers (10 min.).
	5.	Read text pp. 61–68 and library books. SUMMARIZE weathering and erosion forces.
(class.)	6.	Kids find and sort picture examples of forces that bring change. Display. (Open-ended.)
	7.	Haiku poetry on forces that change the earth's surface.

(Front of card)

Materials

Act. 2. Plaster of paris; bean seeds; paper cups.
Act. 3. Shovel; hose. (See custodian.)
Act. 4. MP204; MP206 (AV center).
Act. 6. *Nat'l Geographic, Arizona Highways* back issues; scissors; construction paper; paste.

Assessment

How many examples of weathering and erosion can you find on the school grounds? Find some examples we did not observe on our first tour. Make a record. Also use end-of-section questions, p. 68.

(Back of card)
(continued)

Figure 3–1 *(continued).*

Gen. II. Topsoil is composed of mineral, vegetable, and animal matter; topsoil is conserved in several ways. (Pages 69–77.)

Bridge

What are some reasons farmers might be interested in erosion? How might they guard against soil erosion? What makes up soil? Let's see for ourselves.

Activities

(class.) 1. Small-group analysis of soil samples. Sort objects found. (Open-ended.)
(exp.)   2. Plant seeds in poor and good soil samples, text p. 72. (Open-ended.)
          3. Introduce six study points on soil erosion. See "Conserving Our Soil" videotape.
          4. Read text, pages 69–77, and library books. SUMMARIZE ways to conserve soil.
          5. Possible visit by agent, Soil Conservation Service. (Practice interview and listening skills.)

(Front of card)

Materials

Act. 1. Magnifiers; old spoons; sack of good topsoil; newspapers; clean pint milk cartons.
Act. 2. Bean seeds; sack each of good and bad soil; milk cartons.
Act. 3. SP (set of 6) 117; Vid. 440.1 (AV center).
Act. 5. Bill Johnson, Soil Cons. Service, 555-6600.

Assessment

What are some ways you might prevent erosion on our school grounds? Think about the examples you found before. Discuss these ways with two partners. Then give a report.
We don't live on farms. What difference would it make to us if most farm soil erodes? Also use end-of-section questions, p. 77.

(Back of card)

Gen. III. Lava flows and crustal movements continually build up the earth's surface. (pages 77–84.)

Bridge

Does anyone know what a volcano is? What do you think makes a volcano happen? What is an earthquake? Has anyone been where there was an earthquake? Let's find out some surprising ways the earth's surface changes.

Activities

1. Film: *Earthquakes and Volcanoes* (30 min.).
2. Explore Internet for related information (25 min.).

(meas.) 3. Make clay models of volcanoes, p. 79. Also "seismograph," special project Hone, p. 28. (Art and construction.)

4. Guest speaker with northern California earthquake slides. (or locate earthquake pictures).
5. Use maps to locate active volcanoes.
6. Read text, pages 77–84, and library books. SUMMARIZE how mountains are formed.

(Front of card)

Materials

Act. 1. MP 254 (AV center).
Act. 2. Internet-connected computer.
Act. 3. Two colors of clay; newspapers; rulers; scissors. (Seismograph volunteers, check Hone book for materials.)
Act. 4. Orville McCreedy, 286-6147. (or, past *Nat'l Geographics,* 1989 issues).

Assessment

Children will construct cutaway models of volcanoes and, using the models, explain how volcanoes may happen. Also use end-of-section questions, p. 84.

(Back of card)

(continued)

Figure 3–1 *(continued)*.

Gen. IV. Three kinds of rocks are formed as the earth's surface wears down and builds up.

Bridge

Thank you for bringing so many different rocks. What makes them look different? Which of these might have come from volcanoes? How else might some have been made? Before we find out, let's see how many different properties of these rocks you can observe.

Activities

(comm.) 1. Partners do rock description game. (20 questions—lang. develop.)
(exper.) 2. Crystal growing activity, p. 91. (Open-ended.)
        3. Read text, pages 85–93, and library books.
(class.) 4. Sort rocks as to basic type, p. 90. (Open-ended.)
        5. SUMMARIZE Gen. IV and whole unit.

(Front of card)

Materials

Act. 2. Baby food jars; string; paper clips; sugar; hot plate; teakettle; newspaper.
Act. 4. Children's rock samples—stress variety; heavy paper sacks; several hammers.

Assessment

Children will be able to control the size of "rock" crystals by varying the cooling rates of hot sugar solutions.
Children will be able to identify some properties of rocks and explain how these are clues to the rock's formation.
Also use unit test questions, p. 93.

(Back of card)

Note also the specific assessment section for each of the four main parts of this unit. For generalizations I and II, assessments are stated as questions. For generalizations III and IV, they are stated as student behaviors to observe.

The next step in the planning process is to take your overall unit plan and begin to develop individual lessons. Consistent with the Inquiry Planning Standard found on page 44, individual lessons should promote inquiry in the classroom. Remember the third concept of the Inquiry Planning Standard: "Select teaching and assessment strategies that support the development of student understanding and nurture a community of science learners." To do this, we will need to plan for daily inquiry teaching.

INQUIRY TEACHING

Think back to Mr. Mayernik's comeback can activity. Remember that inquiry teaching and learning is a dynamic process. Students are naturally curious and enjoy inquiry. Your job is to further develop their ability to solve problems, transform information into meaningful knowledge, and become lifelong learners. You, as an elementary or middle school teacher, can convert your classroom into a better learning environment through a variety of inquiry activities. Table 3–1 shows the diversity of inquiry tasks available to you as you plan your activities.

Teacher-Directed Versus Learner-Directed Activities

You will find that variations in the far left column of Table 3–1 require more direction from you as a teacher. They have only one correct answer or one specific pathway to an answer. Variations to the right in Table 3–1 are less teacher directed and more learner centered. These variations are increasingly divergent. They will have more than one answer or pathway to an answer. Let's look at an example. In the following scenarios, both teachers are planning to teach about **food chains.** See whether you notice any differences.

Food chains refer to the organisms in an ecological community that provide a continuation of food energy from one organism to the next as each one consumes a lower member in the chain and is, in turn, preyed upon by a higher member in the chain.

Visit an Inquiry Classroom
Learner-Centered Teaching

View the *Active Learning* video in the "Constructivist Pedagogy" section of the Companion CD. Mr. McKnight, in an active learning situation, questions students about their findings related to earthworms. They are sharing their ideas and proposing explanations and solutions about earthworms consistent with the constructivist learning model.

Review the video and ask yourself the following:
- Why would this video segment be considered an illustration of learner-centered teaching when the teacher is asking questions?
- We suggest that learner self-direction is high in this community of science learners. Do you agree or disagree? Support your viewpoint with specific examples from the video and Table 3–1.

What learner-directed activities have you seen in your field placements? Have you seen any teacher-directed activities that could be changed into learner-directed activities? Explain how these activities could become more learner centered. Record your ideas and the answers to these questions in your portfolio or use the Companion Website to share your ideas.

Table 3–1

Essential Features of Classroom Inquiry and Their Variations

Essential Feature	Variations			
Learner	Self-Direction: Less ──────────────────────────→ More			
Learner engages in scientifically oriented questions	• Learner engages in question provided by teacher, materials, or other source	• Learner sharpens or clarifies question provided by teacher, materials, or other source	• Learner selects among questions, poses new questions	• Learner poses a question
Learner gives priority to evidence in responding to questions	• Learner given data and told how to analyze	• Learner given data and asked to analyze	• Learner directed to collect certain data	• Learner determines what constitutes evidence and collects it
Learner formulates explanations from evidence	• Learner provided with evidence	• Learner given possible ways to use evidence to formulate explanation	• Learner guided in process of formulating explanations from evidence	• Learner formulates explanation after summarizing evidence
Learner connects explanations to scientific knowledge		• Learner given possible connections	• Learner directed toward areas and sources of scientific knowledge	• Learner independently examines other resources and forms the links to explanations
Learner communicates and justifies explanations	• Learner given steps and procedures for communication	• Learner given broad guidelines to sharpen communication	• Learner coached in development of communication	• Learner forms reasonable and logical argument to communicate explanations
Less ↔	Amount of *Learner* Self-Direction		↔	More
More ↔	Amount of Direction from *Teacher* or Material		↔	Less

Source: Adapted from *Inquiry and the National Science Education Standards: A Guide for Teaching and Learning* (p. 29). Copyright © 2000 by the National Academy of Sciences. Courtesy of the National Academy Press, Washington, DC.

Teacher-Directed Example

Mrs. Steen plans her activities to begin with reading *The Magic School Bus Gets Eaten* (Cole, 1996). This story gains student interest and initiates discussion. Next, she asks her students to list the plants and animals found in the story. The students list these in their notebooks. Now, she directs the students to arrange the organisms according to a food chain illustrated on the chalkboard. The students list phytoplankton, zooplankton, anchovies, tuna, and people as a food chain. Mrs. Steen then asks about the source of energy for the food chain.

In this example, students are engaging in questions and activities directed by the teacher. Learner self-direction is low, and teacher direction is high (see Table 3–1).

Learner-Directed Example

Mr. Mitchell plans his lesson to start with reading *What Do You Do When Something Wants to Eat You?* (Jenkins, 1997). The students read about how certain fish, reptiles, amphibians, and other animals escape danger. Mr. Mitchell asks why the animals need to defend themselves in the examples provided in the book. The students respond in a variety of ways, and Mr. Mitchell allows them to ask about examples of animal defenses not found in this story. Soon, students are posing questions about why animals would want to eat one another. Mr. Mitchell continues the lesson by reading *Who Eats What?* (Lauber, 1995). Various food chains are described in the book. The students give other possible examples when prompted by Mr. Mitchell about what food chains may have been a part of their dinners last night.

As the discussion continues, the students come to realize that there are many kinds of food chains, that food chains are part of food webs, that plants are the basis of a food chain, and that the sun is an important part of every food chain. Learners are more self-directed in this example, often asking new questions or providing a variety of answers. The teacher direction is low, as is reflected in Table 3–1.

Convergent and Divergent Questions

In Mrs. Steen's teacher-directed lesson, inquiry is generally focused on one correct answer, such as the sun being the ultimate source of energy. Students are provided specific examples and **convergent questions** related to the food chains for plants and animals. The problem that students are working on is considered closed. Closed problems and activities foster convergent thinking. They converge on a common single response.

Mr. Mitchell's learner-centered lesson encourages students to seek many answers. The correct response is considered open because there is more than one possibility for a correct answer. Students in Mr. Mitchell's class answer **divergent questions** based on their understanding that there are a variety of food chains and these food chains play a key role in ecosystems. Open problems and activities lead to a wide variety of responses and produce divergent thinking. With open problems, answers and other possible experiences diverge from one initial experience, question, or problem. A balance of both open and closed problems and activities are needed for scientific inquiry during the elementary and middle school years.

Convergent questions are asked with predetermined answers in mind.

Divergent questions do not have single answers, are used to promote discussion, and allow for creative thinking.

Closed Activities

Closed activities tend to be short and tightly focused. Open activities are usually longer and branch out into many related questions. Both are appropriate to use in inquiry teaching; however, closed and open activities differ in other ways. To see how, let's study each type in more depth. We begin with some common closed activities involving children. In each case, the students are active; they do things.

Grade 2 Example

In Mrs. Imat's second-grade class, children work on the "Mouth Map" activity from the book *Gobble Up Science* (Johmann & Rieth, 1996). Using sugar, salt, tonic water, and lemon juice, they find the taste buds on their tongues: The tips of their tongues sense sweet, the back of their tongues sense bitter, and they discover salty and sour taste buds on the sides. The activity ends with children discovering what Mrs. Imat knew they would experience.

Grade 4 Example

The AIMS-produced *Fun with Foods* book contains many other food activities that can be adapted for use in the elementary and middle school grades.

In Ms. Bagui's fourth-grade class, children are learning about acids and bases with the "Red-Cabbage Indicator" activity found in the book *Science Experiments You Can Eat* (Cobb, 1994). They find that cabbage juice solution is an indicator and changes color, depending on whether the substance is an acid or a base.

Grade 6 Example

In a sixth-grade class, Mr. Uvah's adolescents learn about variables through the "Popcorn Comparison" activity in *Fun with Foods: A Recipe for Math + Science* (Alfving et al., 1987). Students find that the moisture content of popcorn kernels has an effect on the volume of popped corn that is produced.

Notice that each of these closed activities illustrates some idea or procedure with concrete materials. Working with concrete materials helps the children to form realistic concepts and learn useful investigative techniques. Once a closed activity has made its point, there is no need to continue. Closed activities, when taught well, help children construct a solid subject-matter background that is rooted in experience and often lays the foundation for more open inquiry.

Open Activities

As noted earlier, open activities are usually longer and branch out into many related questions. Students are provided multiple pathways to learning. Let's look at some examples.

Grade 2 Example

Mrs. Bell places a few food items, some balloons, and various other items such as beakers and jars on a table and challenges her second-grade students to blow up a balloon by using the food. This activity is based on the "Blowing Up a Balloon with a Banana" activity found in *Icky, Squishy Science* (Markle, 1996). The activity is a result of informal class discussions after finishing a weather unit by reading *Cloudy with a Chance of Meatballs* (Barrett, 1978) and its sequel, *Pickles to Pittsburgh* (Barrett, 1997). Students were discussing things food could do other than be digested. Mrs. Bell challenged them to try blowing up a balloon with the food items provided. Later, the students will discover some properties of food, including the presence of bacteria.

Food activities are excellent ways to introduce diversity and multiculturalism to elementary and middle school students.

Grade 4 Example

In his fourth-grade class, Mr. Pettis allows students to discover their own ways to cure meat, based on suggestions from the books *More Science Experiments You Can Eat* (Cobb, 1979) and *Silly Science* (Levine & Johnstone, 1995). The students complete this activity based on questions originating with the reading of *Stone Soup* (Brown, 1997), *Eating the Plates* (Penner, 1991), *Corn Is Maize* (Aliki, 1976), and other stories. Their study of the foods eaten by Pilgrims and American Indians generated possible discovery activities that could promote further inquiry.

Use of Open Activities

Most exemplary teachers provide a foundation and then encourage children to try their own ideas about how to investigate and organize objects or events. This is seen in Mr. Mayernik's

"Focus on Inquiry: Divergent Thinking Activity" at the beginning of the chapter. Students are allowed to discover things for themselves. When students are given some autonomy, some suggestions lead to others and there is almost no end to what may be investigated.

Open activities allow students to study objects and events in two very useful ways: (1) observe similarities and differences in the properties of things, and (2) discover conditions that can produce or change properties (thus the name *discovery learning*).

Note the contrast in this pair of questions:

What materials will rust?
In what ways can you get some objects to rust?

When children examine the properties of comparable things, they learn that properties usually exist in varying degrees. As students inspect these variable degrees of properties, they will observe, describe, contrast, measure, and classify them. This is why open-ended investigations of things with comparable properties are so well suited for intuitive-level students and others who lack experience with the materials being examined. A common way to facilitate open activities is through the guided discovery approach.

PLANNING LESSONS

Teacher education students are exposed to lesson planning early in their professional preparation. Planning is an important component of science education. How will you plan a lesson? Will you simply write a page number from a teacher's guide? What are some ways to plan more effectively?

Developing a Lesson Plan

Many models for planning a lesson have been designed. The "objectives, materials, procedure, and evaluation of students" general format is an example of one type of lesson plan. Figure 3–2 presents an enhanced format. It is designed to help you think about the science lesson in a new way. It challenges the teacher to look at the activities from multiple perspectives.

The first part of the lesson model includes an overview of the lesson in your own words, as well as lesson topic, a specific grade level, any curricular objectives, and applicable performance objectives. In this area are the science themes. These originate in the benchmarks (AAAS, 1993). Science themes are needed to see the so-called big picture of science and how the lesson fits into the themes. Specifically, your lesson should support the development of one or more common science themes. These include systems, models, consistency, evolution, scale, and patterns of change. For each lesson, consider how you address one or more of these themes.

Next, provide any applicable standards or benchmarks. Use the *National Science Education Standards,* the *Benchmarks for Science Literacy,* your state standards, or any district standards that may apply.

Scientific process skills—such as classification, observation, measurement, inference, prediction, communicating, and experimentation—should also be addressed as part of the contextual framework. The last thing to consider as part of the contextual framework is the curricular integrations. Think about various ways to integrate social studies, language arts, reading, mathematics, art, music, or physical education into the lesson.

See *http://www.prenhall.com/peters* for a link to the science themes from *Science for All Americans* (1989) by the American Association for the Advancement of Science.

Figure 3–2   Inquiry lesson plan format.

Overview of the Lesson

Science Themes (From *Science for All Americans,* 1989, AAAS)

Standards (Use appropriate standards or benchmarks based on local requirements)
- Science Benchmarks (From *Benchmarks for Science Literacy,* 1993, AAAS)
- Science Standards (From *National Science Education Standards,* 1996, NRC)
- State Science Standards
- District Science Standards

Scientific Process Skills
Curricular Integrations

Materials
Supplies (what, how many, how much, etc.)
Equipment

Procedure
Steps to Follow or Problem to Solve
Closed or Open Questions

Assessment
Student Assessment
Teacher Assessment

Bibliography
Sources for Content Information and Children's Literature

Source: Adapted from Briscoe, Peters, & O'Brien, An elementary program emphasizing teachers' pedagogical content knowledge within a constructivist epistemological rubric. In *Excellence in Educating Teachers of Science,* P. Rubba, L. Campbell, & T. Dana (Eds.). Copyright © 1993 by ERIC Clearinghouse, Columbus, OH.

Materials

The second section in the lesson plan is a listing of materials. Both consumable and non-consumable supplies and equipment should be listed here. Remember to list materials for the teacher demonstration and student participation.

Procedure

The procedure of a direct instruction lesson plan is very specific, whereas a problem-centered lesson will be more generalized in its procedure. A guided discovery lesson is a blend of the two types of lessons. A direct instruction lesson has numbered steps logically arranged to meet time and curricular requirements. Write out and follow every step so that you do not forget anything. Give careful thought to what you want to say and do during the class period. Write these thoughts in an expanded outline form. Specific teacher questions can also be placed here. This ensures that you will not forget to ask something important. In a problem-centered lesson, the procedure may simply be a listing of the problem to solve and sample approaches to a solution.

Visit an Inquiry Classroom
Lesson Materials

View the *Finding and Organizing Materials* video in the "Planning and Management" section of the Companion CD. Mr. McKnight organized his classroom to maximize available workspace and traffic flow. Behind the scenes, he carefully selects appropriate materials and has these available for students in accessible locations. He then arranges the students in workgroups.

Review the video and ask yourself the following:
- How does Mr. McKnight manage the class and materials to ensure that students have what they need to carry out the activities?
- What is the role of the "materials person"?

 Have you observed a teacher engaging students in a lesson involving science materials and/or equipment? Describe the activity and materials and/or equipment needed. How did the teacher manage these materials? Record your ideas and the answers to these questions in your portfolio or use the Companion Website to share your ideas.

Visit an Inquiry Classroom
Pacing a Lesson

View the *Pacing and Time Allocation* video in the "Planning and Management" section of the Companion CD. As Mr. McKnight finishes a science lesson, he allows time for cleanup and begins to ask students about what activities would be appropriate in the future. He provides students with a preview of what they will do in the next lesson.

Review the video and ask yourself the following:
- Given the limited time for science in a busy school day, how can a teacher most effectively plan lessons that include investigations such as the earthworm activities Mr. McKnight plans?
- What is Mr. McKnight's perspective on the limited amount and use of time in the classroom? How does this compare to your view?

Look at a lesson plan used by a teacher in your field placement. How does this lesson's procedure compare with the one described in the text or with Mr. McKnight? Why would there be differences, if any? Record your ideas and the answers to these questions in your portfolio or use the Companion Website to share your ideas.

Assessment

Next, a lesson plan must address assessment. How will you assess your students? Chapter 5 provides an in-depth view on student assessment. Teacher self-assessment should also be considered in this section of the lesson plan, especially for beginning teachers who need to practice reflecting on their instruction. You may want to videotape or audiotape the lesson, have a peer teacher or administrator observe the lesson, seek student feedback in some way, write personal observations in a journal, or use a school-based assessment form.

Bibliography

The lesson plan concludes with a bibliography. All sources used in planning should be listed here, including audiovisual support, computer-based tools, and applicable Internet links. Also include any fiction or nonfiction literature you will make available to students. The Lesson Model: The Planets on page 62 provides an example of a lesson plan.

Visit an Inquiry Classroom
Student Feedback

View the *Feedback* video in the "Planning and Management" section of the Companion CD. Mr. McKnight first uses questioning as a way to check for understanding before continuing with his lesson.

Review the video and ask yourself the following:
- What other ways does Mr. McKnight assess students?
- Is all feedback a form of assessment? Why or why not?

 Does your science methods professor use feedback? Does the professor also provide ongoing assessment? What are some specific examples? Record your ideas and the answers to these questions in your portfolio or use the Companion Website to share your ideas.

Visit an Inquiry Classroom
Planning Integrations

The *Thematic Plan and Integration* video in the "Planning and Management" section of the Companion CD shows students exploring *Your Gross and Cool Body* (*http://yucky.kids. discovery.com/flash/body/*). This videoclip is an expansion of the "Worm World" activities that they were completing as part of their class project (*http://yucky.kids.discovery.com/ flash/ worm/index.html*). Both sites are located at the Discovery Communications *Yuckiest Site on the Internet* (*http://yucky.kids.discovery.com/flash/index.html*). Students will be able to expand their science activities to writing activities about their own body functions as they relate to worms.

See *http://www.prenhall. com/peters* for links related to the use of children's literature in science.

Review the video and ask yourself the following:
- In what other ways could this website be used to expand the earthworm activities?
- Could the "Roach World" (*http://yucky.kids.discovery.com/flash/roaches/*) also be used?

 What other integrations can you think of for an earthworm lesson? Record your ideas and the answers to these questions in your portfolio or use the Companion Website to share your ideas.

Lesson Model
The Planets
(Direct Instruction Lesson Plan Example)

Overview of the Lesson

This lesson centers on the names of the nine planets and their relationship to the sun. The students will be asked to name the planets in order, give an approximation of their size, and be able to understand the concept of a satellite of a planet.

Science Themes

Systems —The solar system is a common example of a system. It is a group of planets and their satellites. It also includes solid, liquid, and gaseous material in an interrelated organization.
Models —The idea of a model is established as students create models of the solar system.
Consistency —The planets rotate in consistent patterns in the solar system.
Patterns of Change —Patterns of change are modeled as stars are formed and the visibility of planets changes throughout the year.
Evolution —There is a lot of verified data on the evolution of the solar system. The launching of new spacecraft to study the solar system and beyond brings relevancy to this topic.
Scale —Scale is established as the various sizes of the planets are compared.

Benchmarks for Science Literacy

By the end of fifth grade, students should know that

- Planets change their positions against the background of stars.
- Earth is one of several planets that orbit the sun, and the moon orbits the Earth. (AAAS, 1993, p. 63)

National Science Education Standards

As a result of their activities in grades K–4, all students should develop an understanding of

- Objects in the sky
- Changes in Earth and the sky (NRC, 1996, p. 130)

Scientific Skills

Classification —Classification activities are promoted as students develop classification systems for the planets (by composition, temperature, and size).
Observation —The students will observe the night sky and record data.
Measurement —The students will measure and re-create a scale model of the solar system.
Inference/Prediction —The students will infer why the temperature of Venus is high, based on that planet's characteristics.

Curricular Integrations

Measurement activities integrate *mathematics* into this lesson.
Art is incorporated into this lesson as students draw planet and star models.
Social studies is integrated into this lesson as students discuss ancient theories of an Earth-centered solar system.
Reading is integrated into this lesson as students read *The Magic School Bus Lost in the Solar System* (Cole, 1990).

Materials

Supplies

Large sheets of paper; crayons, markers, or paints.

(continued)

Equipment

Inflatable planetarium (two large sheets of black painter's plastic with both sides taped together lengthwise to form a large dome). A box fan is taped to one end and turned on to inflate the dome.

Procedure

Steps to Follow

1. Introduce the vocabulary: *Mercury, Venus, Earth, Mars, Jupiter, Saturn, Uranus, Neptune, Pluto, moon, satellite, orbit, asteroid, rotation,* and *revolution.* (Use definitions from end of the chapter and have students repeat the words. Write the definitions on the overhead for them to copy.)
2. Read the chapter on the planets from the student text. Discuss origins of the solar system. Read *The Magic School Bus Lost in the Solar System.*
3. Demonstrate the relative distances between planets by creating a model with students acting as the sun, planets, and satellites (see specific measurements in the text).
4. Demonstrate the rotation of Earth and the moon and their revolution around the sun by using students to represent the sun, Earth, and the moon (see picture in supplemental materials).

Closed Questions

A. What is the center of the solar system? Describe its characteristics.

B. What is the first planet from the sun? Describe its characteristics. (Repeat for the rest of the planets.) What is the difference between the moon and a satellite? (Note: The moon is Earth's satellite. We call other moons by their proper name, *satellite.*)

C. Define an orbit.

Open Questions

A. Which planets are colder? What is a possible cause for their low temperature?

B. Give some possible reasons for Venus being so hot. (Discuss greenhouse effects.)

5. Develop three planet classifications (Monday).
6. Redraw the scale model of the planets from the text, measuring exactly from the book (Tuesday).
7. Draw a picture of the night sky (Wednesday).
8. Find pictures of the winter and summer night sky from other books and magazines (Thursday).
9. Take students into the planetarium and demonstrate the position of the stars and planets by using the portable star projector (Friday).

Additional Homework Activities (select one)

10. Research what causes eclipses of the sun or moon.
11. If you started today and traveled 1000 miles per hour to Jupiter, determine how old you would be when you reached your destination (see adaptation of AIMS activity from *Out of This World*) (Lind et al., 1994).
12. Most people incorrectly believe that the distance from the Northern or Southern Hemisphere of the Earth to the sun causes the seasons. Research the real cause of the seasons.
13. Research the planets on NASA Internet sites.
14. Research and discuss why the International Astronomical Union, the official body for naming astronomical objects, would want to reclassify Pluto as a "trans-Neptunium asteroid" instead of a planet.

Assessment

Student Assessment

1. Design a mnemonic sentence to remember the order of planets (e.g., My Very Excellent Mother Just Served Us Nine Pizzas).
2. Describe in your journal what life would be like on Jupiter. How would it compare to life on the moon?
3. Write to NASA for more information on space exploration and present it to the class.

Teacher Assessment

Videotape the lesson and review it at home.

Bibliography

Branley, F. M. (1987). *The planets in our solar system*. New York: Thomas Crowell.

Cole, J. (1990). *The magic school bus lost in the solar system*. New York: Scholastic.

Lauber, P. (1982). *Journey to the planets*. New York: Crown Publishers Inc.

Lauber P. (1990). *Seeing the Earth from space*. New York: Orchard Books.

Lind, M., Knecht, P., Dodge, B., Williams, A., & Wiebe, A. (1994). *Out of this world*. Fresno, CA: AIMS Education Foundation.

National Geographic Society (Producer). (1987). *The planets* [laserdisc]. Washington, DC: National Geographic Society.

Scholastic. (1994). *The magic school bus explores the solar system* [CD-ROM]. Redmond, WA: Microsoft Corporation.

INSTRUCTIONAL LESSON MODELS FOR INQUIRY TEACHING

Inquiry is seen as a teaching and learning method where students "develop knowledge and understanding of scientific ideas, as well as an understanding of how scientists study the natural world" (National Research Council, 1996, p. 23). Although there are various ways to develop understandings, all inquiry methodologies have essential features as identified by the National Research Council (2000) and shown in Table 3–1. These include the learner doing the following:

- Engaging in scientifically oriented questions
- Giving priority to evidence
- Formulating explanations
- Connecting explanations to scientific knowledge
- Communicating and justifying explanations

As we explore methodologies such as direct instructions learning, guided discovery learning, and problem-centered learning, see if you can identify the NRC's characteristics of inquiry.

Direct Instruction

A common way to engage in closed activities is through **direct instruction.** Direct instruction generally involves carefully sequenced steps that include demonstration, modeling, guided practice, and independent application (Lokerson, 1992). In direct instruction, the teacher employs lectures, worksheets, recitations, demonstrations, or specific-answer type questions in a prearranged sequence. A detailed lesson plan is generally used for a direct instruction experience. The teacher is in control of the lesson and true student inquiry is limited.

Direct instruction is a teacher-centered, well-structured approach to teaching.

Advantages to Using Direct Instruction

One advantage to direct instruction is that the teacher can arrange the sequence of activities ahead of time and thus reduce the number of teaching decisions to be made during a lesson. This is especially helpful for inexperienced teachers who are preoccupied with activity or classroom management issues or who want to be sure they cover a certain curriculum. It is also helpful when introducing a new skill such as classification or engaging children or adolescents in the use of a new piece of science equipment. Direct instruction can also be useful when safety issues must take precedent over student exploration.

A more important advantage is that direct instruction can be used to help students construct a knowledge base for future learning. As noted by Tweed (2004): "Teachers must teach students an experimental design process before students can be asked to conduct their own experiments when studying science concepts . . . Teaching an experimental design process often occurs using an exploratory experiment or using direct instruction, but the teacher should guide the process."

When teaching through a direct approach, teachers can spend as much time as needed to plan beforehand. This allows them to think through which analogies, metaphors, activities, and questions will best support the concept they want to develop before the lesson. The direct approach also allows instruction to continue systematically until the teacher feels comfortable that most students understand some basic concept.

Disadvantages to Direct Instruction

One disadvantage to direct instruction is that students construct their knowledge at an individual pace. Therefore, the teacher's pace may not match the pace of each student. Also, students learn to perform science activities more remotely and are not free to explore topics further on their own. They are subject to what the teacher selects as themes or important concepts. Problem solving and higher order thinking skills are better developed through more independent learning experiences.

Another disadvantage of direct or teacher-centered instruction is that the teacher may have gender, cultural, or other biases that will limit learning for some students. In other words, the students are subject to everything from the teacher's point of view—not their own. For example, if the teacher unconsciously believes that boys are better suited for science than girls, he may call on boys more often to answer a question or to assist in a demonstration. This behavior reinforces the cultural disadvantage girls have in the sciences (Kahle & Meece, 1994).

In review, direct instruction is a method of learning that involves closed activities. Outcomes are predictable and specific. Children follow someone else's ideas or procedures. What should you do to promote children's ideas? To boost children's thinking processes, independence, and creativity, you should offer more open experiences such as guided discovery learning.

See *http://www.prenhall. com/peters* for links related to promoting activities that encourage girls to engage in science learning.

Guided Discovery Learning

Guided discovery learning is a less teacher-oriented and more student-oriented instructional method. It would fall midpoint in the classroom inquiry continuum found in Table 3–1. In this approach, students are guided in exploration of materials. They observe phenomena, gather data on their own, make comparisons, draw inferences, and arrive at conclusions. Teachers follow up on what has been discovered and point out any misconceptions. Students are then free to explore once again. This method is especially valuable in making connections between science vocabulary and scientific concepts.

Remember the lesson plan components from Figure 3–2 on p. 58. The same general procedures are used here as well. Students are provided time to discover concepts based on initial information. In guided discovery, follow-up discussion and questioning is crucial. The direct instruction approach spells out exactly what is to be learned. Guided discovery, in contrast, allows students more time to explore on their own.

In guided discovery activities, it is crucial to follow up after student exploration and determine whether the students have made correct assumptions. The following Lesson Model presents a guided discovery lesson for electricity.

Problem-Centered Learning

Problem-centered learning moves us even further from teacher-control to learner-control lesson models (refer back to Table 3–1). Now, students become more involved in the planning and implementation of lessons. Following the development of an initial question, students continue their investigation until they solve a problem.

> **Problem-centered learning** is a method of teaching and learning that focuses on children's ability to construct their own meaning for concepts.

Start with a Problem

In *Science for All Americans* (AAAS, 1989), there is a message to all science teachers that good teaching starts with questions about nature or explorations of phenomena that are interesting to students and at their level. The authors go on to say that as students become familiar with the things around them, they will begin to question and find answers to these questions. This idea is at the very heart of problem solving in elementary and middle school science. Children are very inquisitive during the elementary and middle school years. Promoting and developing this inherent trait will provide lifelong skills in solving everyday problems. One way to increase problem-solving ability is through problem-centered learning.

Through problem-centered activities, children learn to view science as a meaningful, dynamic activity. They see science as a human endeavor in which they can participate. You will notice that the lesson plan is similar to the other lesson plans, except that its procedure section contains a problem for the students to solve, as opposed to a specific procedure. Generally, a problem-centered lesson will also have more open questions, because the teacher is not presenting specific concepts or definitions that are repeated by the students.

> See *http://www.prenhall.com/peters* for links related to *Blueprints for Reform* (AAAS, 1998).

Problem-Centered Learning: Making Science Relevant

It may not come as a surprise to you that elementary and middle school teachers see a value in their students learning science. What you may not understand is why these same teachers do not teach more science throughout the week. One reason commonly given is increasing pressure from parents and administrators to have students score high on standardized reading and math tests. One way to satisfy both worlds is to teach more science without detracting from reading and mathematics. In other words, integrate other content areas with science as suggested by the National Science Teachers Association (NSTA, 2003) and the authors of the Science Program Standard in the Standards Link box.

Standards Link

Science Program Standard

The program of study in science for all students should be developmentally appropriate, interesting, and relevant to students' lives; emphasize student understanding through inquiry; and be connected with other school subjects.

- **The program of study should include all of the content standards.**

- **Science content must be embedded in a variety of curriculum patterns that are developmentally appropriate, interesting, and relevant to students' lives.**

- **The program of study must emphasize student understanding through inquiry.**

- **The program of study in science should connect to other school subjects.**

(Program Standard B, National Research Council, 1996, p. 212.)

Lesson Model
Guided Discovery Lesson Plan for Electricity

Overview of the Lesson

Electricity has become very important to modern humans. The commonplace nature of electricity makes it an excellent topic of discovery in the elementary or middle school classroom.

Science Themes

Systems —The activity requires the investigator to create a system that includes a power source, a power transmission, and a power consumer.

Models —This activity is done on a small scale but is representative of a much larger system. Through the creation of series and parallel circuits, students will be better able to understand how/where electricity is generated, transported, and used.

Consistency —Electrical systems require consistency. Dry/wet cells are designed to provide a constant voltage so that a device is not damaged by surges or suppressions in current. Likewise, the power derived at power stations requires a feedback system of substations, switching devices, transformers, and monitors to ensure that constant voltage is maintained.

Patterns of Change —Power generation undergoes many changes as new technologies are created to maximize the amount of energy produced from fossil fuels while limiting harmful effects to the environment. Nuclear and solar technologies are changing the way electricity is generated. Batteries are also changing as new materials are being tried to create longer lasting, more powerful, rechargeable, less expensive batteries.

Evolution —The production and use of electricity may have important evolutionary significance. Animals, including humans, may undergo evolutionary change in response to electromagnetic fields, or may have already changed in response to the availability of light and heat from electricity.

Scale —Scale is inherent to a study of electricity. Large-scale generators and transformers produce high-voltage electricity at power stations. Next, the power is transmitted through high-tension lines to substations. From the substations, electricity is scaled down and sent to neighborhoods, where it is again stepped down into a usable voltage for home use. Generally, a house has three wires coming into it. One is a common ground and two are hot wires, at 110 volts each. From there, electricity may go to electrical appliances, where it is further scaled, or transformed, into a much lower voltage, such as 9 volts.

Benchmarks for Science Literacy

By the end of fifth grade, students should be able to

- Make safe electrical connections with various plugs, sockets, and terminals. (AAAS, 1993, p. 293)

National Science Education Standards

As a result of the activities in grades K–4, all students should develop an understanding of

- Light, heat, electricity, and magnetism. (NRC, 1996, p. 123)

Scientific Skills

Classification —Students will be able to classify various types of circuits into either series or parallel.

Observation —Students will observe the various ways that light (or do not light) the bulb.

Measurement —Students check individual batteries to ensure that they are producing a current.

Inference/Prediction —Students will predict various ways to light the bulbs and then test the predictions. Students will infer that their house circuit is a parallel circuit as they discover the differences between the two circuits.

Communication —Communication skills will be developed as students interact in small groups to solve the problem. Communication of results will also occur as groups share their findings.

Experimenting —Students will have to identify the variables that cause the bulb to light up. They will also explore relationships among the batteries, wires, and bulbs. Students will construct hypotheses about the differences between series and parallel circuits. They will have to design a solution to the batteries and bulbs problem.

Curricular Integrations

In *language arts,* numerous stories and poems are based on electricity themes. Most children have experienced the lack of electricity in their homes at one time or another, opening up possibilities for creating short stories.

In *mathematics,* experiences can be related to meter readings/billing and electrical usage, comparisons of electrical usage among appliances, and measuring voltages.

Art can be incorporated into an electricity activity in a variety of ways. Students can draw pictures of their experiences during an electrical blackout.

Music could become part of the lesson as a discussion of how instruments have evolved through the use of electricity.

Social studies is important to the study of electricity. American communities all depend on electricity. A comparison between cultures based on the availability of electricity is important.

Safety is vital to any discussion of electricity. Local power companies are excellent sources for materials on safety topics.

Materials

Supplies

Light bulb–shaped paper for student stories; pamphlets on safety precautions about electricity.

Equipment

Class set of batteries, wires, and bulbs.

Procedure

Steps to Follow

1. The introductory activity/advance organizer includes stories and poems based on electrical themes as a way to introduce the topic. A brief discussion of power outages will also be done as appropriate.
2. The first activity is to light the bulb. Students are provided one battery, one wire, and one light bulb and are instructed to design an investigation that individually would result in lighting the bulb. Guide them in defining a complete circuit and explain the path of electricity through the bulb, if necessary. Remind them that the electrons have to go into and back out of the light bulb for it to function.

Closed Questions for Lighting the Bulb

A. What do you notice about the light bulb? (It has a base, filament, and glass enclosure.)
B. What makes the bulb light? (Electrons flow through the filament.)

Open Questions for Lighting the Bulb

A. What were some probable ways that the light bulb was invented?
B. What are some creative ways to light a bulb?

Steps to Follow (continued)

3. The second activity is to create a circuit with two dimly lit bulbs and another circuit with two brightly lit bulbs. Students are provided two light bulbs, one battery, and four or more wires to produce a series and parallel circuit. Note that the materials only provide for one circuit to be produced at a time. Once the first one is designed, students will have to diagram the finding and then continue with the other circuit. Provide the following diagram if necessary.

(continued)

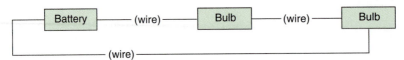

Series Circuit

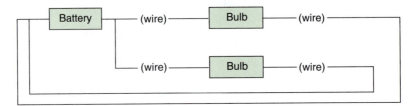

Parallel Circuit

Closed Questions on Circuits

    A.   How are the lights in this room wired? (parallel)
    B.   What happens to the old-style Christmas tree twinkle lights when a bulb is removed? (They all go out because it is a series circuit.)

Open Questions on Circuits

    A.   Why do you think buildings are wired in parallel instead of series circuits?
    B.   What are some ways to create a parallel circuit?

Steps to Follow (continued)

    4.   Science/Technology/Society extension activity on determining appliance power consumption and reading a power meter from power company handout. Discuss how cultures rely on energy.
    5.   Discuss how electricity is produced and various types of fuel. Discuss the impact on the environment (thermal pollution from steam cooling, greenhouse effect from giving off carbon dioxide, acid rain from burning sulfur, electromagnetic fields from electricity transmission).

Closed Questions on Electricity Production

    A.   What form of fuel does our local power company use?

Open Questions on Electricity Production

    A.   If we were to close down all the electrical generation plants that use fossil fuels, what impact would that have on society?
    B.   What are some ways people could conserve energy?
    C.   How did you feel when the power was out last time? How did it change your life?

Assessment

Student Assessment

    1.   Students will complete a written story based on their experiences with electricity.
    2.   Students will go to a hardware store and check types of wire and fuse boxes to determine which would be most appropriate for their house.
    3.   Students will actually make a series and parallel circuit (light the bulbs).
    4.   Students will interview family and friends to see which type of fuel (fossil, solar, nuclear) they prefer when generating electricity and why.
    5.   Students will record in their science notebooks the various ways they lit the bulbs.

Teacher Assessment

Invite a peer teacher to come into the room and observe questioning technique, particularly with regard to teacher dominance of questions versus students' independent inquiry.

Bibliography

Bains, R. (1982). *Discovering electricity.* Mahway, NJ: Troll.
Berger, M. (1989). *Switch on, switch off.* New York: Franklin Watts.
Fife, J. (1996). *Watered-down electricity: Using water to explain electricity.* Huntington, WV: University Editions.
Gosnell, K. (1994). *Thematic unit: Electricity.* Huntington Beach, CA: Teacher Created Materials.
Johnston, T. (1988). *Energy: Making it work.* Milwaukee, WI: Gareth Stevens.
Markle, S. (1989). *Power up: Experiments, puzzles, and games exploring electricity.* New York: Antheneum.
Mayes, S. (1989). *Where does electricity come from?* Tulsa, OK: EDC Publishing.
Siegel, B. M., & Stone, A. H. (1970). *Turned on: A look at electricity.* Englewood Cliffs, NJ: Prentice Hall.

Benefits of a Problem-Centered Approach

When science is done in an integrated, problem-centered format, children begin to value science because they see its relevance. They can read about science in an interesting context. Science activities based on literature build on familiar contexts and further reinforce a positive attitude toward science and other subjects (see Tchudi & Lafer, 1996, for examples). Other advantages for an integrated approach to science are as follows:

- Children learn in a social environment that fosters rich language activities.
- Scientific concepts are put into a meaningful context by connecting them with literature and other content areas.
- More time is spent on learning science because it becomes a part of the normal reading and mathematics curriculum.

Another benefit of an integrated, problem-centered approach to science is that science becomes less of a disconnected collection of facts and more of a "coherent, meaningful body of knowledge" (Keig, 1994, p. 79). Students use their prior knowledge and new experiences to form bridges between the known and the unknown. In *Blueprints for Reform* (AAAS, 1998), the authors indicate that "providing a link to the student's own world through contextual learning can be a powerful motivating factor" (p. 126).

Integrated, problem-centered instruction is also beneficial because it is intrinsically cooperative (Post, Ellis, Humphreys, & Buggey, 1997). Small groups of students are engaged in inquiry, and this can result in a successful learning experience for the group and for each of its members (Jones, 1990). Cooperative methods promote interaction between students. This interaction has the potential to involve students in clarifying, defending, elaborating, evaluating, and even arguing (Tobin, Tippins, & Gallard, 1994). Although cooperative learning may not always lead to the teacher's predetermined learning goal, the consensus building and negotiation are valuable learning tools.

Another benefit of an integrated, problem-centered approach is that this method is a direct application of the multiple intelligence theory provided by Howard Gardner (Charbonneau & Reider, 1995; Sunal et al., 2000). Because children learn in different ways, an integrated curriculum that promotes various approaches to learning will support the various learning styles. Students can benefit from the "multilevel instruction" and "multitasking" inherent in integrated approaches to the curriculum (Roberts & Kellough, 2000, p. 3).

A final benefit of an integrated, problem-centered approach is that it generally includes a variety of children's books. Children's literature is captivating to young people and useful in developing emerging concepts. Children's books help place new vocabulary in a context that makes constructing meaning easier. For example, if a student looks at a selection of dinosaur books, he will begin to develop the concept or scheme of "dinosaurness" or an even more relevant science concept that living things transform over time to adapt to changing environments.

See *http://www.prenhall. com/peters* for the International Reading Association and other links related to the use of children's literature.

Problem-Centered Lessons and Children's Literature

Remember some of the food-related science activities found earlier in this chapter? These activities incorporated the food theme in children's books as an integral part of the lesson. The food topic could have been extended into other content areas to further integrate the lessons and help children and adolescents identify problems to explore that are relevant to their own needs or address their own questions. Consider the following content areas.

- In mathematics, the teacher can read *Spaghetti and Meatballs for All!* (Burns, 1997) as an introduction to geometry, *Each Orange Had 8 Slices* (Giganti, 1992) in order to promote counting skills, or *Gator Pie* (Mathews, 1979) as a means to study fractions.
- Language skills and poetry can be introduced through the story *Never Take a Pig to Lunch and Other Poems About the Fun of Eating* (Westcott, 1994).
- Social studies can be brought in through *Everybody Cooks Rice* (Dooley, 1991) or *The Tortilla Factory* (Paulsen, 1995).
- Other activities can originate from the *Food* (Willrich, 1993) or *Food and Nutrition* (Sterling, 2000) thematic unit books or the countless other children's books related to the food theme.

Although each of the abovementioned books is associated with other content areas, they all support science concepts in one way or another.

When choosing books to use in your science program, keep the following points in mind.

- ***Is the book appropriate for your students' developmental level?***   Do not use a book just because it has the same title as the unit you are currently studying. Check that it is written at an appropriate reading level. If you are not going to read it to the class, make sure that your advanced readers can read it to other students.
- ***Is the content appropriate?***   Before placing a book out for students to read, be sure that the content will not develop further misconceptions about the topic under study. Students have many false notions about scientific phenomena, and you do not want to reinforce these or add to them. Preread each book and note any inconsistencies; eliminate nonsupportive books.
- ***Will the book be interesting to your students?***   Select a wide variety of books (if possible) to ensure that you meet the individual needs of your students. Consider gender and cultural diversity when selecting books. Look for colorful illustrations and a good story line.
- ***Does the book encourage scientific investigation?***   Your purpose for starting with children's literature is to provide a baseline for further knowledge and process skill development. Select books that are good springboards to further learning.

For additional teaching ideas by using children's literature, explore the resources identified in Figure 3–3.

Figure 3–3 Resources for teaching science with children's literature.

Bosma, B., & DeVries, Guth, N. (1995). *Children's literature in an integrated curriculum: The authentic voice.* New York: International Reading Association & Teachers College Press.

Butzow, C., & Butzow, J. (1989). *Science through children's literature: An integrated approach.* Englewood, CO: Teacher Ideas Press.

Butzow, C., & Butzow, J. (1994). *Intermediate science through children's literature: Over land and sea.* Englewood, CO: Teacher Ideas Press.

Butzow, C., & Butzow, J. (1998). *More science through children's literature: An integrated approach (through children's literature).* Englewood, CO: Teacher Ideas Press.

Butzow, C., & Butzow, J. (1999). *Exploring the environment through children's literature: An integrated approach (through children's literature).* Englewood, CO: Teacher Ideas Press.

Butzow, C., & Butzow, J. (2002). *The world of work through children's literature: An integrated approach (through children's literature).* Englewood, CO: Teacher Ideas Press.

Flagg, A., Ory, M., & Ory, T. (2002). *Teaching science with favorite picture books: Grades 1–3.* New York: Instructor Books.

Fredericks, A. (2001). *Investigating natural disasters through children's literature: An integrated approach (through children's literature).* Englewood, CO: Teacher Ideas Press.

Fredericks, A., Meinbach, A., & Rothlein, L. (1993). *Thematic units: An integrated approach to teaching science and social studies.* New York: HarperCollins.

Gertz, S. E., Portman, D. J., & Sarquis, M. (1996). *Teaching physical science through children's literature.* New York: McGraw-Hill Trade.

Hefner, C., & Lewis K. (1995). *Literature-based science: Children's books and activities to enrich the K–5 curriculum.* Phoenix: Oryx.

Jagusch, S. A., & Saul, W. (1992). *Vital connections: Children, science, and books.* Portsmouth, NH: Heinemann.

Keane, N. J. (2002). *Teaching science through literature: Grades 4–6.* Worthington, OH: Linworth Publishing.

Keane, N. J., & Wait, C. (2002). *Teaching science through literature: Grades 6–8.* Worthington, OH: Linworth Publishing.

LeCroy, B., & Holder, B. (1994). *Bookwebs: A brainstorm of ideas for the primary classroom.* Englewood, CO: Teacher Ideas Press.

Shaw, D. G., & Dybdahl, C. S. (1996). *Integrating science and language arts: A sourcebook for K–6 teachers.* Boston: Allyn & Bacon.

An Integrated, Problem-Centered Lesson Example

An example of an integrated, problem-centered lesson is one based on *Bartholomew and the Oobleck* (Geisel & Geisel, 1977). The students' stated problem to solve is to determine and describe the properties and behavior of the cornstarch and water mixture and communicate why the substance behaves in this way.

The teacher begins by reading the story. After the story is read, students receive a mixture of cornstarch and water (made beforehand) for their exploration. The students

Children interact with a cornstarch and water mixture as part of an integrated, problem-centered lesson.

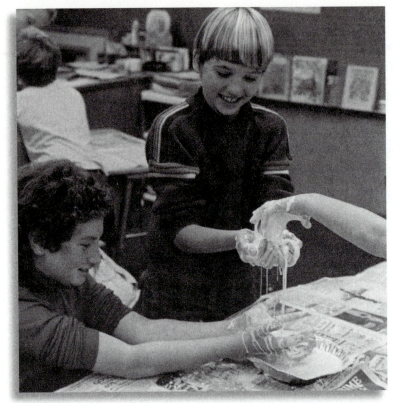

Source: Reprinted from the Great Explorations in Math and Science (GEMS) teacher's guide entitled *Oobleck: What Do Scientists Do?*, copyright by The Regents of the University of California, and used with permission. The GEMS series includes more than 70 teacher's guides and handbooks for preschool through eighth grade, available from LHS GEMS, Lawrence Hall of Science, University of California, Berkeley, CA 94720-5200. (510) 642-7771. *http://www.lhsgems.org*

interact with the mixture and problem-solve to determine its properties. Through this experience, students work on many scientific skills. Students also explore content knowledge as they discuss new words and ideas, as they communicate their results in a small-group social setting. Finally, students develop values and attitudes as they begin to use their natural curiosity to explore scientific phenomena.

Curricular Integration Examples

Mathematics can be integrated by measuring the amounts of water and cornstarch it takes to make a "good" mixture. The subject matter of social studies is integrated in a discussion of kingdoms because the story is based on a king. Art can be integrated when students create mosaics with water-based paints and the cornstarch mixture. The sourcebook for arranging this experience is *Oobleck: What Do Scientists Do?* (Sneider, 1985).

Assessing Integrated, Problem-Centered Experiences

The assessment of this integrated experience should be in keeping with its constructivist nature. Students should be assessed on the product (knowledge), process (skill), and attitude (value) of the experience. Literature/language activities can become an assessment exercise as students write (or orally present) a creative story. Students could also write descriptive adjectives about the mixture. These are used to create poetry, such as cinquains or diamantes.

Scientific attitudes can be assessed as students are asked how they feel about the fact that even scientists cannot agree on why the mixture acts the way it does. Students should also be challenged to come up with their own explanation as to why the material behaves the way it does.

Concept maps (see Chapter 5) would be an appropriate way to determine content knowledge in this case (i.e., the properties of the substance). Students can be provided a key word such as *mixture* and asked to develop links based on what they know. See the Lesson Model for exploring and communicating the properties of a substance.

Misconceptions Occurring During Problem-Centered Lessons

As you think about the various ways to plan and teach lessons, it becomes evident that not every student will learn exactly what you want them to learn. Sometimes students form misconceptions during explorations. Misconceptions are ideas a person has that something is one way but it is really another. This tends to happen in the lessons when students have more control over their learning.

Misconception Examples

In the cornstarch and water lesson, students often think that the material hardens when kneaded in the hands because all of the water is removed by their skin. In fact, just allowing the material to rest in the hands will show that it readily softens again without the skin supplying the moisture.

Here's another example of a misconception. Suppose you ask a child what would happen if an astronaut "dropped" something like a pen on the moon. The child may reply that it would float away. You may then ask why the astronaut does not "float away." Students may answer that the astronaut's heavy boots weigh him down and keep him from floating away. Of course, the moon does have gravity, and this is what keeps the astronaut from floating away. The pen actually does fall toward the moon as it would on the earth. Because the moon has less mass, however, the pen falls with less force than here on the earth. In synopsis, everything on the moon is attracted to it; otherwise, the rocks and dust would also float away.

See *http://www.prenhall. com/peters* for links related to science misconceptions and other specific examples.

Lesson Model

Integrated, Problem-Centered Lesson
for Exploring and Communicating the Properties of a Substance

Overview of the Lesson

Children can become scientists as they explore the world around them. When they encounter a new situation, children can observe, classify, measure, infer, predict, communicate, and experiment to solve problems and gain new information or ideas. Children's curiosity is stimulated as they complete activities. This activity is designed to acquaint children with a substance that does not behave as other substances do. Specifically, the mixture gets harder as it is manipulated and softer when it is left alone. This is in direct opposition to materials such as play dough (flour, water, salt, cream of tartar, dye) or clay.

Science Themes

Systems—The cornstarch and water mixture is a physical/chemical system of molecules that interact with each other and the environment. To understand the nature of the substance, we must consider its behavior as an integrated system of interacting parts and energy.

Models—In considering the way molecules or atoms are arranged in the mixture, students will create pictorial or mental models of the structure of this particular type of matter.

Consistency—Although we can cause temporary changes in the substance by inputting energy in one form or another, students will notice that the system tends to maintain its properties and reorganize itself into the same physical consistency and structure as before the system was disturbed.

Patterns of Change—The cornstarch and water mixture seems to be both solid and liquid at the same time. It can be compared to other substances, and the patterns of change that are represented as liquid and solid states are interchanged.

Scale—The behavior of the mixture may be caused by scale. The sizes of the molecules allow them to interact in ways that a larger substance cannot.

Benchmarks for Science Literacy

By the end of fifth grade, students should know that

- Heating and cooling cause changes in the properties of materials. Many kinds of changes occur faster under hotter conditions.
- When a new material is made by combining two or more materials, it has properties that are different from the original materials. For that reason, a lot of different materials can be made from a small number of basic kinds of materials. (AAAS, 1993, p. 77)

National Science Education Standards

As a result of the activities in grades K–4, all students should develop

- Abilities necessary to do scientific inquiry
- Understanding of properities of objects and materials (NRC, 1996, pp. 121, 123)

Scientific Skills

Classification—Students will compare this substance and other materials in an attempt to classify it according to its properties.

Observation—Students will use all their senses to observe the substance (provide a caution against tasting the material).

Inference/Prediction—Students will infer from the collected data such non-observable properties of the mixture as what it is made of or how the atoms might be arranged.

Communication—Students will communicate their findings to the group. They will also communicate with each other when developing theories of why it behaves the way it does.

Experimenting—Students will design and carry out experiments to alter the mixture, to find its properties, and to explain its behavior.

Curricular Integrations

For *language arts,* the teacher can record the words used to describe the mixture and discuss descriptive adjectives. Descriptive poetry, such as cinquains or diamantes, can be developed.

Mathematics activities can be developed as students compare densities of other substances to that of the mixture. Art can be integrated into this lesson as students experiment with water-based paints and the mixture.

Physical education is promoted as students act out the behavior of a substance's molecules.

Social studies is a natural integration as kingdoms are discussed. Also, the interaction between science and society can be stressed.

Safety during the activity is stressed when using heating devices. Also, caution against eating the substance or getting it on clothing.

Materials

Supplies

Two or three boxes of cornstarch; green food coloring; water; small objects such as marbles, coins, rubber stoppers; other common substances or materials that can be used to explore. (Note: Prepare the mixture by placing one or two boxes of cornstarch in a mixing bowl and mixing in small amounts of green-colored water. Continue until the consistency is like a thick plaster.)

Equipment

Thermometers, heat source (microwave), balance, graduated cylinders

Procedure

Problem to Solve

1. The problem to be solved is (1) determine and describe the properties and behavior of the cornstarch and water mixture, and (2) successfully communicate a theory as to why the substance behaves the way it does. Record the words used to describe the properties of the mixture in a concept map.

[Note: While students explore, walk around the room, questioning students about what they are doing, why they are doing it, and what else they can do to gain information about the mixture.]

Closed Question

A. What happens to the mixture as you continue to squeeze it in your hands? (It hardens.)

Open Questions

A. What did you find out about the mixture?
B. What do you think causes the mixture to behave this way? Have students explain why it behaves as it does and suggest what materials it might be made from.
C. What possible explanations do you think scientists give for the behavior of the substance? Discuss scientific theory and why scientists cannot completely agree on why it behaves as it does. Discuss the tentative nature of science theoretical models and their use, and the scientific search for explanations.
D. How could the king have eliminated this material from the kingdom?

2. Extension activity. Problem: Can you find other materials that behave the same way as the mixture?

(continued)

Open Question

    A.   What other substances do you think behave like this substance?

    3.   Art/PE extensions. Problem: Why would it be unlikely that this material would cover an entire kingdom?

Closed Question

    A.   What is a kingdom?

Open Question

    A.   Since America is a democracy and not a kingdom, would we handle the situation differently than the king did in the story?

Assessment

Student Assessment

1. Develop a concept map on the properties of the mixture.
2. Assign group reports that explain why the mixture behaves as it does. Require such items as a hypothesis, data collected, a summary of the data, and conclusions.
3. Write a story about your own day in the kingdom as the messy substance fell. What did you find out?
4. Take a small amount home and ask a parent or friend to provide thoughts on the mixture.
5. Find out more about Newtonian and non-Newtonian fluids.
6. Leave the mixture out for 1 week. What effect does this have on the substance? Explain why this happens.
7. Use descriptive adjectives to develop poetry, such as cinquains or diamantes.

Teacher Assessment

Audiotape the lesson and review it with the following questions in mind: How did the students react to the investigation? What percentage of the time was I dominating the discussion and how often were students actively discussing the mixture?

Bibliography

Geisel, T. S., & Geisel, A. S. (1977). *Bartholomew and the Oobleck.* New York: Random House. (original work published in 1949 by Dr. Seuss)

Kerr, D. A. (1983). Quick clay. *Scientific American,* 209(5), 132–142.

Sneider, C. I. (1985). *Oobleck: What do scientists do?* Berkeley, CA: Lawrence Hall of science.

Walker, J. (1978). The amateur scientist. *Scientific American,* 239(5), 186–198.

Walker, J. (1982). The amateur scientist. *Scientific American,* 246(1), 174–180.

Summary

- When planning a unit, the main things you must know are (a) how to determine which generalizations to use, (b) how to gather more activities to teach each generalization, and (c) how to introduce, or bridge into, each generalization's sequence of activities.
- Closed problems and activities lead to a single response. They foster convergent thinking. Open activities and problems lead to a wide variety of responses. They produce divergent thinking.
- Children can be taught using direct instruction, guided discovery, or problem-centered lessons. As you reduce teacher control and increase student autonomy, students are required to take charge of their learning. More meaningful relationships can be formed with problem-centered learning.

Reflection

Companion CD

1. Look at the "Earthworm Family" lesson linked to the *Thematic Plan and Integration* video on the Companion CD. Can you identify aspects of this lesson that are high in "teacher direction"? How could you modify the lesson to make it more learner centered?

2. Look at the "Earthworm Waste" lesson linked to the *Curiosity and Interest* video on the Companion CD.

How could you make this lesson into more of a "guided discovery" format?

3. Look at the "What Is Vermicomposting" lesson linked to the *Teacher Attributes* video on the Companion CD. How could you make this lesson into more of a "problem-centered" lesson format?

Portfolio Ideas

1. Take a lesson plan that you have recently completed and rewrite it in the form of a problem-centered lesson to share in your portfolio and with the class.

2. Search the Internet for some lesson plan databases. A good starting point is to use the key words *lesson, plan, elementary,* and *science*. Record findings in your portfolio.

3. Observe the next five science lessons while at your practicum site. Note in your portfolio the use of open and closed activities. How could more open activities be incorporated?

4. Ask several adults one of the misconceptions questions. Do you notice any pattern in their answers? Did your classmates have similar experiences? Record findings in your portfolio.

5. Read *Multiple Intelligences in the Classroom* (Armstrong, 1994, Alexandria, VA: ASCD),

Teaching with the Brain in Mind (Jensen, 1998, Alexandria, VA: ASCD), or *Use Both Sides of Your Brain* (Buzan, 1989, New York: Plume) and research ways that curriculum and planning can be modified to better meet students' needs. Enter findings in your portfolio.

6. Integrate multiple intelligences activities into your curriculum by using a resource such as *Celebrating Multiple Intelligences: Teaching for Success* (Faculty of the New City School, 1994, St. Louis, MO: Author), *Succeeding with Multiple Intelligences: Teaching Through the Personal Intelligences* (Faculty of the New City School, 1996, St. Louis, MO: Author), or *If the Shoe Fits . . . How to Develop Multiple Intelligences in the Classroom* (Chapman, 1993, Arlington Heights, IL: IRI/Skylight). Compile a listing of activities in your portfolio.

References

Alfving, A., Eitzen, L., Hyman, J., Patron, R., Holve, H., & Nelson, P. (1987). *Fun with foods: A recipe for math + science*. Fresno, CA: AIMS Education Foundation.

Aliki. (1976). *Corn is maize*. New York: HarperCollins.

American Association for the Advancement of Science (AAAS). (1989). *Science for all Americans*. Washington, DC: Author.

American Association for the Advancement of Science (AAAS). (1993). *Benchmarks for science literacy*. New York: Oxford University Press.

American Association for the Advancement of Science (AAAS). (1998). *Blueprints for reform*. New York: Oxford University Press.

Barrett, J. (1978). *Cloudy with a chance of meatballs*. New York: Aladdin Paperbacks.

Barrett, J. (1997). *Pickles to Pittsburgh*. New York: Atheneum Books.

Briscoe, C., Peters, J., & O'Brien, G. (1993). An elementary program emphasizing teacher's pedagogical content knowledge within a constructivist epistemological rubric. In P. Rubba, L. Campbell, & T. Dana (Eds.), *Excellence in educating teachers of science* (pp. 1–20). Columbus, OH: ERIC Clearinghouse.

Brown, M. (1997). *Stone soup*. New York: Aladdin Paperbacks.

Burns, M. (1997). *Spaghetti and meatballs for all! A mathematical story*. New York: Scholastic.

Charbonneau, M., & Reider, B. (1995). *The integrated elementary classroom: A developmental model of education for the 21st century*. Boston: Allyn & Bacon.

Cobb, V. (1979). *More science experiments you can eat*. New York: HarperTrophy.

Cobb, V. (1994). *Science experiments you can eat* (Rev. ed.). New York: HarperTrophy.

Cole, J. (1996). *The magic school bus gets eaten*. New York: Scholastic.

Dooley, N. (1991). *Everybody cooks rice*. Minneapolis, MN: Carolrhoda Books.

Geisel, T. S., & Geisel, A. S. (1977). *Bartholomew and the Oobleck*. New York: Random House.

Giganti, P. (1992). *Each orange had 8 slices: A counting book*. New York: Mulberry Books.

Jenkins, S. (1997). *What do you do when something wants to eat you?* Boston: Houghton Mifflin.

Johmann, C., & Rieth, E. (1996). *Gobble up science.* Santa Barbara, CA: Learning Works.

Jones, R. (1990). *Teaming up!* LaPorte, TX: ITGROUP.

Kahle, J., & Meece, J. (1994). Research on gender issues in the classroom. In D. Gabel (Ed.), *Handbook of research on science teaching and learning* (pp. 542–557). Arlington, VA: National Science Teachers Association.

Keig, P. (1994). Introducing elementary teachers to thematic science instruction. In L. Schafer (Ed.), *Behind the methods class door: Educating elementary and middle school science teachers* (pp. 79–88). Columbus, OH: ERIC Clearinghouse.

Lauber, P. (1995). *Who eats what?* New York: HarperCollins.

Levine, S., & Johnstone, L. (1995). *Silly science: Strange and startling projects to amaze your family and friends.* New York: John Wiley.

Lokerson, J. (1992). *Learning disabilities: Glossary of some important terms.* Arlington, VA: The ERIC Clearinghouse on Disabilities and Gifted Education.

Markle, S. (1996). *Icky, squishy science.* New York: Hyperion.

Mathews, L. (1979). *Gator pie.* Littleton, MA: Sundance.

National Research Council (NRC). (1996). *National science education standards.* Washington, DC: National Academy Press.

National Research Council (NRC). (2000). *Inquiry and the national science education standards: A guide for teaching and learning.* Washington, DC: National Academy Press.

National Science Teachers Association (NSTA). (2003). *Science education for middle school students. A position statement.* Washington, DC: Author. Retrieved October 1, 2004, from *www.nsta.org/positionstatement&psid=20*

Paulsen, G. (1995). *The tortilla factory.* New York: Voyager Books.

Penner, L. R. (1991). *Eating the plates: A pilgrim book of food and manners.* New York: Aladdin Paperbacks.

Post, T., Ellis, A., Humphreys, A., & Buggey, L. (1997). *Interdisciplinary approaches to curriculum: Themes for teaching.* Upper Saddle River, NJ: Merrill/Prentice Hall.

Roberts, P., & Kellough, R. (2000). *A guide for developing interdisciplinary thematic units* (2nd ed.). Upper Saddle River, NJ: Merrill/Prentice Hall.

Sneider, C. I. (1985). *Oobleck: What do scientists do?* Berkeley, CA: Lawrence Hall of Science.

Sterling, M. (2000). *Food and nutrition.* Westminster, CA: Teacher Created Materials.

Sunal, C., Powell, D., McClelland, S., Rule, A., Rovegno, I. Smith, C., & Sunal, D. (2000). *Integrating academic units in the elementary school curriculum.* New York: Harcourt College Publishers.

Tchudi, S., & Lafer, S. (1996). *The interdisciplinary teacher's handbook: Integrating teaching across the curriculum.* Portsmouth, NH: Heinemann.

Tobin, K., Tippins, D., & Gallard, J. (1994). Research on instructional strategies for teaching science. In D. Gabel (Ed.), *Handbook of research on science teaching and learning* (pp. 45–93). New York: Macmillan.

Tweed, A. (2004). Direct instruction: Is it the most effective science teaching strategy? *NSTA Reports.* Arlington, VA: National Science Teachers Association.

Westcott, N. (1994). *Never take a pig to lunch and other poems about the fun of eating.* New York: Orchard Books.

Willrich, L. (1993). *Food.* Westminster, CA: Teacher Created Materials.

Suggested Readings

Eby, J., & Martin, D. (2001). *Reflective planning, teaching, and evaluation for the elementary school: A relational approach* (3rd ed.). Upper Saddle River, NJ: Merrill/Prentice Hall. (a book that promotes reflective thought in the planning process)

Freeland, K., & Hammons, K. (1998). *Curriculum for integrated learning: a lesson-based approach.* New York: Delmar. (a guide to K–8 integration based on an integrated lesson plan structure)

Mason, C., & Markowsky, J. (1998). *Everybody's somebody's lunch: Teacher's guide.* Gardiner, ME: Tilbury House. (a book of activities and information on food chains, predators, and prey)

National Science Teachers Association (NSTA). (1996). *Pathways to the science standards: Guidelines for moving the vision into practice.* Arlington, VA: Author. (a practical guide to help put the national standards into practice during teaching and assessment)

Shymansky, J. A. (1996). Transforming science education in ways that work: Science reform in the elementary school. In J. Rhoton & P. Bowers (Eds.), *Issues in science education* (pp. 185–191). Arlington, VA: National Science Teachers. (discusses curriculum and instruction in the light of science education reform)

CHAPTER 4

DEVELOPING INQUIRY SKILLS

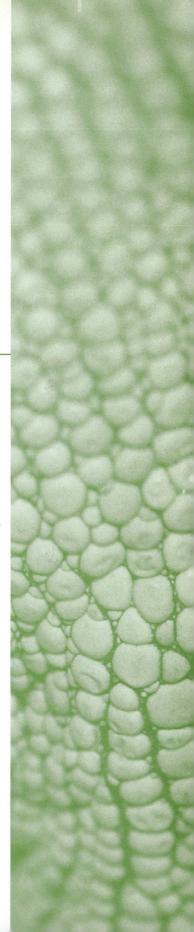

FOCUS QUESTIONS

- How can an "active" approach to science make it more meaningful?
- What are the components of the learning cycle?
- What are the scientific skills?
- What are some examples of scientific attitudes?

Focus on Inquiry

Scientific Skill Development

Dr. George E. O'Brien, Miami,
Florida International University
Angela M. Alexander,
Pine Villa Montessori School, Dade County (Florida) Public Schools

Picture a small community school just 30 miles from downtown Miami but in a rural, farm region of south Florida. This particular day, Ms. Alexander has arranged her students into cooperative learning groups, and they are excited, curious, and anxious about what is going to happen in the science lesson.

Each group receives plastic gloves, dissecting needles, hand lenses, and an oval-shaped object wrapped in aluminum foil. Can the students predict and/or infer what the objects are? They unwrap the foil from the objects carefully and inspect the objects. An initial reaction from many students is, "Wow, I don't know if I really want to touch this." These reactions fade fast. The students use dissecting needles to separate parts that make up the oval-shaped objects and then to record observations and make inferences concerning what the objects or their contents might be and why they think so. Quickly, some students discover or infer that they are working with bones. Some say they are working with wishbones, and one student says these are hog bones (because hogs have a lot of bones). Some students think they can make out a bird's head, and one student thinks she can see parts of a hamster. Some students guess that they are working with dinosaur teeth, human teeth, or some kind of fossil.

The students from each group sort the bones. The task of sorting and organizing the bones into recognizable entities is a problem-solving challenge. The challenge of discovering the mystery objects piques the students' curiosity. Although on this day no one infers the objects to be owl pellets, the pieces of bones lead to more discoveries about the animals that are consumed by barn owls.

At the University

Back in Miami, Dr. O'Brien, a professor of elementary science methods at the university, sets up the activity in the same way as Ms. Alexander. He leads his students through the same challenge of identifying the contents of owl pellets. As bones are uncovered and carefully removed and placed to the side on sheets of plain white paper, university students use dichotomous keys (classification) to identify skulls removed from the barn owl pellets. There is much debate and negotiation (communication) in the cooperating groups concerning the identity of the skulls. As skulls of small mammals, including moles and shrews (Order Insectivora), and rats, voles, and mice (Order Rodentia) are identified, the students take pride in their individual and group accomplishments. As a follow-up activity, the students are to diagram food webs with a barn owl at the highest trophic level and grass seeds at the lowest level. The sequence of activities helps the students construct knowledge of diets of barn owls and other birds of prey, food webs showing that energy passes from one organism to another on a higher level through consumption of that lower organism, and other ecological concepts.

Learning Science Is an Active Process

In the fourth-grade classroom, Ms. Alexander brings books for her students to research owls. Can the students identify the contents of the owl pellets? Yes. In much the same ways that the university students identified prey, the children are able to identify the skulls of different animals. All the students—at the elementary school and university—solved the mystery of finding out the contents of the pellets. The students, by collecting information from the evidence (in this case, produced by barn owls about 12 hours after consuming a meal by casting, or regurgitating, indigestible hair and bones as a pellet) and using science process skills (in this activity, analyzing, communicating, observing, inferring, classifying, predicting, extrapolating, synthesizing, evaluating, measuring, interpreting information, and making conclusions) enjoyed participation in the active, intellectual process of science. Science surveys and interviews conducted by the instructors, after these lessons emphasized hands-on, inquiry-based science, revealed positive attitudes toward science (in both groups) and positive attitudes toward science teaching (in the university group).

Teachers of science—whether at the elementary school or the university—should believe that learning science must be an active process. Learning science is something students do, not something that is done to them. When an instructor focuses on actively engaging students in doing science, then a natural connection of learning concepts, scientific skills, and attitudes follows. In such classrooms, a focal question in planning science lessons is, "What will the students be doing?" They will be observing, classifying, measuring, predicting, inferring, collecting data, graphing, experimenting, and/or communicating. The better the teacher understands the level of skill development that the students have, the better she can choose activities to match the needs of her students.

Making Connections

Just as it is important for students to be active in their learning, it is equally important for the teacher to be an active inquirer and a visible partner to the students during the instructional process. Following are comments from Ms. Alexander, who taught the lesson on owl pellets.

"I approach teaching science in a way that empowers the students. The students will be given the power to create their own learning environment, and these ideas on what to teach come from discussions I have with my students many times a day."

"When the children are working on activities that require an experimental design, I go to each group to discuss how they will set up the experiment. While the students are working on this task, I go from group to group and question the groups on why they chose to set up their experiment this way. Some experimental setups will be better than others. Each group of students will be working from what their group knows. They will be exposed to all the other groups' experiments, which will encourage them to consider other variables in their next exploration. I feel it's also important for the students in the group to self-evaluate their group's experiment. This helps me to know where the group is in the learning process and what they should be focusing on in the next experiment."

"Before they begin the experiment, the groups predict what they think will happen; they may also predict why they think it will happen. When the children start the experiment, I go from group to group, asking each questions about their experiment so I can understand their thinking and/or explanations. I keep notes on each group and record their responses to questions and any misconceptions that I detect. Each group devises a plan and collects data according to that plan. Then the students explain what they think happened in the experiment and share any data collected and recorded with other groups."

"In my class, I feel the students are in charge of their own learning. The teacher sets up and manages situations in which the students can discover and invent on their own to reach understanding. Science process skills are important in my classroom, as is development of critical thinking. The students are encouraged to reach understandings that allow them to be better able to explain their theories. I encourage students to reconsider any misconceptions they might have, and I have students discuss different opinions to see if a consensus can be reached."

The classroom setting Ms. Alexander describes includes the following characteristics:

- Students are engaged in a motivating classroom environment that provides encouragement and frequent student–teacher interaction.
- Students can integrate science processes and problem-solving skills.
- Students are encouraged to actively construct knowledge and explanations.
- Students can use familiar objects in real-life settings.
- Students are given the opportunity to encounter natural phenomena through firsthand experiences.
- Students are involved in varied classroom settings, including individualized instruction, cooperative learning, whole-class demonstrations, and interest centers.
- Students employ risk taking, divergent thinking, and self-initiated questioning.
- Student activities are developmentally appropriate and capitalize on student interest.
- Students are encouraged to create a learning community where everyone's opinions, questions, and conceptions are valued.

Obviously, an elementary or middle school teacher preparing a science lesson has to focus on the question, "What will the students do?" Just as important, however, the teacher needs to be aware of other vital factors, including the selection of instructional materials, physical limitations of the students (e.g., in using manipulatives), choice of management strategy, assessment techniques, cognitive developmental levels of the students, decisions on prerequisites and hierarchy of tasks, and relevant or related science misconceptions. The selection of the overall instructional strategy (e.g., learning cycle or constructivist learning model) is also an important part of inquiry-based hands-on/minds-on science (Flick, 1993).

MAKING ACTIVE SCIENCE MEANINGFUL

The Focus on Inquiry: Scientific Skill Development discusses how the use of scientific skills makes science active and meaningful. What did you notice about the use of the skills of observation, classification, measurement, communication, inference, prediction, and experimentation?

In 1929, John Dewey noted that education emphasized the learning of *fixed conclusions* rather than the advancement of intelligence as a *method of action*. He went on to say that schools *separate knowledge from the very activities that would give the knowledge meaning*. By this, he meant that teachers concentrated on teaching facts and conclusions. They were not teaching concepts through experimentation. Students were not developing the skills necessary to investigate facts or to develop new knowledge.

In a more recent discussion of how science should be taught, National Research Council (NRC) members explain the necessity and interaction of activities and content even more specifically. Their views are summarized as follows:

> Those developing the national standards were committed to including inquiry as both science content and as a way to learn science. Therefore, rather than simply extolling the virtues of "hands-on/minds-on" or "laboratory-based" teaching as the way to teach "science content and process," the writers of the *Standards* treated inquiry as both a learning goal and as a teaching method. (NRC, 2000, p. 18)

In this millennium, educators should take seriously the NRC's suggestion and Dewey's advice. Teachers need to continue the practice of inquiry teaching in their own classrooms. As the authors of both *National Science Education Standards* (NRC, 1996) and *Benchmarks for Science Literacy* (American Association for the Advancement of Science [AAAS], 1993) indicate, inquiry teaching is essential to scientific literacy for all students.

Standards Link

Science Inquiry Standard

As a result of activities in grades K–8, all students should develop

- **Abilities necessary to do scientific inquiry**
- **Understandings about scientific inquiry**

(Content Standard A, National Research Council, 1996, pp. 121, 143.)

See the Chapter 4 Web Destinations on the Companion Website (*http://www.prenhall. com/peters*) for links from the National Research Council on the application of the standards in teaching and learning.

CW

The Goal of a Science Program

The goal of all science programs should be problem solving and developing the inquiry skills necessary for competing effectively in the global marketplace. Scientific ventures such as genetic engineering, drug research, telecommunications, nuclear fusion, and environmental monitoring are increasingly done as cooperative ventures between many nations. Today, more than ever, educators must prepare a diverse workforce capable of scientific research, investigation, and informed decision making.

To paraphrase Dewey, intelligent action is the lone definitive resource of humankind (1929). This action of education refers to such entities as the science process skills. These are what scientists, adults, and children use to do science.

What skills were being taught in the owl pellet activity? How would you use this activity in your classroom? Are the instructional strategies consistent with the Science Inquiry Standard, as listed in the Standards Link box? Is the strategy consistent with the constructivist learning model as presented in Chapter 2? What is the **learning cycle** approach to inquiry mentioned in the owl pellet activity? How could the learning cycle be used in teaching skills to children?

Teaching Tips The assumption behind the learning cycle is that it is consistent with the ways students learn and can modify false beliefs (see Rosenthal, 1993).

Learning cycle is an inductive approach to instruction involving exploration, concept introduction, and concept application phases.

USING THE LEARNING CYCLE

The learning cycle is based on an *inquiry* approach to learning consistent with the standards (see the Science Inquiry Standards Link) and an effective strategy for bringing explorations and questioning into the classroom (National Science Teachers Association [NSTA], 2004; Karplus & Their, 1967; Odom & Settlage, 1996). The learning cycle helps students develop a quest for knowledge, data, or truth. All students are naturally curious, and this approach to learning scientific skills leads to a *conceptual understanding* (Karplus, 1977). An advantage of the learning cycle is that it is a methodology that can translate the skills and vocabulary used by scientists into a more meaningful learning experience for students.

Barman (1989) has modified the original terminology of the learning cycle to make it more understandable for elementary and middle school teachers. He suggests the following three phases.

1. *Exploration Phase. The first phase of the cycle is student centered; the teacher plays the role of a facilitator, observing, questioning, and assisting students as needed. The students interact with materials and each other during this phase.*

In our owl pellet story, this phase occurred when the students were interacting with the owl pellets. For example, they were observing the contents of the owl pellets, classifying the bones with a key, and communicating with each other what they had found. In both the elementary and university classrooms, students were actively involved in inquiry, with the teacher playing the role of facilitator.

2. *Concept Introduction Phase. This teacher-centered phase is characterized by naming things and events. The teacher's function is to gather information for students that pertains to their explorations in the first phase. The teacher works with students to develop vocabulary and to introduce pertinent information.*

During the owl pellet activity, Ms. Alexander brings in books for the students to begin naming things and events surrounding the formation of the pellet. Dr. O'Brien's class also engages in learning new names such as Rodentia and Insectivora as students continue the lesson.

3. *Concept Application Phase. This activity-oriented phase is, again, student centered and allows students to apply freshly learned information to new situations. The teacher presents a new problem to solve, allowing more time for the students to apply what they have learned.*

The university students depict this phase as they diagram food webs to illustrate the barn owl's diet. They are applying what they have found out in the second phase. The fourth-grade students also begin to apply what they have learned as they further research the characteristics of the owl through children's literature and nature books.

As shown in Figure 4–1, this cycle also has an evaluation and discussion aspect. This is an interactive component throughout each phase. The evaluation and discussion help identify current false beliefs and prevent the construction of new misconceptions. In each of the phases, the teacher may rely on various means of assessment (see Chapter 5) to assist in student understanding. Clearly, the cycle is supported by a continuous evaluation. That way, there can be a return to a previous phase, when needed, or an appropriate further application in a new phase.

In the previous examples, both Ms. Alexander and Dr. O'Brien facilitated discussions throughout the owl pellet activity. They were careful to monitor what the students were

See the Chapter 4 Web Destinations at *http://www.prenhall. com/peters* for links to programs that use the learning cycle.

See the Chapter 4 Web Destinations at *http://www.prenhall. com/peters* for additional learning cycle links.

Figure 4–1   The learning cycle.

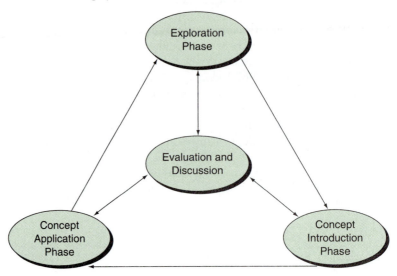

Source: Adapted from a figure by Charles Barman in "A Procedure for Helping Prospective Elementary Teachers Integrate the Learning Cycle into Science Textbooks," *Journal of Science Teacher Education,1*(2), p. 22.

saying and to ask pertinent questions wherever they thought misconceptions were present. The ongoing assessment allows for a holistic, or complete, approach to evaluation that includes activity-based evaluation. Consider other possible evaluation strategies as we further explore the three phases.

Exploration Phase

Exploration phase of the learning cycle allows children the opportunity to experience events to initiate their thought processes.

As we discussed earlier, the **exploration phase** is a student-oriented phase. Remember the constructivist model presented in Chapter 2? The exploration phase of the learning cycle is similar to the exploration component of the constructivist learning model in which students are *actively engaged*. The teacher's function in either model is to scaffold the learning environment based on the concepts she believes are important for the students to learn at that time.

Students can be involved in observing, classifying what they have observed, measuring, making informal inferences based on their observations, conducting experiments, collecting and organizing data, and communicating their findings to their peers in the learning cycle exploration phase. It is important for you as the facilitator to build the foundation by making the connections between the activities and the students' everyday lives.

Exploration Example

For example, if you want to develop an understanding of floating and sinking, you could first discuss the students' trips to a pool or the beach by asking, "What floated on the water? What sank?" Next, have the students observe pictures of various objects either floating or sinking. Then, ask a series of questions designed to engage the students in a discussion of the phenomena. Students will begin to make inferences about why objects float or sink. It is important for you to identify students' inferences, noting similarities and differences in their perceptions or explanations. The students could even test several objects during this

Visit an Inquiry Classroom
The Learning Cycle—Exploration

View the *Exploration* video in the "Model Inquiry Unit" section of the Companion CD. Mr. McKnight moves throughout the classroom facilitating student interaction as they observe earthworms and record their findings.

Review the video and ask yourself the following:
  • What specific examples show this is a "student-oriented" phase of the learning cycle?
  • What is Mr. McKnight's role in this lesson?

CW   Reread the owl pellet activity at the beginning of this chapter. Compare and contrast Mr. McKnight's explorations with those of Ms. Alexander. Record your ideas and the answers to these questions in your portfolio or use the Companion Website to share your ideas.

phase and make a chart of which ones float or sink. Assessment during this phase could be as informal as open questions or as structured as individual student interviews.

Concept Introduction or Invention Phase

During the **concept invention phase,** the teacher is a facilitator. She begins to focus the questioning, to organize the information, and to guide the class into an agreed-upon concept. This process of making connections and sense of things is termed *concept invention.* The teacher assists the students in naming the objects and concepts (vocabulary development) and in experimenting with the newly formed concepts, relating them to the experiences from the exploration phase. In terms of the constructivist model, students are now in the "proposing explanations and solutions" phase and are looking for ways to construct new explanations.

Concept invention phase of the learning cycle allows children the opportunity to determine relationships among the objects or events that they explored in the exploration phase.

Concept Invention Example

In the floating and sinking example, the teacher would introduce terminology and concepts such as *weight, surface tension,* and *density.* Specific definitions would accompany these terms and relate to the students' explorations. Questioning why the students think some objects float and some sink would be based on both the new vocabulary and definitions and the explorations. Students would measure various densities in support of concept development. Finally, the students would construct the notion that objects that are denser than water will sink in water and those that are less dense than water will float in water.

Concept Application Phase

Now it is time for the students to apply their new knowledge and skills in the **concept application phase.** Students are provided similar situations and challenged to implement their new concepts. In terms of the constructivist model, the students are now taking action on what they have learned. They make decisions about the new explorations and apply newly learned knowledge and skills.

Concept application phase of the learning cycle allows children the opportunity to apply the concept or skill that they developed in the concept invention phase.

Visit an Inquiry Classroom
The Learning Cycle—Concept Invention

View the *Concept Invention* video in the "Model Inquiry Unit" section of the Companion CD. Mr. McKnight questions the students and helps them to think about their earthworm explorations and to form concepts. Notice how students are making connections between their current activities and past observations and experiences.

Review the video and ask yourself the following:
- What concepts are the elementary or middle school students forming?
- What is the role of teacher questioning in a student's concept development?
- Many times, elementary or middle school teachers have students engage in a fun science activity but then do not follow up with concept invention. Why is the concept invention stage so important?

 In the NSTA's *Position Statement on Scientific Inquiry* (2004), the authors make the statement, "Scientific inquiry is a powerful way of understanding science content." Explain what they mean by this statement and the role that the concept invention stage of the learning cycle might play in supporting scientific inquiry and understanding science content. Use specific examples from the video on the Companion CD. Record your ideas and the answers to these questions in your portfolio or use the Companion Website to share your ideas.

Concept Application Example

In terms of the floating and sinking example, the teacher may provide new items for students to hypothesize about and test. The teacher may also complete a performance-based evaluation (see Chapter 5) at this point, checking how many objects the students can correctly identify as "floaters" and "sinkers." Different experiments may test the new knowledge or lead back to the exploration phase of the cycle. For example, the teacher may ask the students to float a paper clip in a cup of water. The students know that the paper clip is denser than water, so now they have to experiment with surface tension, bringing them back to the exploration phase.

A Variation of the Learning Cycle

One way to make the learning cycle more complete is through the addition of stages to capture the students' attention and assess what the students have learned after instruction (Staver & Shroyer, 1994). A variation of the learning cycle with these additions is the five-stage model developed by BSCS (Bybee et al., 1989). This five-stage model incorporates the engage, explore, explain, elaborate, and evaluate stages. The *engage stage* is matched with the invitation stage of the constructivist learning model. Students observing surroundings and looking for interesting phenomena are characteristics of both models. Here, teachers begin with questions to capture students' attention.

The *explore, explain,* and *elaborate stages* are equivalent to the original learning cycle. The added *evaluate stage* provides additional opportunity for assessment. It allows the teacher to find out what the students have learned and sets the stage to begin the cycle once again.

The Learning Cycle and Textbooks

In many elementary and middle schools, a textbook series makes up the science program. Such books contain many activities whose purpose is to illustrate ideas presented in the

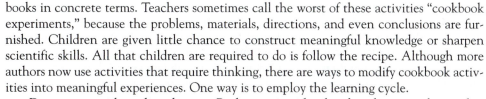

Visit an Inquiry Classroom

The Learning Cycle—Concept Application

View the *Concept Application* video in the "Model Inquiry Unit" section of the Companion CD. Students gather again to discuss their newly developed concepts with Mr. Mc-Knight. Later, they will engage in further earthworm activities to apply their knowledge in new ways.

Review the video and ask yourself the following:
- What activity would you do as a follow-up to the discussion shown in this video segment?
- As the students finish their study of earthworms, how could you transition into a study of round worms or flat worms as a way to apply what they have learned in previous explorations?

In the article, "Less Is More: Trimming the Overstuffed Curriculum," Fratt (2002) supports the American Association for the Advancement of Science's Project 2061 position that teachers should teach fewer topics but teach them in greater depth to promote better understanding. Do you think that the learning cycle approach supports the idea of promoting better understanding? Explain your answer and include specific examples from the video on the Companion CD. Record your ideas and the answers to these questions in your portfolio or use the Companion Website to share your ideas.

books in concrete terms. Teachers sometimes call the worst of these activities "cookbook experiments," because the problems, materials, directions, and even conclusions are furnished. Children are given little chance to construct meaningful knowledge or sharpen scientific skills. All that children are required to do is follow the recipe. Although more authors now use activities that require thinking, there are ways to modify cookbook activities into meaningful experiences. One way is to employ the learning cycle.

Do not start with reading the text. Rather, start with related explorations designed to invite students to want to explore more. Try an experiment out of the book as a discovery activity and not as a set of directions to follow. Then, use the text to develop the related language and reinforce the concepts. Finally, try some associated experiments from the text or supplemental materials.

If you are involved in selecting the textbook for your science program, pay attention to the ways authors lead into the activities and the comments following them. Look for questions that are posed before the experiment, with extending information following the experiment. This enables you to use the author's questions to explore beforehand, and then introduce the experiment, and finally use the book's information to extend the children's learning after the experiment is completed.

The Learning Cycle and Skill Development

In short, we want to use the learning cycle to develop students' scientific understandings and skills. The learning cycle is generalized as a *do-talk-do* cycle (Ramsey, 1993). In the "do" parts of the cycle, skills are being used. What specifically are the scientific skills? Which skills are appropriate for the elementary or middle school students? What are other ways to develop these skills?

In preparing for your own first elementary or middle school science unit, like the authors of Focus on Inquiry: Scientific Skill Development you may decide to use owls as a theme. You will want to focus on scientific skills. You will probably begin to ask yourself the following questions about skills.

How will the scientific skills fit into my elementary or middle school curriculum?
Do I fully understand the skills?
Am I prepared to teach scientific skills to children?
What are some examples of activities I can do to promote specific scientific skill?

SCIENTIFIC SKILLS

The learning cycle explains *how* you will teach scientific skills. In their respective publications, the NRC (1996) and the AAAS (1993) explain *why* you need to teach the how-tos of teaching scientific skills. Now we look at the *what* question. What are the scientific skills of observation, classification, measurement, communication, inference, prediction, and experimentation? Let's begin with observation.

Observing

Observation is defined here as carefully exploring the properties of an object or phenomenon, such as texture, color, sound, taste, smell, length, mass, or volume.

The process of **observation** is the taking in of sense perceptions. It is our job to help students use all their senses when they observe similarities, differences, and changes in objects or events. Students can learn that each of the senses is a gateway to observing different properties of objects. Seeing allows them to notice properties such as size, shape, and color of objects and how the objects may interact. Hearing makes knowable properties of sounds, such as loudness, pitch, and rhythm. Touching teaches the meaning of texture and is another way to discover sizes and shapes of objects. Tasting shows how labels such as bitter, salty, sour, and sweet can be used to describe foods. Smelling allows students to associate objects with odors, such as smells "like perfume" or "like cigar smoke."

Properties enable children to compare and describe likenesses and differences among objects. This leads to explorations that require several of the other processes, such as classifying and communicating. You can ask broad and narrow questions to guide learning in such science processes as observation.

See the Chapter 4 Web Destinations on the Companion Website at *http://www.prenhall.com/peters* for links related to owl pellet availability and activities.

In keeping with our owl theme, you may want to begin with a children's literature approach to the study of owls. *Owl Eyes* (Gates, 1994) is a good starting point. This story describes a Mohawk legend in which animals can choose their own colors and body form. It assists the students in observations of the owl and its characteristics. *Owl Moon* (Yolen, 1987) is another story rich in observation that describes a walk in the woods in search of owls. *Good-Night Owl!* (Hutchins, 1972) is a story about animal noises and would be a good introduction to student observations of animal sounds in the schoolyard.

As you begin to explore the owl pellets with children in a primary-level class, invite everyone to observe by saying, for example:

What do you notice about the object wrapped in foil?
Does it make any noise?
What do you think you will see inside?
Is what you see inside different from what you expected to see?

Later, pose more questions:

How does the object feel?
How many bones did you find?
What do the bones look like?
What does it smell like?

An owl rests in its natural habitat as children observe its characteristics.

In a middle-level class, begin to make observations more specific:

What animal skeletons in the guide compare to the skeletons that you found?
How many animal remains did you find in the pellet?

In an upper-level class, explore with even more specific observations:

In what specific ways are the bones alike?
How do the skulls that you found compare with the ones shown in the guide?

Classifying

Most primary students can select and group real objects by some common property. **Classification** imposes order on collections of objects or events through characteristics such as color, shape, and size. Dichotomous classifications divide objects or events into two groupings. Elementary students should be proficient at dichotomous classification and multigroup classifications in which they observe and group items on the basis of different properties.

Classification is seen as constructing an order based on similarities and differences between objects or events.

With our owl lessons, we can introduce *The Book of North American Owls* (Sattler, 1995) and *Owls* (Kalman, 1987). The students can classify the owls on the basis of habitat or physical features. Through reading *Town Mouse & Country Mouse* (Brett, 1994), the students can set up a dichotomous key listing comparisons of the two types of habitats that the mice—and accompanying owl and cat—live in as presented in the story.

Primary-Level Example

In a primary-level class, students can look over the contents of the pellet and sort them by properties. The teacher can prompt the students with the following:

> Think of one property, such as hardness. Sort all the objects that have that property into one pile. Leave what's left in another pile.

Later, to expand on the activity, the teacher can say:

> What other properties can you use to sort your objects?

In another primary-level class, students look over the contents of the pellet and sort them into animal and plant remains.

Middle- and Upper-Level Examples

Many middle-level students can classify an object into more than one category at the same time and hold this in mind. In a middle-level class, some students have classified owls into three groups, based on the geographic range of their habitat, with two subgroups each: urban and rural. They completed this independently in response to their teacher's question:

> How can you group owls by habitat?

Next, the teacher will explore owl coloration subgroups. Some upper-level students can also reclassify according to other properties that fit their purposes. In an upper-level class, students have a collection of pictures of animals that owls may prey upon. They start off by dividing them into groups by order but then decide that this will not fit their purpose. They have to reclassify according to the prey's location on the food chain. This example demonstrates a major point about classification: It is done to fit a purpose. What works to fulfill the intent of the classifier is what counts. Objects can be classified in many ways.

Measuring

Measurement is the specific determination of the length, mass, volume, speed, time, or other property of an object or event. See the Companion Website for additional information.

Thinking about properties in a quantitative way naturally leads to measuring them. **Measurement** is used to compare things. At first, at the primary level, children may be unable to compare an object with a standard measuring tool, such as a meterstick or yardstick. Instead, they find out who is taller by standing back to back. They find out which of two objects is heavier by holding each object in their hands. Eventually, they begin to use nonstandard measuring devices, such as paper clips or lengths of string, to measure their desks.

There is good reason to start off measuring in this way. Remember that primary students may not conserve several concepts that deal with quantity. Changing the appearance of an object still fools them. Children who think that merely spreading out some material gives them more, for example, have to be taught differently than children who conserve quantity. Most young children find it difficult to work meaningfully with standard units of measurement such as centimeters and inches until about age 7.

Primary students can build readiness for working with standard units by using parts of their bodies or familiar objects as arbitrary units to measure things. A primary child may say, "The classroom is 28 of my feet wide."

Concrete Referents and Improvised Tools

One way to improve the ability of children to measure and estimate accurately is to have numerous concrete objects in your classroom for them to refer to as needed. Metersticks, yardsticks, and trundle wheels are useful for thinking about length. Containers marked with metric and English units are good for measuring liquid volumes.

Similar references are needed for other concepts involving quantity. A kilometer is a round trip from the school to the police station. A mile is the distance from the school to the post office. Meanings associated with time can be developed by many references to water or sand clocks (containers with holes punched in the bottom) and real clocks. Temperature differences become meaningful through using several kinds of thermometers.

Measurement Motivators: From Dinosaurs to Decimals (Palumbo, 1989) and *Measurement: 35 Hands-On Activities* (Garcia, 1997) can be helpful resources when developing meaningful measurement experiences with your students. The concept of measurement as a part of everyday life is also seen in *How Big Is a Foot?* (Myller, 1990), in which a foot is used to measure a bed. As students become interested in more detailed information, refer to such sources as *The World of Measurements* (Klein, 1974). This source contains details on units, their history, and their use.

By the time they leave elementary school, most children will have had some experience with a variety of measuring instruments such as the ruler, meterstick, yardstick, balance, clock, thermometer, graduated cylinder, protractor, directional compass, and wind gauge. When possible, children themselves should choose the right measuring tool for the activity underway. Sometimes they can make their own tools when they need them. Inventing and making a measuring instrument can be challenging and interesting.

Measurement and the Metric System

Scientists everywhere have long used the metric system because, like our number system, its units are defined in multiples of 10. The three basic units most commonly used in the metric system are the meter, liter, and gram.

A meter is used to measure length, a liter is used to measure liquid volume, and a gram is used to measure weight or mass. Strictly speaking, the terms *mass* and *weight* mean different things in science. Mass is the amount of material or matter that makes up an object. Weight is the gravitational force that pulls the mass. On the moon, for example, an astronaut's weight is only about one sixth of what it is on the earth, but the astronaut's mass stays unchanged.

The Celsius (C) thermometer, named after its inventor, Anders Celsius, commonly measures temperature in the metric system. It has a scale marked into 100 evenly spaced subdivisions.

Prefixes are used in the metric system to show larger or smaller quantities. The three most common prefixes and their meanings are as follows:

- *milli-:* one thousandth (0.001)
- *centi-:* one hundredth (0.01)
- *kilo-:* one thousand (1000)

Take a closer look at Figure 4–2 to see how prefixes are used in combination with basic units.

Before your students use different metric standards, have them consider the right standard for the job. Children will usually discover that the metric system is easier to use than the English system. Conversions from or to the English system should be avoided because they are confusing. If your curriculum calls for work with both metric and English measures, give your students a lot of practice with concrete materials for both systems. Try to treat each system separately instead of shifting back and forth. For example, when the students are comparing indoor and outdoor Fahrenheit temperatures as part of a weather

Figure 4–2   Comparison of length, volume, weight, and temperature.

Length

1 millimeter (mm)	= The diameter of paper clip wire
1 centimeter (cm)	= The width of a formed paper clip
1 meter (m)	= 1000 millimeters (mm)
1 meter (m)	= 100 centimeters (cm)
1 kilometer (km)	= 1000 meters (m)
1 kilometer (km)	= About the length of nine football fields
1 kilometer (km)	= About six tenths of a mile

Volume

1 milliliter (ml)	= About one fifth of a teaspoon
1 liter (l)	= 1000 milliliters (ml)
1 liter (l)	= 100 centiliters (cl)
1 liter (l)	= Slightly over a quart
1 kiloliter (kl)	= 1000 liters (l)

Weight (Mass)

1 milligram (mg)	= About 1/1000 of the mass of a paper clip
1 gram (g)	= 1000 milligrams (mg)
1 gram (g)	= 100 centigrams (cg)
1 kilogram (kg)	= 1000 grams (g)
1 kilogram (kg)	= About 2.2 pounds

Temperature

0 degrees Celsius	= Freezing point of water
100 degrees Celsius	= Boiling point of water

activity, do not automatically ask what the temperature would be in degrees Celsius. Instead, at a later time, develop a chart of Celsius temperatures outside over the period of a month and discuss the temperatures and any temperature changes.

The story *A Toad for Tuesday* (Erickson, 1998) can be a starting place for measurement activities related to the owl theme. Potential measurement activities could include the distance of the toad's journey through the woods before meeting the owl, the time the owl waits before changing his mind about his vow to eat the toad, the potential temperatures of the woods, the relative sizes of the toad and owl, and the appropriate weights of the owl and toad.

Communicating

Communication is the sharing of information through written or spoken means such as an oral report, charts, graphs, reports, and publications.

Communication is putting the information or data obtained from our observations into some form that another person can understand or some form that we can understand at a later date. Children learn to communicate in many ways. They learn to draw accurate pictures, diagrams, and maps; make proper charts and graphs; construct accurate models and exhibits; and use clear language when describing objects or events. The last of these activities is usually stressed in elementary science.

It is important to say things or show data in the clearest possible way. We can help our students learn this by giving them many chances to communicate and by helping them to evaluate what they have said or done.

The book *The Man Who Could Call Down Owls* (Bunting, 1984) is a good introduction to communication. *Turtle in July* (Singer, 1989) also involves month-by-month communication from animals' points of view, including a poem from an owl.

Think of a primary-level class where some students are seated on a rug. They are viewing a series of pictures of the life cycle of an owl from an LCD projector. The teacher has scanned the pictures into the computer from *See How They Grow: Owl* (Ling, 1992) and is projecting them for all the students to see. She suggests a game in which a child communicates the properties of a life stage, such as "I am fluffy, hunched over, and my eyes are closed." Others try to identify the stage. The child who identifies the growth period first gets to be the new describer. Reminding the children to carefully consider the description discourages guessing. After each student's identification, the teacher asks questions, for example:

What did she say that helped you figure out this stage?
What else would be helpful to say?
Did anyone get mixed up?
How do you think that happened?

The teacher summarizes the communications activity by reading *Owl Babies* (Waddell, 1994) and having the children describe the owlets.

In an upper-level class, the students want to find out the locations of owls. They are collaborating with students from throughout the region via the Internet. Students are collecting real-time data on sightings of owls and hearing owls' screeches. Together they will make maps, charts, and graphs on their findings and communicate the results.

See the Chapter 4 Web Destinations on the Companion Website at *http://www. prenhall.com/peters* for links related to graphing and graphing activities.

In another upper-level class, students want to find out the warmest time of the day. Temperature readings are made on the hour from 10 A.M. until 3 P.M. for 5 days in a row and then averaged. They decide to record their results on a line graph, but they do not know whether to put the temperature along the side (vertical axis) or along the bottom (horizontal axis) of the graph. Is there a "regular" way? The teacher helps them see how graphs are arranged in their mathematics text. Scientists call the change being tested the *manipulated variable*. In this case, time is usually placed along the horizontal axis. The change that results from the test is called the *responding variable*. In this situation, temperature is the responding variable and is placed along the vertical axis.

Defining Operationally

Defining operationally is a subprocess of communicating, usually introduced after the primary grades. To define a word operationally is to describe it by an action (operation) rather than by other words. For example, suppose you invite some students to hold an evaporation contest: Who can dry water-soaked paper towels fastest? They begin to speculate excitedly. But there is just one thing they will have to agree on before the fun begins: How will everyone know when a towel is "dry"? This question stumps the students, so you pose another open question that hints at *actions* they could take: What are some things they could do to the towel to tell if it is dry? Now, they start coming up with the following operations (actions) to try.

Squeeze the towel into a ball and see if water comes out. Rub it on the chalkboard; see if it makes a wet mark. Tear it and compare the sound to a dry towel you tear.

Hold it up to the light and compare its color to an unsoaked towel.

See if it can be set on fire as fast as an unsoaked towel. Put an unsoaked towel on one end of a balance beam; see if the other towel balances it.

The children agree that the last operation is easiest to observe and the least arguable. It is stated as an operational definition: "A towel is dry if it balances an unsoaked towel from the same package." Now the activity can begin.

Had the open question not worked, a narrow question such as, "How would squeezing the towel show if it is dry?" could have been posed, followed with a broad question such as, "What else could you do to the towel to tell if it is dry besides squeezing it?"

When operational definitions are not used, it is easy to fall into the trap of **circular reasoning:** What is the condition of a dry towel? It contains no moisture. What is the condition of a towel that contains no moisture? It is dry. Or, to borrow from children's humor, consider this example:

> He is the best scientist we've ever had.
> Who is?
> He is.
> Who is "He"?
> The best scientist we've ever had.

There are some predictable times when the need for operational definitions will come up. Watch the children's use of relative terms such as *tall*, *short* (How tall? short?), *light*, *heavy*, *fast*, *slow*, *good*, and *bad* (What is "bad" luck?).

Creating a Record of Activities

Recording is another subprocess of communicating. When activities require time to gather data (e.g., growing plants over many weeks) or when there are many data to consider (e.g., discovering how much vitamin C many juices contain), it is often sensible to make a record of what is happening. Without a record, it is difficult to remember what has happened and to draw conclusions. In a way, recording can be considered communicating with oneself. Many teachers ask their students to make records in a notebook or data log. Records can be in picture or graph form, as well as in writing. Whichever way the data are recorded, they should be clear.

In a primary-level class, some children are recording the growth of their plants with strips of colored paper. Every other day, they hold a new strip of paper next to each plant and tear off a bit to match the plant's height. They date the strips and paste them in order on large paper sheets. A growth record of the plants is clearly visible to all the students.

Other children in the class have drawn pictures of their plants at different stages, from seed to mature plant. These pictures are made into record booklets at the teacher's suggestion. The children describe each picture for the teacher, who swiftly writes their short statements on paper slips. The children paste these beneath their pictures. The result is a "My Plant Storybook" for each child, who can proudly read it to impressed parents.

In a middle-level class, five groups are at work with narrow strips of litmus paper. (This chemically treated paper changes color when dipped into acidic or basic liquids.) The children want to find out whether five mystery liquids in numbered jars are acidic, basic, or neutral. Each group has a recorder who notes the findings on a data sheet. At the end of the work session, the teacher asks how the results of all the groups should be recorded on the chalkboard. It is decided as outlined in Table 4–1. Notice that by having a code (A: Acid, B: Base, N: Neutral) written to one side, the teacher cuts down on the time needed to record the findings. The data are now compared, differences noted, and possible reasons discussed. Careful retesting is planned to straighten out the differences.

In an upper-level class, some students want to find out whether there is a pattern to the clouds passing over the city in the spring. They have made a chart that has three columns: one each for March, April, and May. In each column is a numbered space for each day of that month. Next to about half of the days, the students have drawn the weather

Circular reasoning is like a specious argument where the child's answer is plausible to a child but the argument has a logical flaw.

Table 4–1

Acidity of Mystery Liquids

Group	1	2	3	4	5	
Miranda	A	B	N	B	A	A: Acid
Tasha	A	B	N	B	A	B: Base
Evan	A	A	N	A	A	N: Neutral
Brian	A	B	N	A	A	
Britton	B	B	N	B	B	

bureau cloud symbols for the cloud cover, if any, on those days. Even though the record chart is only partly completed, a sequential pattern is taking shape. After the chart is completed, the students will compare it with data gathered by the local weather bureau office for the same months in previous years.

Inferring

The usual meaning of **inference** is to interpret or explain what we observe. If Wallie smiles when she greets us (observation), we may infer that she is pleased to see us (explanation). The accuracy of our inferences usually improves with more chances to observe. Several like observations may also lead us to the *prediction* that the next time we see her, Wallie will smile (observation) because she will be pleased to see us (explanation). For convenience, then, view the process of inferring as having two parts: We may make an *inference* from what we observe, and we may predict an *observation* from what we infer. Let's now look at children explaining observations and then, later, in another section, predicting them.

> **Inference** is an explanation of an observation based on the available information.

Inferring as Explaining

In at least three common ways, we as educators can help children infer properly from observations. Primary-level students, however, may have a very limited overall understanding of this process.

First, we can get students to distinguish between their observation and an inference. In a middle-level class, two children are looking at a picture of shoeprints in the snow. One set of prints is much smaller than the other (observation). One child says, "One of these sets of shoeprints must have been made by a man and the other by a boy" (an inference). The other child says, "That's true" (another inference). Hearing this, the teacher asks an open question to make them aware of other possibilities:

> In what other ways could these prints have been made?

They think for a moment and come up with other inferences: Perhaps two children made the prints—one wore his father's shoes; or maybe it was a girl and her mother; or it could have been a girl and her older brother.

The teacher points out that what they have observed is still the same but that there is more than one way to explain the observation. If the children look at the tracks closely, they may conclude that one of their inferences is more likely than the others. A *conclusion* is simply the inference in which one has the most confidence after considering all the evidence.

Second, we can get students to interpret data they have observed or recorded. Remember the students who were using litmus paper to identify mystery liquids? When several groups recorded their data, they noticed that some data were inconsistent. Some liquids were labeled both acidic and basic. The children inferred from this that the litmus test was done incorrectly by one of the groups. After the tests were redone, all the data became consistent. So, the children inferred that their final labeling of the mystery liquids was probably correct.

Recall the cloud data study. The sequential pattern the children saw when they examined their data was an inferred pattern. Later, when they compare their pattern with the weather bureau's report, they will be able to evaluate the quality of their inference.

Third, we can let students observe and interpret only indirect evidence or clues. Scientists must often depend on clues rather than clear evidence in forming possible inferences. For example, no scientist has visited the middle of the earth, yet earth scientists have inferred much about its properties.

Children can learn to make inferences from incomplete or indirect evidence, and they can also learn to become wary of hasty conclusions. In a primary-level class, some students are working with two closed shoeboxes. One box contains a smooth-sided, cylindrical pencil; the other box contains a six-sided, cylindrical pencil. The children's problem is, "Which box contains which kind of pencil?"

They tip the boxes back and forth and listen intently, inferring correctly the contents of the two boxes. When the teacher asks students what made them decide as they did, one child says, "You could feel which one was the bumpy pencil when it rolled." The other child says, "The bumpy one made more noise."

Later, the teacher puts into the boxes two pencils that are identical except for length. The students now find that correct inferring is more difficult, so they become more cautious. What observations must they rely on now?

In the middle and upper grades, students can do an excellent job of inferring the identity or interactions of hidden objects from indirect observational clues. In science, this way of inferring is called *model building*.

Explore owl inferences with your students. Why is the owl's beak a particular shape? Why are the feathers of one owl different than those of another? How do owls differ from eagles or other birds of prey? Read *A First Look at Owls, Eagles, and Other Hunters of the Sky* (Selsam & Hunt, 1986) to follow up on your inferences.

Predicting

> **Prediction** is an estimate of a future observation.

A **prediction** is a forecast of a future observation based on inferences from the available data. The more data that are available, the more confidence we have in the prediction; the reverse is also true. We can be confident that spring will follow winter, but not at all confident that spring fashions this year will be exactly like those of a year ago. Without some data, we can only guess about future observations; to predict is impossible. When students put their data in graph form, they usually have many chances to predict.

Upper-level students measure and record on a graph the time candles burn under inverted glass jars. After they have recorded the times for 100-, 200-, and 300-milliliter jars, the teacher asks, "How long do you think the candle will burn under a 250-milliliter jar?"

Notice that predicting the time for a 250-milliliter jar would require the students to read the graph between the current data—they have the times for a 200- and a 300-milliliter jar. This is called *interpolating*. If the teacher had asked the students to predict the candle-burning time of a 400-milliliter jar, the students would have needed to go beyond the current data. This is called *extrapolating* from data. Using these processes to predict is more accurate than guessing.

Children often need assistance when predicting. Simple diagrams can help them reason through data. If they cannot calculate precise predictions, just asking them to predict the direction of change is useful to them. Primary-level students might be asked, "Will more or less water evaporate when the wind blows?" Middle-level students might be asked, "Will a *higher, lower,* or the *same* temperature result when these two water samples of different temperatures are mixed?"

Experimenting

Experimentation is the quintessence of inquiry teaching. Authors of the Inquiry Teaching Standard in the Standards Link box list investigations, inquiry, accessibility of science resources, and the learning environment as important teaching considerations. When we think of inquiry, we often think of experiments. But just what is involved with an "experiment"?

To a child, experimenting means "doing something to see what happens." Although this definition is overly simple, it does capture the difference between experimenting and the other six science processes. In experimenting, we change objects or events to learn how nature changes them. This section is about how children can discover the various conditions of change. Experimentation builds on the concept of open investigations.

Experimenting is often called an *integrated* process skill because it may require us to use some or all of the other process skills: observing, classifying, inferring and predicting, measuring, and communicating. That is one reason some curriculum writers may reserve experimentation for upper-grade activities; but experimental investigations can vary in difficulty. With guidance, even primary students will benefit from experimentation. This does not mean any hands-on activity may properly be called experimenting. Two generally accepted criteria that separate hands-on activities from experimentation are as follows:

Experimentation is finding a conclusion to a hypothesis through the integration of all the scientific skills.

Children should have an idea they want to test (hypothesizing).
Children should vary only one condition at a time (controlling variables).

To many educators, almost any investigation is experimenting, as long as the child changes an object for a purpose and can compare its changed state to the original one. This is the position taken in this book.

Hypothesizing

How do we get students to form ideas they want to test before they manipulate objects? There are several ways of getting children to state operations that they want to try. For elementary students, stating operations as questions such as, "Will dropping a magnet make it weaker?" or "Does adding salt to water make objects float higher?" is a clear and easy way

Students discover the properties of a parachute as part of an extension to a parachute lab.

for them to state hypotheses. It makes them focus on what they want to do to produce some effect, or on what effect to observe and connect to a cause.

In science, a hypothesis is often stated in an "if–then" manner: If I do this, then I believe this will happen. If a magnet is dropped, then it will get weaker. You may want to use the if–then form with upper-level students. For most children, however, stating a hypothesis as an operational question is easier and more understandable.

Allowing students to explore the properties of real objects stimulates them to suggest their own ideas for changing the properties. Their curiosity usually prompts them to state operations they want to try or to be receptive to broad or narrow questions that you ask. For example, in a primary-level class, some children have been making and playing with toy parachutes. They tie the four corners of a handkerchief with strings and attach these to a sewing spool. Some release their parachutes while standing on top of the playground slide and watch them fall slowly to the ground. Others simply wad the cloth around the spool and throw their parachutes up into the air.

A few children have made their parachutes from different materials. They are quick to notice that some parachutes stay in the air longer than others. After they go back to the classroom, they discuss their experiences. Then, the teacher says:

> We have plenty of materials to make more parachutes on the science table. How can you make a parachute that will fall more slowly than the one you have now?

The children will respond in different ways: "Make it bigger," "Make it smaller," "Use a lighter spool," or "Make it like Martha's." These are the children's hypotheses. Some children may say nothing, but peer intently at the materials. They are hypothesizing, too, only nonverbally. The children's ideas need testing so that they can find out what works. Now the children have purposes for doing further work with parachutes.

Where did the children's hypotheses originate? When the children were first observing their parachutes in action, they did much inferring. ("Jimmy's parachute is bigger than mine. It stays up longer." "Corinne has a big spool. Her chute falls fast.") It is natural for people to be curious about the correctness of their inferences. *Hypotheses are simply inferences that people want to test.*

Exploring the properties of concrete materials provides the background that most children need to construct new concepts. They may not be able to offer broad explanatory hypotheses to test concepts or theories. This calls for additional scaffolding and prior knowledge and experience. For this reason, some *what* questions (What makes a ship float?) are difficult for children to answer. Instead of broad, general hypotheses, elementary students are likely to offer limited hypotheses based on the objects they have observed or manipulated.

Primary students are far more limited in this ability than upper-elementary or middle school thinkers. Scaffolding is more effective with real materials to think about during their discussion, instead of relying on discussion alone. Most primary students can only think about one variable at a time. This limits the experimenting they can do, because they are unlikely to control other variables that might affect the outcome. So, primary-level investigations usually lean more heavily on the other six science processes.

Controlling Variables

To find out exactly what condition makes a difference in an experiment, we must change or vary that condition alone. Other conditions must not vary; in other words, they must be controlled during the experiment.

Suppose you think that varying the size of a parachute will affect its falling rate. A good way to test the variable is to build two parachutes that are identical in every way except size. These could then be released at the same time from the same height. After repeated trials, you can infer whether size makes a difference in the test.

Grade 2 Example

Do not expect primary-level students to reason in this way. They will not think of the many variables or conditions that can influence their experiment. They may unwittingly change several variables at the same time. Their intent is simply to make a parachute that will fall more slowly than another, not to isolate variable conditions. Older children, in contrast, will grasp the need to control some variables. Typically, they will insist on releasing their parachutes from the same height and at the same time. Otherwise, "It won't be fair," they will tell you.

The parachute experiment is more than just a trial-and-error activity. The children have observed parachutes and have done some inferring about their observations. The changes they try will reflect thinking we can call hypothesizing. And although they may not think of controlling all the possible variables, they are conscious of some. This is the nature of children. How well they do and how fast they progress is influenced by how we as teachers scaffold their experiences. Following are more examples of teachers helping their students construct the idea of experimentation.

Grade 4 Example

In Mr. Li's fourth-grade class, the children have worked with seeds and plants for about 2 weeks. The teacher says:

> We've done well in getting our plants started. But suppose we didn't want our seeds to sprout and grow. Sometimes in nature seeds get damaged or conditions are not right for seeds to grow. What could you do to keep seeds from sprouting and growing?

Figure 4–3   Things that may keep a seed from growing.

Squashing it	Cutting it in half
Chewing it	Not watering it
Freezing it	Watering it with saltwater
Boiling it	Microwaving it

The children begin suggesting operations to try, as shown in Figure 4–3. These are their hypotheses; at this point, they need not be framed as operational questions. The teacher writes all of these on the chalkboard, regardless of content. The teacher then has the class screen the hypotheses for those that may have possibilities:

> With which conditions might the seed have some chance to live? Suppose Matoteng squashed his seed just a little. Would the seed sprout? Would the plant look squashed? Would this happen with any kind of a seed? How about some of the rest of these conditions?

This mixture of broad and narrow questions is posed slowly to give the children time to think. The children discuss a number of possibilities. After a while, the teacher says:

> How can we test our ideas?

It soon becomes obvious that some children are going to do several things at one time to their seeds, so the teacher says:

> Suppose Hongmei squashes her seed and also freezes it. How will she know which one stopped the seed from growing?

The children decide to change just one condition at a time. Pairs of children quickly form operational questions from hypotheses they want to test:

> Will squashing a bean seed keep it from sprouting? Will cutting a bean seed in half keep it from sprouting?

Interest is high as experimenting begins.

Grade 6 Example

In Ms. Xu's sixth-grade class, students are working in pairs. They are testing their reaction time by catching dropped rulers. In each pair, one student holds the ruler just above his partner's hand. When he releases the ruler, the partner catches the ruler between her thumb and forefinger. The ruler number closest to the top of her pinched fingers is recorded. This is her "reaction time." After a few minutes, the teacher asks the students to give their reaction times. He writes these on the board in the form of a histogram, as shown in Table 4–2. Histograms are used to classify data in a way that encourages thinking about the differences in the data.

After a few moments, in a discussion with the students on how the scores are distributed, Ms. Xu says:

> Suppose everything and everyone were the same in our experiment. How would the histogram look? Well, are there differences that may have given us these results? What conditions might affect reaction time?

The students start forming hypotheses:

> Not everybody did it the same way.
> Some people have faster reaction times.

Table 4–2

Reaction Time Histogram

```
                              X
                              X
                              X
                    X         X
                    X    X    X    X
          X         X    X    X    X
          X         X    X    X    X    X    X
 X        X         X    X    X    X    X    X         X
 1    2   3    4    5    6    7    8    9   10   11   12
```

Some kids have more practice.
I was tired today.

After a discussion to narrow down and clarify different ideas, Ms. Xu says:

How are you going to test your ideas?

The students state their ideas as operational questions: Will people have the same reaction time if they do the experiment in exactly the same way? Does practice give you a faster reaction time? Do people who feel "tired" (defined as having fewer than 8 hours of sleep) have slower times than when they don't feel tired? Everybody agrees that they must do the experiment in the same way each time to control the test variables. Then each question is tested separately under the controlled conditions.

Experimentation and Scientific Attitudes

According to the National Science Education Leadership Association (2001), "Teachers should base their teaching of elementary science on process and inquiry skills such as observing, classifying, measuring, interpreting data, proposing hypotheses and conclusions." Experimentation incorporates all of the process and inquiry skills. Another positive outcome of promoting experimentation and scientific skills in your classroom is in the area of student attitudes toward science.

SCIENTIFIC ATTITUDES

As seen in the Inquiry and Attitudes Standard in the Standards Link box, an important part of inquiry is acquiring positive scientific attitudes. Experimentation and other skills are not fully developed if they are completed in a negative framework or only finished to "get it over with." Science is different from such activities as learning to spell, in which the task is simple and there is only one correct answer. Science includes developing attitudes and

Teaching Tips

Exploring your students' attitudes and resolving any negative attitudes toward science will assist in positive teaching experiences throughout the school year.

questioning those attitudes. The development of these attitudes is part of the job for elementary and middle school teachers. We will consider five categories related to attitudes.

Curiosity

"To be a child is to touch, smell, taste, and hear everything you can between the time you get up and when your parents make you go to bed. I don't have to teach curiosity. It's there already." The kindergarten teacher who made this statement about curiosity echoes the feeling of many of her elementary school colleagues. Yet, in some classes, there are children who lack interest in science.

Walk into two adjoining classrooms: one with a hands-on science program and another where students just read and do worksheets during science time. Handing concrete materials to children is like rowing downstream or cycling with the wind at your back. Making children sit still and be quiet for long periods is like rowing upstream or riding into the wind: You can do it, but it is better to avoid it. Children lose much of their curiosity unless they are allowed to do what comes naturally.

Teachers who maintain or spark students' curiosity apply science to everyday life. These teachers also use several open-ended investigations during a teaching unit. As you can see, we often use children's literature as a way to initiate curiosity about a topic. For example, reading *Poppy* (Avi, 1995) explores the relationship between an owl and a deer mouse. Students will immediately begin to wonder about the relationship between these two animals.

> ### Standards Link
>
> #### Inquiry and Attitudes Standard
>
> Teachers of science develop communities of science learners that reflect the intellectual rigor of scientific inquiry and the attitudes and social values conducive to science learning. In doing this, teachers:
>
> - **Display and demand respect for the diverse ideas, skills, and experiences of all students.**
>
> - **Enable students to have a significant voice in decisions about the content and context of their work and require students to take responsibility for learning of all members of the community.**
>
> - **Nurture collaboration among students.**
>
> - **Structure and facilitate ongoing formal and informal discussion based on a shared understanding of rules of scientific discourse.**
>
> - **Model and emphasize the skills, attitudes, and values of scientific inquiry.**
>
> (Teaching Standard E, National Research Council, 1996, pp. 45, 46.)

Inventiveness

Fluency refers to the number of ideas a child gives when challenged with a problem. We can promote fluency by asking open-ended questions.

To be inventive is to solve problems in creative or novel ways. This is contrast to simply taking a known solution and applying it to a problem at hand: It's good to apply what you know about a car jack to change a flat tire, but what do you do when there's no jack? Inventive people may apply their knowledge to solve problems much as other persons do, but they are more likely to show **fluency, flexibility,** and **originality** in their thinking.

Flexibility is the inclination to shift one's focus from the usual.

Critical Thinking

Originality is shown when children generate ideas that are new to them. We can promote originality by encouraging children to use their imagination and combine others' ideas in new ways, and by withholding evaluative comments until we have all the ideas.

To think critically is to evaluate or judge whether something is adequate, correct, useful, or desirable. A judge does this when she decides whether the evidence is adequate to find guilt; the judge has a standard in mind against which she makes a judgment. This is the key to critical thinking: Know the accepted standard and decide whether or to what degree it is being met.

Visit an Inquiry Classroom
Curiosity

View the *Curiosity and Interest* video in the "Nature of Science" section of the Companion CD. Mr. McKnight asks students questions to stimulate their curiosity. More importantly, however, he has the students identify questions that they would like to explore.

Review the video and ask yourself the following:

- Why doesn't Mr. McKnight simply provide a written question and have all the students explore that question?
- Mr. McKnight does not readily answer the question of "how do they have babies" but instead tells Josh, "When you learn the answer, you won't believe it." Why didn't he simply provide a brief answer to this question?

Novak (1977) suggested that inquiry is a student behavior that involves activity and skills, but with the focus on the active search for knowledge or understanding to satisfy students' curiosity. Explain why you agree or disagree with this idea.

 Record your ideas and the answers to these questions in your portfolio or use the Companion Website to share your ideas.

A problem we face as teachers of elementary and middle school children is the numerous standards of behavior in science. Many are highly sophisticated. Let's see if we can reduce them to a manageable few and restate them on a level that makes sense to young minds.

Science has three overall standards for critical thinking that most children can gradually understand and learn to assimilate: open-mindedness, objectivity, and willingness to suspend judgment until enough facts are known.

The *open-minded* person listens to others and is willing to change his mind if warranted. An *objective* person tries to be free of bias, considers both sides in arguments, and realizes that strong personal preferences may interfere with the proper collecting and processing of data. Someone who *suspends judgment* understands that additional data may confirm or deny what first appears. Looking for further data improves the chances for drawing proper conclusions.

Try having several groups work on the same activity and then report and compare findings. The degree of open-mindedness soon becomes obvious when people refuse to listen to others, push their own ideas, or jump to conclusions before all groups have their say.

Critical and creative thinking go hand in hand—it is artificial to separate them. When problem solving or experimenting, for example, children should be encouraged to generate several possibilities, rather than just consider the first idea suggested. You also want them to appraise all the ideas critically so that they can tackle what looks most promising. Controlling variables in experimenting gives students another chance to generate suggestions, but they must also think: "Will these controls do the job?" Later, if groups come up with different findings, critical thinking is again needed to answer why. Perhaps one or more variables were not controlled after all. You can see that creative and critical thinking are different sides of the same coin.

When students seek information, a variety of sources are available to them, including each other, printed matter, audiovisual materials, electronic information, and knowledgeable adults. Certainly, students can be cautioned to check copyright dates and agreement with what is known, to consult more than one source, and to note conflicts in fact. This is especially important when exploring the Internet, where information can be posted from anyone who has access to it. Children often do not critically appraise information. As educators, we can help children learn ways to consult these sources efficiently and to understand what the sources say.

Spend time reading fictional materials with your students. *Owls in the Family* (Mowat, 1981) is a humorous tale of two owls. Critical thinking is promoted as students begin to separate fact from fiction in this story.

Persistence

Most elementary and middle school science activities can be completed within a short time, but some require a sustained and vigorous effort. To do our best work often takes persistence. Children sometimes lack the persistence to stick with a worthwhile goal. Primary-level students often want instant results. Their short attention span and need for physical activity can easily convert into impatience. You can combat this impatience by arousing children's interests with meaningful science activities.

Uncertainty

Another important attitude to develop is the ability to understand or accept uncertainty. Much of this attitude centers on students understanding the nature of elementary statistics. Some events can be predicted well; some cannot. We do not always know all the variables in a given situation, nor do we always have representative data of a population. For instance, the weather announcer on television only predicts rain tomorrow on the basis of the percentage of times it has rained with similar weather conditions (e.g., air pressure, wind patterns, cold and warm fronts).

Elementary and middle school students should be aware that evidence is not always complete and that therefore predictions may not always be precise. Experiments are influenced by the lack of an accurate observation, missing information of compounding factors, or a model to explain the variables effectively. Scientists do not always have all the answers, but must theorize on the observations and experimental results they do have.

Visit an Inquiry Classroom
Teacher Modeling of Attitudes

Watch *Glen McKnight's Perspective with the Teacher Attributes* video in the "Nature of Science" section of the Companion CD. What does Mr. McKnight specifically say that indicates he possesses positive scientific attitudes and passes these on to his students?

Review the video segment and ask yourself the following:
- If I were being interviewed, what would I say about my attitudes toward science?
- We state that "early learning of attitudes begins with imitation" and that "the open-minded, accepting teacher who reflects positive attitudes is more likely to influence students in positive ways." From your own experiences, do you find this to be true? Provide specific examples.

Corsaro (2003) discusses how we as a society may be losing our parental influences on children and that more influence may come from the school environment. If he is accurate with this idea, what would that suggest to you as a future elementary or middle school science teacher? Record your ideas and the answers to these questions in your portfolio or use the Companion Website to share your ideas.

Developing Attitudes

Early learning of attitudes begins with imitation and later comes from experiences with the consequences of having or not having the attitudes. The open-minded, accepting teacher who reflects positive attitudes is more likely to influence students in positive ways than one who lacks these qualities.

Open-ended activities bring out positive attitudes. Success in science is bound up with curiosity, inventiveness, critical thinking, persistence, and tolerance for uncertainty. Children learn, in a more limited way, the same habits of mind as scientists and other reflective people. Successfully practicing these attitudes helps build self-esteem.

Summary

- In *observing,* students learn to use all their senses, note similarities and differences in objects, and become aware of change.
- In *classifying,* students group things by properties or functions. Students may also arrange them in order of value.
- *Measuring* teaches students to use nonstandard and standard units to find or estimate quantity. Measurement is often applied in combination with skills introduced in the mathematics program.
- *Communicating* teaches students to put observed information into some clear form that another person can understand.

- By *inferring,* students interpret or explain what they observe. When students infer from data that something will happen, usually the term *predicting* is used. When people state an inference they want to test, usually the term *hypothesizing* is used. Therefore, predicting and hypothesizing are special forms of inferring.
- In *experimenting,* we often guide students to state their hypotheses as operational (testable) questions and help them control variables within their understanding.

Reflection

Companion CD

1. Look at "The Earthworm's Body: Digging It" lesson linked to the *Learning to Think* video on the Companion CD. Can you rewrite this lesson to be more consistent with the learning cycle?
2. Look at "The Earthworm and Water" lesson linked to the *Cognitive Apprenticeship* video on the Companion CD. How could you modify the "Extended Practice" section to have students apply their new knowledge and skills as part of the concept application phase?
3. Look at "Mechanics of the Digestive System" lesson linked to the *Scientific Method* video on the Companion CD. Observation is not identified as a skill to be taught in this lesson. In what ways could you modify this lesson to include developing observational skills?

Portfolio Ideas

1. Safety is an important consideration when experimenting or developing other scientific skills in the elementary and middle school classrooms. Purchase a copy of *Safety in the Elementary Science Classroom* (National Science Teachers Association, 1997, at http://www.nsta.org) and identify potential safety hazards in your practicum classroom. Record these in your portfolio and discuss them with the teacher. Also visit the Companion Website (http://www.prenhall.com/peters) for more safety information.
2. What other scientific skills can you think of to teach children? What approaches could you take to develop these skills in elementary or middle school students? Record findings in your portfolio.

3. How well do you know the science processes?
    Experiment with one of the activities from the books
    listed in the Suggested Readings. Repeat your
    experiment with students at your practicum site,
    document findings in your portfolio, and compare
    their results with those of your classmates.
4. Interview an elementary or middle school student
    and compare her scientific attitudes with those in
    this chapter. Share these results in your portfolio and
    with the class or your instructor.
5. Try some activities in *Floaters and Sinkers* (Cordel &
    Hillen, 1995) as an initial source to learning cycle
    activities related to mass, volume, and density. Enter
    findings in your portfolio.
6. A fun way to introduce the metric system is to have a
    classroom or schoolwide Olympics. The book *Math
    & Science: A Solution* (Ecklund & Wiebe, 1987) has

metric measurement activities related to the
Olympics. *Olympic Math* (Vogt, 1996) also has
measurement and graphing activities. The *Math
Counts* series (Pluckrose, 1995) has titles that relate
to introductory measurement, such as length, weight,
time, and capacity, that can assist students in
identifying concepts as part of the Olympics
experience. Record how your event turned out in
your portfolio.

7. Try using the "Deliver Woodsy's Message" activity in
    the *Woodsy Owl Activity Guide* (Children's Television
    Network, 1977) as a communication activity.
    Students can make posters, create mobiles, write
    poetry, or perform a play based on a "lend a hand—
    care for the land" theme. Record what you find in
    your portfolio.

References

American Association for the Advancement of Science (AAAS).
    (1993). *Benchmarks for science literacy*. New York: Oxford
    University Press.

Avi. (1995). *Poppy*. New York: Orchard Books.

Barman, C. R. (1989). A procedure for helping prospective elementary
    teachers integrate the learning cycle into science textbooks.
    Journal of Science Teacher Education, 1(2), 21–26.

Brett, J. (1994). *Town mouse & country mouse*. New York: G. P. Putnam.

Bunting, E. (1984). *The man who could call down owls*. New York:
    Macmillan.

Bybee, R. W., Buchwald, C. E., Crissman, S., Heil, D. R., Kuerbis, P. J.,
    Matsumoto, C., & McInerney, J. D. (1989). *Science and technology
    education for the elementary years: Frameworks for curriculum and
    instruction*. Washington, DC: National Center for Improving
    Science Education.

Children's Television Network. (1977). *Woodsy Owl Activity Guide*.
    Washington, DC: USDA Forest Service.

Cordel, B. & Hillen, J. (1995). *Floaters and Sinkers*. Fresno, CA: AIMS
    Educational Foundation.

Corsaro, W. A. (2003). *We're friends, right?: Inside kids' culture*.
    Washington, DC: National Academy Press.

Dewey, J. (1929). *The quest for certainty: A study of the relation of
    knowledge and action*. New York: G. P. Putnam.

Ecklond, L. & Wiebe, A. (1987). *Math & Science: A Solution*. Fresno,
    CA: AIMS Educational Foundation.

Erickson, R. E. (1998). *A toad for Tuesday*. New York: Lothrop, Lee &
    Shepard Books.

Flick, L. B. (1993). The meaning of hands-on science. *Journal of Science
    Teacher Education, 4*(1), 1–8.

Fratt, L. 2002. Less is more: Trimming the overstuffed curriculum.
    District Administrator, 38(3). Retrieved December 23, 2004, from
    www.districtadministration.com/page.cfm?p=228

Garcia, A. (1997). *Measurement: 35 hands-on activities*. Cypress, CA:
    Creative Teaching Press.

Gates, F. (1994). *Owl eyes*. New York: Lothrop, Lee & Shepard Books.

Hutchins, P. (1972). *Good-night owl!* New York: Macmillan.

Kalman, B. (1987). *Owls*. New York: Crabtree.

Karplus, R. (1977). Science teaching and the development of reasoning.
    Journal of Research in Science Teaching, 14(2), 169–175.

Karplus, R., & Their, H. D. (1967). *A new look at elementary school
    science: Science curriculum improvement study*. Chicago: Rand
    McNally.

Klein, A. (1974). *The world of measurements*. New York: Simon &
    Schuster.

Ling, M. (1992). *See how they grow: Owl*. New York: Dorling Kindersley.

Mowat, F. (1981). *Owls in the family*. New York: Bantam.

Myller, R. (1990). *How big is a foot?* New York: Dell.

National Research Council (NRC). (1996). *National science education
    standards*. Washington, DC: National Academies Press.

National Research Council (NRC). (2000). *Inquiry and the national
    science education standards: A guide for teaching and learning*.
    Washington, DC: National Academies Press.

National Science Education Leadership Association. (2001). *Elementary
    science education. Position statement*. Raleigh, NC: Author.
    Retrieved December 23, 2004, from www.nsela.org/
    nselapositionpapers.pdf

National Science Teachers Association. (1997). *Safety in the elementary
    science classroom*. Washington, DC: Author.

National Science Teachers Association (NSTA). (2004). *Scientific
    inquiry. A position statement*. Washington, DC: Author. Retrieved
    October 1, 2004, from www.nsta.org/positionstatement&psid=43

Novak, J. (1977). *A theory of education*. Ithaca, NY: Cornell University
    Press.

Odom, A. L., & Settlage, J., Jr. (1996). Teachers' understandings of the
    learning cycle as assessed with a two-tier test. *Journal of Science
    Teacher Education, 7*(2), 123–142.

Palumbo, T. (1989). *Measurement motivators: From dinosaurs to decimals*.
    Torrance, CA: Good Apple.

Pluckrose, H. (1995a). *Math counts: Capacity*. Chicago: Childrens Press.

Pluckrose, H. (1995b). *Math counts: Length*. Chicago: Childrens Press.

Pluckrose, H. (1995c). *Math counts: Time*. Chicago: Childrens Press.

Pluckrose, H. (1995d). *Math counts: Weight*. Chicago: Childrens Press.

Ramsey, J. (1993). Developing conceptual storylines with the learning cycle. *Journal of Elementary Science Education, 5*(2), 1–20.

Rosenthal, D. (1993). A learning cycle approach to dealing with pseudoscience beliefs of prospective elementary teachers. *Journal of Science Teacher Education, 4*(2), 33–36.

Sattler, H. R. (1995). *The book of North American owls*. New York: Clarion Books.

Selsam, M. E., & Hunt, J. (1986). *A first look at owls, eagles, and other hunters of the sky*. New York: Walker.

Singer, M. (1989). *Turtle in July*. New York: Macmillan.

Staver, J. R., & Shroyer, M. G. (1994). Teaching elementary teachers how to use the learning cycle for guided inquiry instruction in science. In L. Schafer (Ed.), *Behind the methods class door: Educating elementary and middle school science teachers* (pp. 1–11). Columbus, OH: ERIC Clearinghouse.

Vogt, S. (1996). *Olympic math*. Grandview, IL: Good Year Books.

Waddell, M. (1994). *Owl babies*. Compton, CA: Santillana.

Yolen, J. (1987). *Owl moon*. New York: Philomel Books.

Suggested Readings

Council for Environmental Education. (1992). Owl pellets. In *Project WILD K–12 activity guide* (pp. 144–145). Bethesda, MD: Author. (a guide to owl pellet activities)

Gabel, D. L. (1993). *Introductory science skills* (2nd ed.). Prospect Heights, IL: Waveland Press. (a comprehensive workbook of scientific skill development and assessment)

Goldsworthy, A., & Feasey, R. (1997). *Making sense of primary science investigations*. Hatfield, Herts., UK: Association for Science Education. (a guide to primary science investigations and the skills involved)

Ostlund, K. (1992). *Science process skills*. Menlo Park, CA: Addison-Wesley. (ways to assess each of the science processes, with material lists and reproducible worksheets)

Ostlund, K., & Mercier, S. (1996). *Rising to the challenge of the national science education standards: The process of inquiry*. Fresno, CA: S & K Associates. (36 activities that promote the processes of science inquiry)

Rezba, R. J., Sprague, C., Fiel, R. L., Funk, H. J., Okey, J. R., & Jaus, H. H. (1995). *Learning and assessing science process skills* (3rd ed.). Dubuque, IA: Kendall/Hunt. (a workbook of scientific skill development and assessment)

Ruchlis, H. (1991). *How do you know it's true? Discovering the difference between science and superstition*. Buffalo, NY: Prometheus Books. (an easy-to-follow account of how scientific theories are based on facts and observations)

Smith, B. (1989). *Measurement motivators: From dinosaurs to decimals*. Torrance, CA: Good Apple. (a book of measurement activities)

ASSESSMENT

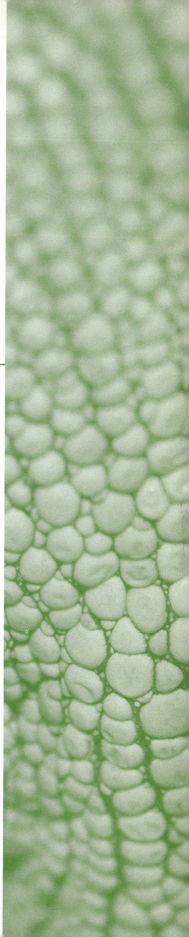

FOCUS QUESTIONS

- How is assessment different today than when you were in elementary or middle school?
- What are some types of authentic assessment?
- How can you effectively assess attitudes in the science classroom?

Focus on Inquiry

Portfolios

Christine Peters,
Harborcreek School District, Pennsylvania

During the last several years, I've been using portfolio assessment more and more. At first, I felt somewhat uncomfortable with the notion. I worried whether I'd find the time in our hectic day to collect, sort, choose, meet, and interview. Now that I've been using this form of individualized assessment, I see that my students are the ones who are responsible for the selection process. This is actually the most important aspect of using portfolios. By involving the children in the decision-making process, they achieve a deeper sense of pride, a feeling of ownership about their work, and a desire for excellence.

In building portfolios, I am concentrating on the process of the child's learning, as well as the product. My students are better able to focus on a specific goal, rather than on a letter grade. I am also promoting a closer relationship with my students because my assessment focuses on the development of a student's work over time. Not only do my students feel a great sense of pride, but I feel like the world's best teacher when I compare one of their spelling assessments from September with one from May, or when I listen to one of my student's oral reading cassettes from the first week of school—when she knew very few words and didn't have enough skills to sound them out—and compare it with the middle or end of the tape when she is able to read anything she picks up from the library.

The toughest part of using portfolio assessment is deciding when to fit the interviewing and selection process into your day. I have tried many approaches, and what I like the best is what I call "free choice time." Every other Friday afternoon, the boys and girls in my classroom are free to do what they would like to do. Of course, I give them some guidance in choosing options, and if there is any unfinished work for the day or week, that must be completed first. I will often invite one or two other adults into my classroom to help with the interviewing and selection process. Administrators, instructional and learning support teachers, and parents have all been involved in this process in my classroom in the past. It is valuable to use the same volunteers so that little time will be respent on "training," even though this is not always possible.

A typical free choice time in my classroom will look like this:

- A small group works in the science center on a food pyramid with pictures they've cut out of magazines; several children play *Pictionary* using the sand trays and shaving cream boards in the corner; a group of children make numbers out of clay to take to another classroom; two children tape themselves reading one of the big books our class wrote, entitled *Ten Black Dots;* and several children read books from our classroom library that they will then present to their classmates by using puppets or posters.

- At the same time, I and my adult volunteers will meet individually with each of my 22 students. Before the students are individually interviewed, they are told what materials are required for their meeting. They have an idea of which works (products) they will want to place into their portfolios, and they have thought about why they have chosen such pieces. During their interviews, I go over the selected pieces and together (later in the year, the students fill this out independently) we write out a "Portfolio and Goals Survey." This survey states the date, the title of the piece, why the piece was chosen, the favorite part of the piece, what the piece shows, what the child has learned so far, what he wants to learn next, and things that will help him learn better.

- If I have several adult helpers and if time permits, then I also find it valuable to go over one of my checklists with each child. One week, I may share each child's oral reading checklist with him or her, and the next week I'll share the writing or cooperative learning checklists. These are forms that I keep in students' portfolios to record learning skills and behaviors that I observe in their daily work and in how they work with each other.

I love using portfolios in my elementary classroom! The students enjoy having a collection of their work that progresses throughout the year. Even my students with learning difficulties can't help but see the progression of skill in their work. They all feel successful and are always trying to do their best, hoping that what they are currently working on will be added to their portfolio. Parents are even excited about the portfolio assessment going on in my classroom. They can see their child's learning in concrete terms and become partners in the learning process. Parents are invited in often to view their child's works, and a few times a year, the portfolio is sent home along with a letter in which the parents are encouraged to give feedback.

It doesn't take much preparation to begin using portfolios in your classroom. All you need are some file and pocket folders, composition books, cassette and/or videotapes, large manila envelopes, and lots of stick-on notes. To store the portfolios, I use a large plastic crate. A cardboard box would even fit the purpose.

Some of the items that go into my students' portfolios are my observations; their writing samples; journals; reading, writing, math, and cooperative learning inventories; artwork; parent surveys; rubrics; book evaluations; and child-selected samples of daily work.

Portfolio assessment teaches students how to learn and teaches teachers how to slow down, get to know each student and his or her strengths and needs, and develop a curriculum that appeals to each student's multiple talents. It encourages students—and teachers—to strive for excellence in all they do.

THE CHANGING PRACTICE OF ASSESSMENT

The portfolio process discussed in the Focus on Inquiry: Portfolios is representative of **assessment** practice changes in our schools. To better understand the need for these changes, let's use an industry metaphor.

Throughout most of the 20th century, school, like industry, was conceived of as a manufacturing process in which raw materials (students) were operated on by the machinery (teachers). Some of the products were worked on for longer periods of time than others, but in the end, we molded a finished product (a literate citizen).

Education in the 20th century certainly moved beyond the agrarian practices of the 19th century. Students were no longer in one-room schoolhouses where education was planned around harvest and planting seasons. Children of this era learned in unison as they progressed through the assembly line (curriculum). The primary process used to shape the final product was expository teaching. The bosses (school administrators) told the workers how to run the assembly line under rigid work rules (behavioral aims, goals, and objectives) that gave them little or no stake in the process (see Rubba, Miller, Schmalz, Rosenfeld, & Shyamal, 1991).

Assessment practices, the "quality control" of the educational allegory described above, were consistently used to seek out the degree of factual knowledge students were able to absorb. It is well documented that educators of this generation were in the "we teach what we test" mode. Unfortunately, tests of this nature were "fundamentally incompatible" with reform efforts such as those we now associate with constructivism (Resnick & Resnick, 1989).

Assessment involves the collection and interpretation of information about what students know and can do as it relates to the curriculum.

See the Chapter 5 Web Destinations on the Companion Website (*http://www.prenhall.com/peters*) to explore current assessment research and practice.

Assessment Today

This chapter reflects the view that the primary purpose of assessment is to improve opportunity to learn and the student's construction of knowledge and that quality assessments should be designed to reflect excellence in science curriculum and instruction (National Science Teachers Association [NSTA], 2001). One way to do this is to match the assessment with the learning paradigm of constructivism. We hope to make the linkage between what we want students to know and the assessment tool used to find the answer. Assessment should not be something we do *to* children, but something we can do *with* children. Look at the Consistency of Assessment Standard in the Standards Link box. This standard is a good beginning example. Does this standard cause teachers to think about assessment in a different way? Why would they use one procedure or another? What question would they hope to answer through the data collected? How will they analyze the data collected? Is the scoring rubric fair and consistent? Will this approach be helpful to the students and lead to good instructional decisions?

As you read this chapter, think about your own assessment practices. Consider how your beliefs and practices may be different from what you find here and why you and your students should be more involved

> ### Standards Link
>
> #### Consistency of Assessment Standard
>
> Assessments must be consistent with the decisions they are designed to inform.
>
> - **Assessments are deliberately designed.**
> - **Assessments have explicitly stated purposes.**
> - **The relationship between the decisions and the data is clear.**
> - **Assessment procedures are internally consistent.**
>
> (Assessment Standard A, National Research Council, 1996, p. 78.)

in assessment. A good starting point is to see why we use assessment, what assessment involves, and how it is changing.

Assessment of Science Learning

The following are good reasons for using assessment in your classroom:

For many beginning teachers, it is easier to concentrate on two assessment areas—the knowledge and skills of the students.

- Monitoring students' progress
- Increasing communications with students
- Improving instruction and the learning environment
- Determining the best science program and opportunities to learn
- Enhancing teacher accountability

You will find that assessment techniques can check students' process skill development, factual knowledge, conceptual knowledge, problem-solving ability, and higher level understanding.

Knowledge Objectives

Knowledge objectives, the content and concepts of science, can be overwhelming if you concentrate on discrete facts and definitions. Instead, work toward encompassing concepts and generalizations. For example, instead of focusing on learning every item that a magnet will attract, work toward the generalization that magnets attract objects made of iron and steel.

Skill Objectives

Skill objectives, or the process skills of science referred to in Chapter 4, are also easier to work with if they are kept to a manageable level. During the elementary and middle school years, focus on observation, classification, measurement, inference, prediction, communication, and experimentation.

Changing Emphasis

In keeping with the standards-based reform efforts, assessment is one of the most important revisions to the learning environment. The authors of *National Science Education Standards* sought a changing emphasis in the area of assessment (National Research Council [NRC], 1996). They envisioned less emphasis on assessing discrete or scientific knowledge and more emphasis on assessing scientific understanding, reasoning, and well-structured knowledge.

Today, this means we no longer place as much importance on teacher-tested vocabulary and definitions related to a topic under study. Rather, we look for teacher- and student-assessed genuine understanding. We look at how the phenomenon under study fits into the child's current and future thought processes. With changing assessment procedures, we no longer look at what students do not know, but what opportunities students have had to learn and what they do know or have achieved. We can build on the knowledge that our children already have, and thus expand the possibilities.

Look at the Achievement and Opportunity to Learn Standard in the Standards Link box. The authors make an interesting point that assessment of the **opportunity to learn** is as important as assessing the learning itself. This means that assessment should be an ongoing process. Meaningful connections should take precedence over "covering the curriculum." In *Benchmarks for Science Literacy* (American Association for the Advancement of Science [AAAS], 1993), authors call for reducing the amount of material being covered

Opportunity to learn is the concept that assessment should go beyond individual achievement and include the teacher's presentation of the content and skills through quality instructional delivery.

Visit an Inquiry Classroom
Ongoing Assessment

View the *Ongoing Assessment* video in the "Model Inquiry Unit" section of the Companion CD. Mr. McKnight uses an "investigation record" as a tool for assessing his students.

Review the video and ask yourself the following:
- What evidence is there in the video that this form of assessment is working?
- Would you want to rely solely on the investigation record as an assessment tool? If so, justify your answer. If not, what other types of assessment would you use?

In the year 2000, the National Assessment of Educational Progress presented a survey of fourth- and eighth-grade student achievement in *The Nation's Report Card: Science* (2003). The authors noted that between 1996 and 2000, there was no statistically significant difference observed in the average science scores of fourth- or eighth-grade students. Given the national testing requirements under No Child Left Behind, do you think there is an increase in the average science scores in 2005? Why or why not? Record your ideas and the answers to these questions in your portfolio or use the Companion Website to share your ideas.

in science classes. Their goal of "teaching less, but teaching it better" does not mean to teach science less often. It means to teach fewer unrelated facts and to spend more time making connections, refining skills, and providing in-depth study of a topic. Part of this goal is to spend time before, during, and after instruction on assessment, including identifying and resolving misconceptions.

This assessment picture can be more difficult but provides a better indication of the true learning occurring in your classroom. To see how assessment can be more student centered and related to understanding, follow along with the students as they study the effects of water on the environment.

Mr. Correa's Water Lesson

Mr. Correa reads *A Drop of Water* (Wick, 1997) to his fifth-grade class and sparks an interest in how water travels through the water cycle. The next day, a student follows up the discussions by telling the class about a book she recently read called *Water Dance* (Locker, 1997). The student tells the class the story of how water travels throughout the environment.

Later in the week, Mr. Correa facilitates from the *Project Learning Tree* an activity called "Water Wonders" (American Forest Foundation, 1996). Students become drops of water and cycle through clouds, mountains, oceans, streams, plants, animals, and groundwater stations set up in the classroom. At each stop, they pick out a slip of paper that leads them to the next randomly selected station. They keep track of their journey by taping the slips of paper

> **Standards Link**
>
> ### Achievement and Opportunity to Learn Standard
>
> Achievement and opportunity to learn science must be assessed.
>
> - **Achievement data collected focus on the science content that is most important for students to learn.**
> - **Opportunity-to-learn data collected focus on the most powerful indicators.**
> - **Equal attention must be given to the assessment of opportunity to learn and to the assessment of student achievement.**
>
> (Assessment Standard B, National Research Council, 1996, p. 79.)

Children experiment at a laboratory streambed as part of their river erosion activities.

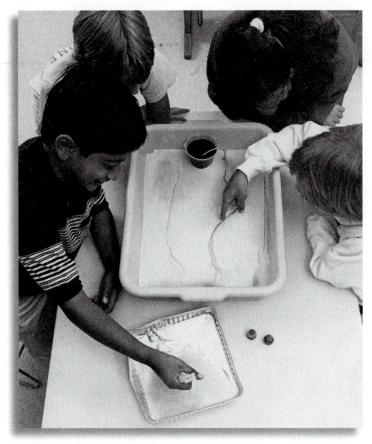

Source: Reprinted from the Great Explorations in Math and Science (GEMS) teacher's guide entitled River Cutters, copyright by The Regents of the University of California, and used with permission. The GEMS series includes more than 70 teacher's guides and handbooks for preschool through eighth grade, available from LHS GEMS, Lawrence Hall of Science, University of California, Berkeley, CA 94720-5200. /(510) 642–7771. http://www.lhsgems.org

they select at each station onto a scorecard. After they finish, students each tell a story about their adventures. In the follow-up discussion about streams, one student mentions a stream near his house. He informs the class of hearing his father's concern over a new tax to assist the county with erosion and drainage problems. Taking the discussion a step further, Mr. Correa decides to model the situation with the students.

Teaching Tips

River Cutters is one in the Great Explorations in Math and Science (GEMS) series of thematic activity books based on a hands-on/cooperative learning format (see *http://www.prenhall.com/peters* for the link to GEMS materials).

He engages the students in an activity from *River Cutters* (Lawrence Hall of Science, 1989). The students work together to set up a streambed with diatomaceous earth inside. They place a rubber tube connected to a water source that allows drops of water to flow onto the surface. They carefully observe this model of the effects of water on the earth.

Next, students draw pictures of what happens with the models. Using tags that Mr. Correa places alongside specific features, students label the streams, rivers, valleys, and other features that form in the diatomaceous earth. They discuss the features in the streambeds with their small groups and later with their teacher. Mr. Correa asks the students what other experiments they could do with the streambed apparatus.

Mr. Correa now looks on as the students generate ideas for further study. They write a description of what they would like to find out, propose ways to model the situation, and predict outcomes. They want to demonstrate what is occurring near Ninth Street. The students begin to work with the streambeds. They are adjusting the water flow to create the correct model of their neighborhood.

Where has the assessment occurred with the stream activities? What type of assessment was done? Could Mr. Correa have employed **authentic assessment** as part of his water lessons? To answer these questions, let's look further into what is meant by authentic assessment.

> **Authentic assessment** is seen as measuring or testing what the student really knows about a concept or skill, as opposed to testing something inconsistent with what was taught or the goals of the science program.

The Use of Authentic Assessment

When you were asked about the water cycle and erosion in elementary and middle school, was it similar to how Mr. Correa assessed his class? If so, you participated in authentic assessment. The authors of the *National Science Education Standards* (NRC, 1996) and Project 2061 (see AAAS, 1998) indicate that assessment should be authentic or genuine. They want the data to measure what they are supposed to measure. This view of assessment is indicated in the Quality of the Data and Interpretations Standard, as described in the Standards Link box.

Assessment should be "similar in form to tasks in which [students] will engage in their lives outside the classroom or are similar to the activities of scientists" (NRC, 1996, p. 83). The term *embedded assessment* refers to how assessment should be "part of the activities that naturally occur in a lesson or a logical extension of the lesson's central activity" (National Science Resources Center, 1997, pp. 103, 108). Examples of authentic assessment are included in Figure 5–1.

You can infer from the different types of assessment practices noted in Figure 5–1 that assessment is not just for assigning a grade. In fact, there are two types of assessments according to the Project 2061 authors (AAAS, 1998): *internal purpose assessments* and *external purpose assessments*.

Internal purpose assessments are administered to convey expectations about what is important to learn, to provide information on progress, to help students judge their learning, to guide and improve instruction, and to classify and select students (AAAS, 1998). Examples are the child-developed, teacher-made, and textbook series–provided assessment tools used by teachers as part of the normal classroom experiences.

External purpose assessments include examinations given to provide information for accountability, to guide policy decisions, to gather information for program evaluation, to

> **Standards Link**
>
> ## Quality of the Data and Interpretations Standard
>
> The technical quality of the data collected is well matched to the decisions and actions taken on the basis of their interpretation.
>
> - **The feature that is claimed to be measured is actually measured.**
>
> - **Assessment tasks are authentic.**
>
> - **An individual student's performance is similar on two or more tasks that claim to measure the same aspect of student achievement.**
>
> - **Students have adequate opportunity to demonstrate their achievements.**
>
> - **Assessment tasks and methods of presenting them provide data that are sufficiently stable to lead to the same decisions if used at different times.**
>
> (Assessment Standard C, National Research Council, 1996, p. 83.)

> **Internal purpose assessments** are classroom-based assessments used by the teacher to measure the progress of students within their class.

> **External purpose assessments** are standardized assessments generally initiated by a school district or state to compare intact classes within a larger system.

Figure 5–1   Examples of authentic assessment practices.

- Student observations
- Student interviews
- Written reports or journals
- Portfolios
- Performance measurements
- Concept or vee maps
- Multiple-choice tests
- Essay tests
- Short-answer tests
- Attitude surveys
- Creative assessments
- Projects and laboratory experiences

See the Chapter 5 Web Destinations at the Companion Website (*http://www.prenhall. com/peters*) for links related to National Board Certification.

sort and classify people for admissions, and to certify or hire (AAAS, 1998). This is the standardized type of assessment resulting from achievement, placement, or certification tests such as the Iowa Test of Basic Skills, Scholastic Aptitude Test, or a standardized state exam for elementary or middle school students.

Today, both internal purpose and external purpose forms of assessment are receiving much attention. Internal purpose assessment is a key to the reform effort, because the assumption "we teach what we test" still holds true in many classrooms. External purpose assessment is likewise becoming increasingly important for teachers at a personal level. Suggested initiatives such as linking assessment results to teacher performance portfolios, or teacher pay raises, are now being proposed or implemented in some states. The ability to provide quality assessment is also a consideration in National Board Certification (National Board for Professional Teaching Standards, 1997). In either internal purpose or external purpose assessment situations, it is important to understand what good assessment is and the many forms of authentic assessment.

Characteristics of Good Assessment

A good rule of thumb for assessment is that it is *reflective*, not *reflexive*. Assessment should not be an automatic, end-of-the-chapter reflexive routine. It should be an everyday experience that is increasingly indistinguishable from the classroom learning activities themselves. It is not a multiple-choice test that comes at the end of the chapter, waiting for our response. Rather, it is a *teacher- and student-selected* means to show that learning has occurred.

Standards Link

Sound Inferences Standard

The inferences made from assessments about student achievement and opportunity to learn must be sound.

- **When making inferences from assessment data about student achievement and opportunity to learn science, explicit reference needs to be made to the assumptions on which the inferences are based.**

(Assessment Standard E, National Research Council, 1996, p. 86.)

Assessment data should support reasonable conclusions of learning that has occurred as seen in the Sound Inferences Standard in the Standards Link box. The information should help both teacher and students reflect on what they have or have not learned. It should also help the teacher reflect on what future lessons or activities will assist in student understanding of the concepts being learned. Appraisal of learning should account for the students' individual differences and varied experiences. Figure 5–2 contains some good assessment characteristics.

Figure 5–2 Characteristics of good classroom assessments.

- They indicate an opportunity to learn.
- They allow for the student to select the best approach to a task.
- They are relevant to the student and are not just a correct answer.
- They accommodate the student's developmental level.
- They account for the student's prior knowledge.
- They are consistent and reliable for the student.
- They generally take more time to complete than tests.
- They are relevant to the learning goal.
- They promote transfer of learning into new situations.
- They produce measurable evidence of learning.
- They include both individual and group efforts.
- They are a continual process.

TYPES OF AUTHENTIC ASSESSMENT

Essay Items

Essay items provide a bridge between traditional assessment procedures and authentic assessment practices. Essay questions are useful in evaluating whether students are able to express personal ideas clearly. This type of question can be designed to assess higher order thinking, the ability to solve problems, or the capability to reason about the interrelationships between concepts.

As a caution, essay questions can be very subjective because there is not one right or wrong answer. The questions may be too vaguely worded for students to understand exactly what answer the teacher wants. Or, they may be too obvious for students and so the questions are not effective in measuring learning.

Also keep in mind that disabilities, language differences, and cultural diversity will affect students' abilities to answer questions, as pointed out in the Fair Assessment Standard in the Standards Link box. Students with poor language skills will often do poorly on these items, regardless of content knowledge. Likewise, students with good language skills may be able to bluff through answers that they do not fully understand. Cultural differences are also an important consideration.

As with other tests, careful construction of items will help make the test more meaningful. Compare the following two test items:

> What are the phases of the moon?
> Explain what we would observe here on Earth as the moon goes through its phases.
> Explain why it appears this way to us on Earth.

The first item is open for your students to interpret. They could respond by just listing "new, first quarter, full, last quarter." The second item requires your students to provide an explanation for why the phases occur and what they would look like, as well as the names of the phases. Essay tests that are well constructed match what was learned in class. They also ask well-defined, explicit questions that are understandable to all students. Additionally, good essay questions indicate, either in writing or through discourse, exactly what the teacher is looking for as an acceptable response.

 Teaching Tips Creating a rubric for essay test questions provides a fair and consistent method when grading essay items.

Visit an Inquiry Classroom
The Teacher's Role in Assessment

View the *Teacher Withitness* video in the "Planning and Management" section of the Companion CD. At the beginning of the video sequence, Mr. McKnight works with groups of students as they complete the activities. He asks questions and allows students to fill in their investigation record. This is his form of authentic assessment.

Review the video and ask yourself the following:
- Are there other ways Mr. McKnight could assess students?
- Will the investigative records show that Mr. McKnight's students are learning? Explain your answer.

In *Classroom Assessment and the National Science Education Standards* (NRC, 2001), the authors define *authentic assessment* as "assessments that require students to perform complex tasks representative of activities actually done in out-of-school settings." Explain what they mean and include the teacher's role in the assessment process. Record your ideas and the answers to these questions in your portfolio or use the Companion Website to share your ideas.

The teacher should set and communicate to the students his expectations for length, detail, and spelling prior to the test. A grading rubric should also be developed that lists the specifics of what is expected. Use of a checklist will eliminate most subjectivity.

Are essay questions and other paper-and-pencil tests the best indication of learning? Could the students actually *do something* as part of the assessment?

Standards Link

Fair Assessment Standard

Assessment practices must be fair.

- Assessment tasks must be reviewed for the use of stereotypes, for assumptions that reflect the perspectives or experiences of a particular group, for language that might be offensive to a particular group, and for other features that might distract students from the intended task.

- Large-scale assessments must use statistical techniques to identify potential bias among subgroups.

- Assessment tasks must be appropriately modified to accommodate the needs of students with physical disabilities, learning disabilities, or limited English proficiency.

- Assessment tasks must be set in a variety of contexts, be engaging to students with different interests and experiences, and not assume the perspective or experience of a particular gender, racial, or ethnic group.

(Assessment Standard D, National Research Council, 1996, p. 85.)

Performance-Based Assessment

Reflecting back on Mr. Correa, his students are being assessed as they complete the activities. How? The students are challenged to create a model streambed that is consistent with the severe erosion patterns in their neighborhood. Their *performance* on this task is one form of authentic assessment.

A performance-based assessment will generate an answer by the students. This type of assessment will also indicate the process used by the students to arrive at that answer. Performance-based assessment is often associated with the phrase "know and be able to do" (Ochs, 1996). Because students are doing something, we can assess the procedure as well as the product. There are ways to assess the procedure a student uses to arrive at an answer. This procedure is often more important than the answer itself. In fact, many times more than one answer will be correct.

The streambed example, as in other performance-based measures, provides three basic steps to follow (McMillan, 1997). The first step is *to construct the performance task* for students. In our example, Mr. Correa wanted his students to apply what they learned about erosion, so he asked the students themselves to generate or identify an idea for a task. Brainstorming ideas leads into the second step, which is *to develop a task description*. This is often done as a group effort but can also be completed individually. Third, with Mr. Correa's assistance, the students were asked *to write a task question*. Their specific "problem to solve" was to model what was going on in their neighborhood.

Assessment of the performance task can be done through teacher observation, student interviews, a written outline for the students to complete, or daily journal entries.

Was this the best question to explore? It was meaningful to the students, but other questions are certainly possibilities. Other examples of products that could be developed through this type of assessment include models based on scientific concepts, written material, or a formal decision. Products could also be applications of process skills, such as experiments with definite or undetermined conclusions.

When used, journals should be written in daily and checked often so that a dialogue can occur between the student and the teacher. This will indicate whether the student has misconceptions or whether the teacher needs to adjust instructional practice in any way or to encourage students to explore further.

Assessing Process Skills

Process skills should also be addressed. Assessing these operations requires students to be placed in contexts that allow them to gather and process data. To help yourself better track your students' achievement of process skills, develop a recording chart similar to the one in Figure 5–3.

In its purest form, a performance measure has a child demonstrate process skills with concrete materials. For instance, the inquiry may ask the child to measure several irregularly shaped rocks to find the one with the greatest volume. Materials for this task include various types of rocks, a wide-mouthed clear plastic cup, a spoon, a marking pen, and a container of water. To demonstrate this process, the child could partly fill the cup and mark the water level with the pen. Next, he will carefully submerge each of the various rocks into the cup with the spoon, taking care each time to mark the water level and not spill any water. If the process is performed properly, the child identifies the rock with the highest water level as having the most volume.

See the Chapter 5 Web Destinations on the Companion Web (*http://www.prenhall.com/peters*) for links related to assessing student performance in science.

Another example of a performance measure is to ask a child to infer the identity of three unknown leaves by consulting a chart with descriptions of leaves. A variation of the task is to ask the child to classify a small collection of leaves. Can the child put them into two or more groups and state the observable property or properties used to group them? Will the groupings be consistent with the stated properties?

Working with concrete materials may not always be possible. Performance-based measures can also use representations of things. For instance, students can classify pictures

Figure 5–3   **Process skill checklist.**

Name	Classify	Observe	Measure	Infer	Communicate	Experiment
ROSE	(A-C-T)	(A-C-T)	(A-C-T)	(A-C-T)	(A-C-T)	(A-C-T)
DAVE	(A-C-T)	(A-C-T)	(A-C-T)	(A-C-T)	(A-C-T)	(A-C-T)
NINA	(A-C-T)	(A-C-T)	(A-C-T)	(A-C-T)	(A-C-T)	(A-C-T)
JOSH	(A-C-T)	(A-C-T)	(A-C-T)	(A-C-T)	(A-C-T)	(A-C-T)

Note: A = Achieved Skill, C = Continuing to Improve, T = Trouble Applying

of leaves or animals. Another idea is to supply a chart that shows data from an investigation and to ask the child to interpret the data and draw a conclusion.

When children are capable writers, some performance measures may be completed entirely with words. For experimenting, this problem might appear as follows:

> Suppose you want to find out whether bean plants will grow faster with fertilizer A or fertilizer B. How could you set up an experiment to find out?

The problem could also address a specific part of the experiment:

> What variables do you need to control in the plant experiment?

In either instance, it is important to place an emphasis on assessing the performance of the students. But if you have a good science program, isn't that enough?

Using Performance-Based Assessment

Some teachers with active, hands-on/minds-on science programs bypass performance measures. They believe that they get all the assessment data they need by observing their students at work and interacting with them during regular activity times and follow-up discussions. This may be possible with a wide array of process-rich activities and systematic observing; but mandated performance explorations are becoming more prevalent at school district, state, and national levels. Avoiding them entirely in the regular science program may cause students to do poorly on such assessments. Reliability of your personal assessments may also be affected if you leave out **performance-based assessment.** This could be due to bias of your observations of certain students because of their personality or prior success. One way to complete this type of assessment and decrease bias is through an instrument such as the example in Figure 5–4.

Note that the particular checklist in Figure 5–4 is for a small-group assignment. You will have to modify the checklist to use on an individual basis or in different learning situations. Also, if you are working with early grades, you will find that teacher observation is the primary means of gathering assessment data. In these situations, it is important that you track progress over longer periods of time and record progress as students develop new skills.

Project-Based Science Assessment

Whether exploring on an individual basis or as a small group, **project-based science** assists students in investigating authentic questions based on scientific phenomena. The principle behind project-based science is that young learners engage in exploring important and meaningful questions through a process of investigation and collaboration (Krajcik, Czerniak, & Berger, 1999). The result of this approach is that students learn fundamental science concepts and principles that they can apply to their daily lives.

It's a good idea to view science projects as normal and regular extensions of concepts and generalizations studied by the whole class. Projects can be individual self-directed activities, similar to a science fair project. They can also be small-group projects during which students collaborate in learning. One way or the other, they make assessment simpler, less formal, and more frequent. Extended investigations can be useful in pursuing knowledge in greater depth or in focusing on a particular area of interest. But what makes a good project?

Characteristics of a Good Project

An ideal project usually requires self-assessment from start to finish. If guidelines are simple and your comments regarding success are consistent, students will develop judgment in assessing their efforts during projects and when reporting them. The components of a good project are found in Figure 5–5.

Performance-based assessment is a form of testing that requires students to perform a task rather than select or provide answers on a test. The teacher then judges the quality of the student's work based on an agreed-upon set of criteria. An example would be asking a student to generate scientific hypotheses.

Project-based science organizes science experiences around an authentic question. The students focus on all of the class activities to answer this driving question.

See the Chapter 5 Web Destinations Companion Website (*http://www. prenhall.com/peters*) for a link to project-based science and the PIViT software from the University of Michigan.

Figure 5–4 **Performance-based assessment checklist (upper elementary).**

Completed by the Student

Student Names
(List the names of the students in your group.)

Problem to Be Solved
(State the problem you are investigating in your own words.)

Method or Strategy
(How will you go about solving the problem?)

Skills
(Identify how you used the following skills while investigating this problem: classifying, observing, measuring, inferring/predicting, communicating, and experimenting)

Results
Written Response
   What did you find from your investigation?
Pictures
   Can you illustrate your findings?

Verification and Communication
Did you compare your answer with other groups? Did you verify it with the teacher?

Teacher Checklist

_____ Students understood the problem.
      (0—no; 1—somewhat; 2—completely)
_____ Students developed a method/strategy to solve the problem.
      (0—no; 1—somewhat; 2—completely)
_____ Students used scientific skills in solving the problem.
      (0—no; 1—somewhat; 2—completely)
_____ Students were able to come to a conclusion.
      (0—no; 1—somewhat; 2—completely)
_____ Students communicated and verified their results.
      (0—no; 1—somewhat; 2—completely)
_____ Total (possible 10)

Remember that good projects also give students many chances to display the scientific attitudes of critical thinking, such as persistence, inventiveness, curiosity, and questioning techniques. Sample questions for you to keep in mind during the assessment process are as follows:

1. Are the parts of the report or presentation logical and consistent?
2. Does the display or model show evidence of learning?
3. Is there evidence that the child overcame difficulties or was successful at problem solving?
4. Was the child resourceful in substituting materials as needed?
5. Does the child or other children ask further questions based on the project?

When you notice behaviors like these and give positive comments, you will reinforce the students' success at projects. Returning to our situation with Mr. Correa, he plans to continue the learning situation with individual projects.

As a springboard for ideas, next week, Mr. Correa's students will independently read a variety of children's literature, including *Bringing the Rain to Kapiti Plain* (Aardema, 1992), *Mendel's Ladder* (Karlins, 1995), *Peter Spier's Rain* (Spier, 1997), *A Rainy Day* (Markle, 1993), and *The Rains Are Coming* (Stanley, 1993). These and other books related to rain will help initiate creative ideas for individual projects. Keep in mind that as the students design the projects, they can also design complementary assessment procedures.

Peer or Individual Assessments

Do you want your students involved in the assessment process? Try experimenting by allowing your students to design an authentic assessment procedure. Of course, student assessments may not be as elaborate as some procedures that you may design, but they have certain advantages. Often, students will become more involved in the learning process if they are included in the evaluation and decision making that occur in the classroom. Additionally, students are creative and can develop some interesting and useful assessments.

There are some considerations to keep in mind with regard to individually created assessment procedures. First, consider that this is a **low stakes assessment.** By this, we mean that it is only one piece of the assessment package for that student. In contrast, a **high stakes assessment** affects a student's future to a much higher degree. A student's final grade should be determined through a combination of procedures, including different forms of teacher-based assessments.

A second consideration in peer- or self-constructed assessment procedures is to be clear with the directions that are given related to the assessment. Make sure that everyone knows what is required. Ask questions to ensure that your students understand the requirements. Provide guidance to be sure that the students are not undertaking a procedure they cannot complete. Finally, encourage the students and assist them in reaching their goals. A follow-up interview may assist in clarifying the assessment procedure and results.

Interviews

Are you having learning or assessment difficulties with your students? Interviews are an effective way to get information directly. They can be especially useful with early elemen-

Low stakes assessment is a tool to assist in finding out what a student knows, in determining future curricula, or in diagnosing a student's skills.

High stakes assessment is used to determine passing or failing, to place a student in a remedial or advanced program, to decide on graduation, or otherwise to compare students, classrooms, schools, districts, states, or even nations.

Figure 5–5   Components of a good project.

- **Title:** Name of the investigation that is being considered.
- **Problem:** A brief description of the problem to be solved. The student or teacher can determine the problem.
- **Materials:** A listing of what is needed for the investigation.
- **Hypothesis:** A statement that explains what will happen during or as a result of the investigation.
- **Experiment:** The steps that will be taken to investigate the hypothesis. Includes specifics on variables and how measurements will be taken.

- **Data:** An organized listing of the data collected in charts and graphs.
- **Results:** A data-specific explanation of what happened as a result of the experiment.
- **Conclusion:** An explanation of what happened in your own words.
- **Research Results:** A summary of the background information collected as part of the investigation.
- **Communication of Investigation:** A report, display, presentation, or other means to share the results of the investigation.

tary students who cannot express their thoughts in writing. Interviews are also helpful for assessing students with special needs. Keep in mind that the specific answers provided by the children are less important than the reasons why they responded as they did. Try to look for trends in thinking patterns and to identify misconceptions.

When using interviews as an assessment tool, keep in mind that you should be accepting of all answers and value each child's thoughts and opinions. Put yourself in the child's perspective and ease the sometimes uncomfortable situation by using the following techniques:

Know and use the child's name.

Select nonconflicting times to interview.

Sit at floor level.

Talk in a cheerful tone.

Inform the child before the interview what you are doing.

Intervene only as necessary to keep the discussion focused on the topic. Ask questions such as the following to promote further discussion:

What can you tell me about . . . ?
What do you think about . . . ?
How do you feel about . . . ?
Can you explain why . . . ?
How would you describe . . . ?
How did you discover . . . ?

Maintain the discussion with questions such as the following:

What else can you say about . . . ?
What if you were to . . . ?
How is this related to . . . ?
Is there another way to explain . . . ?
How could we change . . . ?
What question should I ask the next student about . . . ?

General questions should be prepared ahead of time; nevertheless, ask additional clarifying questions as needed. Also make sure to provide enough time for the interview.

Try to make students feel relaxed with the interview process. Allow them to create illustrations or to use models as needed. Some early elementary students may even want to "speak" through a teddy bear or other object if they are too shy to speak directly to you. Do not mistake a child's being afraid to speak as a sign that he or she is unfamiliar with the concept discussed.

 Teaching Tips If you are using other students or parent volunteers as interviewers, make sure that you have a checklist of interview questions for them to fill out.

Another use for interviews is to supplement regular testing for culturally and linguistically diverse students. For instance, you can do these things:

Provide additional clues to failed test items.

Change the language of test items in an interview.

Ask probing questions in the student's own dialect.

Focus on how the student is attempting to solve a problem. (Gonzalez, Brusca-Vega, & Yawkey, 1997)

Using interviews to help meet the needs of diverse students will not only allow you to better find their strong and weak areas but also will be a boost to their self-confidence when

A child composes her daily notes as part of her science journal.

they can understand the assessment procedure. Complement interview discussions with journal writing as the students are able to express themselves with written discourse.

Journals

Do you remember keeping a science notebook when you were in school? Journals similar to the one you may have kept can assist students in recording observations, outlining procedures, drafting hypotheses, developing inferences, writing the results of experiments, or reflecting on what they have done. You know that recording data in a notebook or log is usually necessary when observations occur over time. Doing so makes it more likely that the students will keep track of changes, observe more carefully, and think about what they are doing. Teachers may also ask their students to respond in writing to questions in activities for similar reasons. These recordings are best kept in a journal.

Notice how often questions appear in properly constructed activities. This practice is typical of elementary school science. Students can appraise their recordings by comparing them with those of other group members. It's natural for students to pursue reasons, when experimental data conflict. Journals can be a way to develop this dialogue with students who want to learn more about a topic. Remember to be flexible and consider that not every journal should look the same.

Today the concept of writing to learn is applied in all subjects. It holds much value for science. Many teachers have their students keep science journals. A journal offers opportunities to improve science learning and to practice important writing skills at the same time. Writing requires thinking, which changes with different purposes.

Descriptive writing can be used, among other possibilities, to identify things:

Can you describe an animal (plant, habitat, etc.) so well, without naming it, that your partner can tell what it is? Make a chart that shows the properties of these rocks. Can your partner match the rocks to your descriptions?

Assessing these writings is straightforward. If a problem with a conflicting answer arises, the partners can work together to figure out a solution.

Defining concepts in writing, before and after instruction, enables children to assess for themselves what they have gained from their studies. The questions, "What is soil, and what is it made of?" may yield quite different results before and after lessons.

Creative writing should also be linked to concepts being studied. If your students are writing stories about an imaginary visit to an outer planet, you might ask them to use recently learned words correctly, such as *orbit, acceleration,* and *zero gravity.*

Teaching Tips Use cooperative learning groups in judging whether concepts are used correctly in journals or creative writing activities. Your students should consult with you as needed.

You can also ask students at different developmental levels to write summaries of what they have learned in a lesson, give opinions and defend them, write persuasive letters, and compose interview questions. Each form can be assessed for clarity, logic, and completeness. Journals are also a valuable tool with students who are too shy to express answers publicly. Journals provide a secure channel of communication with the teacher.

It is important to have your students assess their own writing as much as possible through clear directions and standards. You should evaluate or sample their writing often, but at the same time allow them to do most of the work. The following methods will help you provide guidance for them to self-evaluate their work:

How would you describe your level of participation in the activity?

What contributions did you make to the solution of the problem?

What best describes your role in the group (leader, recorder, materials manager, maintenance crew, liaison, or bystander)?

How effectively do you manage time while completing tasks?

What are you learning in science?

One way we use journals in our own work is to include them as part of a folder or three-ring notebook that is a student's **portfolio.**

Portfolios

Portfolio is a sampling of work over time that gives observable evidence of knowledge, processes, and attitudes gained by a student over one or more subject-matter units.

Would you like to cultivate more self-assessment abilities like those described in the Focus on Inquiry: Portfolios at the beginning of the chapter? Would you like to motivate your students to increase their effort in learning? Can you show parents tangible and understandable evidence of what their children are learning? If you would like to improve your assessment procedures, consider a portfolio for each child. A portfolio is a "container of evidence of someone's knowledge, skills, and dispositions" (Collins, 1991, p. 293).

The collection can be a student or personal portfolio where children show accomplishments and learning over a long period of time. An example is a graduation portfolio or a yearlong, grade-level portfolio. Another type is the project portfolio where a student demonstrates the sequence of steps that go into a project or independent study. Other examples are graded portfolios, integrated portfolios, cooperative group portfolios, multiyear portfolios, multiple intelligences portfolios, portfolios of intelligent behavior, class profile portfolios, school profile portfolios, time capsule portfolios, and district portfolios (Williams, 2000).

Visit an Inquiry Classroom
Authentic Assessment

View the *Authentic Assessment* video in the "Constructivist Pedagogy" section of the Companion CD. Students share their findings from the earthworm activities.

Review the video and ask yourself the following:
 • Based on what you have learned thus far, is this representative of authentic assessment? Explain your answer.
 • Could Mr. McKnight use the computer in other ways to assess students?

In *Classroom Assessment and the National Science Education Standards* (NRC, 2001), the authors state, "Journals kept by the students become the stimulus for regular reflections on learning and the connections between their topic to the bigger picture." Explain what they mean in this statement. Record your ideas and the answers to these questions in your portfolio or use the Companion Website to share your ideas.

Mr. Correa, from our streambed example earlier in this chapter, uses project portfolios as part of the evaluation of his students. In his view, project portfolios are good assessment tools during the 4-week study of the water cycle.

What should go into a portfolio? Both the child and you should select items, or **artifacts,** for the portfolio. When the child selects artifacts to demonstrate learning, he can also jot down why he selected the item. This will make the learning and assessment more relevant. You will also find that to have diverse student portfolios, you must have diverse learning opportunities in the classroom. Otherwise, the portfolio becomes a collection of the standard science tests and vocabulary sheets. Collins (1991) warns:

> There is no guarantee that portfolios always will be a mode of authentic assessment; they can become folders in which teachers plunk the same tired stuff they have been doing because they have been instructed by the administration to use portfolios for assessment. (p. 299)

Mr. Correa avoids the misuse of portfolios discussed in this quote by having students select artifacts to include in the portfolios. Following are examples of artifacts that Mr. Correa's students will include:

* Tests—end of lesson, unit, performance
* Activity log pages
* Project or book reports
* Concept maps, vee maps, other graphic organizers
* Charts
* Graphs
* Science journal pages
* Creative stories
* Science words learned
* Artwork
* Out-of-class assignments
* Computer resources or data
* Videotaped resources or data
* Cartoons and analysis or explanation

Artifacts   are typical products or results of a student's learning, such as a student story, lab report, or picture of a scientific phenomenon.

Figure 5–6   Portfolio artifact form.

Name: _____

Date: _____

Portfolio Artifact: (name of item)

I am including this item because . . .

_____

_____

_____

This is how the item shows what I learned . . .

_____

_____

_____

The next time I do this activity, I will change . . .

_____

_____

_____

_____

In addition to items that the students will include in their portfolios, Mr. Correa will have his students include an artifact form, as shown in Figure 5–6, for some of the items. The form will assist the students in determining what items to place in their portfolios.

What are some other points to keep in mind? Everything should be dated so that items in a category can be put in order by time and progress observed. Guide the children to look for improvements in their work and to discuss with their groups the examples they have selected. Encourage them to pair an original effort with an improved version when possible; this can make them more conscious of their progress and help develop a sense of pride in their work.

How should the artifacts be arranged? Materials may be stored in a standard expandable folder or a larger folder cut from poster board. Storage considerations may prompt you to consider electronic portfolios. The advantage of electronic portfolios is that they can be easily stored on disk, reducing the amount of paper in the classroom. The disadvantage is that students' keyboarding skills may be inadequate or computer access may be limited in the elementary classroom.

Should the science portfolio be separate? Or is it better to reserve a section for science in a more comprehensive portfolio? Primary-level teachers lean more toward comprehensive portfolios. Upper elementary and middle school teachers generally arrange portfolios by content area. Either type gets overstuffed and difficult to store or manage

Teaching Tips

To help your students set goals for themselves, periodically have them review and think carefully about the work samples they include in their portfolios. This can be done monthly or at the end of a unit.

Figure 5–7   Parent or guardian portfolio assessment rubric.

Parent or Guardian Name: _____

Date: _____

Portfolio Assessment Questions

The item I think is my child's best work is . . .

_____

_____

The item I think my child could improve on is . . .

_____

_____

Overall, I see evidence of my child learning because . . .

_____

_____

_____

I would like to see my child . . .

_____

_____

unless some material is sent home periodically or discarded. Some teachers ask their students to write thoughtful responses to these two questions:

What do I feel good about?

What do I want to improve?

Responses to the second question can make it easy to set goals with children. At the next periodic review, they can examine their portfolios for evidence that shows whether the goals were met. Also have parents assist in evaluating portfolios. This assistance helps develop better teacher–parent, teacher–child, and parent–child communications. A form such as the one in Figure 5–7 can be used for parent portfolio assessments.

Teacher scoring of the portfolio is also a consideration. Figure 5–8 shows a typical scoring method for elementary science portfolios.

See Chapter 5 Web Destinations at the *http://www.prenhall.com/peters* Companion Website for links related to the public domain concept map software from the Institute for Human and Machine Cognition at the University of West Florida.

Concept Maps

One message from researchers in human learning is especially clear: Organization and meaning go together. The better we are able to relate new information to what we already know, the easier we are able to remember and use it. Science programs now commonly employ several different graphic organizers to help children construct meaningful relationships among the facts and concepts they learn. The **concept map** is probably the most used organizer, and an excellent means to assess conceptual knowledge.

Concept maps are hierarchical graphic organizers of a person's concepts.

Nodes are the specific locations where the concepts contained on the map are located.

Links or cross-links are the relationships between concepts in different nodes of the concept map.

Figure 5–9 shows a concept map that was developed by a student independently studying chameleons. It was generated with a computerized concept map program. As you can see from the map, it contains **nodes** representing the individual concepts and **links** connecting the concepts in a meaningful way. This type of assessment provides a richer view of the student's knowledge than typical objective tests.

Figure 5–8 Portfolio assessment scoring rubric.

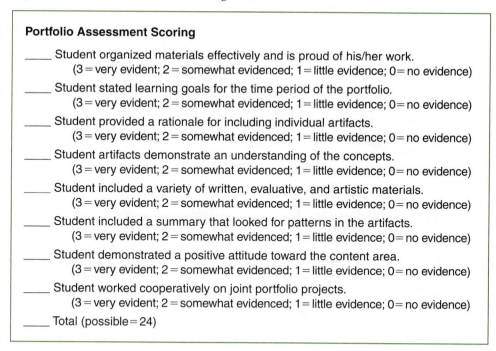

A concept map, according to Novak and Gowin (1984), is a "schematic device for representing a set of concept meanings embedded in a framework of propositions" (p. 15). The **propositions** are used to link the concepts, and the map in its entirety is like a snapshot of the person's conceptual understandings. Concept maps can be used before, during, or after a learning activity to assess development of understandings. They encourage reflective thinking and foster development of scientific concepts (Mason, 1992).

Concept maps are also an effective small-group project. When done by groups, communication and negotiation among members help in identifying student misunderstanding. Working together, they can resolve their misconceptions.

How can you get your students started with concept mapping? So that students can see how concepts maps are formed, it may be good to start with showing students maps related to the context you are teaching. Next, provide the students maps in which some of the words are already filled in. Have the students complete these maps by filling in other words of their choice. Later, provide just the words for them to use in developing their own concept map. For example, Mr. Correa could have provided the following words:

water cycle

clouds

streams

oceans

mountains

plants

animals

groundwater

Propositions are the connecting words, such as *has, can be,* or *is part of.*

Figure 5–9   Concept map.

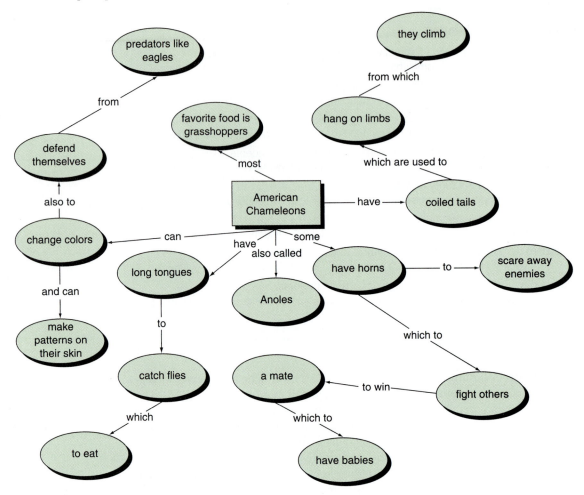

Beginning students could map just these words. Advanced students could add more words as appropriate to complete the concept map. In time, students will be proficient at reflecting their knowledge with concept maps with little assistance from the teacher.

Note that students often make different concept maps after receiving the same instruction. This happens even when they understand all the concepts in the way that you intend. They may simply view relationships among the concepts differently. It is important for them to compare their maps on a regular basis with partners and to interact with you to more fully assess what they have learned.

Vee Maps

Vee maps are similar to concept maps but have two sides: a conceptual side (the "knowing" side that may contain a concept map) and a methodological side (containing results and actions).

Vee maps, similar to concept maps, are useful in developing and conducting investigations. They are a less-structured approach to activities, likened to a "road map showing the route from prior knowledge to new and future knowledge" (Roth & Verechaka, 1993, p. 25).

Vee maps are arranged with the "knowing" words and phrases about a topic on the left and the "doing" or skills and activities on the right. In the center is a large V that represents the interplay and interdependence between the knowing and doing. The following quote summarizes the use of vee maps:

The left and right sides of the Vee emphasize two interdependent aspects of science learning: knowing and doing, respectively. What students know at any one moment—their existing conceptions, the investigative tools available to them, and their ideas—will determine the quality and quantity of the questions they ask. Conversely, the answers students obtain to their questions will affect what they know, by changing, adding to, refining, or reconfiguring their knowledge. The Vee should lead students to discover the relationship between doing and knowing science. (Roth & Bowen, 1993, pp. 28–32)

Teacher Observations

The job of teaching is inexact at best. We view it as a series of consecutively developed hypotheses. That is, each thing we do or say is a kind of hypothesis that we are uncertain will be accepted (learned) by the children. If much teaching takes place before receiving specific feedback, learning has occurred, and then we can make many unwarranted assumptions about what has been learned by the children.

We can observe, and often help students stay on track, in whole-class settings, but the most productive times are likely to be in individual and small-group situations. There are many chances for informal teacher–child contacts during the activity times in lessons. Notice what your students say and do when they interact with you, a partner, or other members of a small group. What you observe gives you data for fast self-correction or for assisting individual students, if needed.

The quickest way to find out whether students understand the concepts and processes being taught is to ask questions and listen carefully to their responses. Forming follow-up questions to responses may help in detecting misconceptions so that you can quickly address these errors in thinking.

Open-Ended Questions

An open-ended question has more than one correct response or pathway to a response (Carter & Berenson, 1996). The response may be an answer to a question, a procedure to arrive at a solution to a problem, or an opinion about something. The value of this type of question is that each student can answer it differently.

> **Teaching Tips**
> Open-ended questions are useful in identifying misconceptions or in promoting divergent thinking.

Assessment of open-ended questions often lies in the completeness of the response. A clear, complete response that includes accurate information and/or the student's opinions is desirable. A rubric for scoring this type of question could simply be a six-point scale based on information provided by the student, as shown in Figure 5–10.

Following are guidelines for writing open-ended questions:

- Make sure that the question is understandable to students.
- Do not lead students to an answer; let them construct one on their own.
- Make the questions interesting when possible.
- Match each question with the content or process being studied.
- Allow sufficient wait time for students to respond.
- Allow multiple students time to answer and ask further questions before going on to another question.
- Attempt to get at deeper levels of understanding through increasingly complex questions.
- Maintain students' interest through meaningful, thought-provoking questions.

Figure 5–10   **Open-ended question scoring rubric.**

Use the following list of five areas to assess a student's response to an open-ended question.

- Understands the question
- Provides a complete response
- Provides accurate information
- Justifies the response as needed
- Provides additional information as requested

Award one point for each objective demonstrated by the student. The scoring ranges from one to five points for each response, as follows:

Scoring rubric:

5—all five areas complete
4—one of the above five is missing
3—two of the above five are missing
2—three of the above five are missing
1—four of the above five are missing
0—five of the five are missing or no response

Weather Concepts

Name	Sunshine	Wind	Rain	Snow	Hail	Hurricane	Tornado
Bonnie							
Total:____	____	____	____	____	____	____	____
Doug							
Total:____	____	____	____	____	____	____	____
Shirley							
Total:____	____	____	____	____	____	____	____
Jonathan							
Total:____	____	____	____	____	____	____	____

ASSESSING ATTITUDES

Recall that scientific attitudes of children are often shown by their behaviors in four broad categories: curiosity, inventiveness, critical thinking, and persistence. The sample behaviors listed under these categories are the kinds of actions you look for when you appraise growth in attitudes. Good times to assess attitudes are during hands-on activities and discussions. Remember, though, that broad attitudes cannot be developed quickly. Positive attitudes are a long-range by-product of the quality of learning activities and general atmosphere of your classroom.

Take time to sample attitudes periodically and, if necessary, develop an informal attitude inventory. It should include items like the following:

Are you curious about nature or scientific phenomena?
Do you enjoy science as much as other subjects?
Do you complete science activities outside class time?
Do you watch science-related shows at home on videotapes or television?
Have you read any science-related books lately?
Do you know a scientist in your neighborhood or community?

Visit an Inquiry Classroom
Modeling Positive Attitudes

View the *Cognitive Apprenticeship* video in the "Constructivist Pedagogy" section of the Companion CD. Mr. McKnight interacts with students as they form and test hypotheses related to earthworms and their behavior.

Review the video and ask yourself the following:
- How is Mr. McKnight modeling positive attitudes toward science?
- Which of the four broad categories, *curiosity, inventiveness, critical thinking,* and *persistence,* are modeled in the video? Explain your answer.

In *Changing and Measuring Attitudes in the Science Classroom,* Kobella (1989) asserts, "Teachers realize the importance of how students feel about science subjects and courses; nevertheless, they place little emphasis on affective objectives. The affective domain is often neglected because teachers have difficulty designing strategies to develop positive attitudes among students and documenting their development." How would you react to this statement? What strategies could you personally use to create better attitudes toward science when you become the classroom science teacher? Record your ideas and the answers to these questions in your portfolio or use the Companion Website to share your ideas.

Do you like to answer questions during science class?

Have you considered a career in a science field?

When students cannot read, try using smiling, neutral, and frowning faces on a scoring sheet. The students can respond to items as you read them. What about attitudes toward scientists?

Attitudes and Stereotypes Related to Scientists

A good way to assess attitudes toward scientists is with the Draw-a-Scientist Test (Mason, Kahle, & Gardner, 1991). In this test, children are provided a blank sheet of paper and asked to "draw a scientist." The test is scored by counting the number of stereotypical indicators, such as lab coats, pencils and pens in a shirt pocket, male gender, facial hair, and glasses. A high score on this test indicates that the student has a stereotypical or negative image of a scientist. Try this out with your students to see what their image of a scientist is like.

See the Chapter 5 Web Destinations at the Companion Website (*http:www. prenhall.com/peters*) for links related to the Draw-a-Scientist Test.

Summary

- Assessment is no longer something we do *to* students, but something we can do *with* students. Assessment should be reflective, not reflexive. With changing assessment procedures, we are no longer looking at what students do not know. Instead, we want to know what opportunities they have had to learn and what they do know or have achieved.
- Internal purpose assessments are administered to convey expectations about what is important to learn, to provide information on progress, to help students judge their learning, to guide and improve instruction, and to classify and select students. External purpose assessments include examinations that are given to provide information for accountability, to guide policy decisions, to gather information for program evaluation, to sort and classify people for admissions, and to certify or hire.
- Essay and open-ended questions are useful in evaluating whether students are able to express

personal ideas clearly and can be designed to assess higher order thinking, the ability to solve problems, or the capability to reason about the interrelationships between concepts.

- A performance-based assessment not only will generate an answer by the student but also will indicate the process by which the student arrived at that answer.
- Project-based assessments assist students in investigating authentic questions based on scientific phenomena and allow young learners to engage in exploring important and meaningful questions through a process of investigation and collaboration.
- Peer or individual assessments allow students to creatively become involved in the assessment and learning process.

- Interviews and teacher observations are an effective way to get information directly, to identify misconceptions, and to provide the reasons for student responses.
- Journals can assist students in recording observations, outlining procedures, drafting hypotheses, developing inferences, writing the results of experiments, reflecting on what they have done, and developing a dialogue between students and teachers.
- A portfolio is a sampling of work over time that gives observable evidence of knowledge, processes, and attitudes gained by the students over one or more science units.
- Concept maps and vee maps assess conceptual knowledge through graphic representations.

Reflection

Companion CD

1. Look at the "Earthworm's Cousin—Nightcrawler" lesson linked to the *Teamwork* video on the Companion CD. How could you rewrite this lesson plan to make better use of performance-based assessment?
2. Look at the "Earthworm's Cousin—The Bearded Worm" lesson linked to the *Pacing and Time Allocation* video on the Companion CD. How could

you rewrite this lesson to focus on scientific skill development and assessment? Include a rubric for assessing the skills.
3. Look at the "Earthworm's Cousin—Planaria" lesson linked to the *Feedback* video on the Companion CD. Suppose that you were to use concept mapping as an assessment tool with this lesson. What would a sample student concept map look like for this lesson?

Portfolio Ideas

1. Next time you are at your practicum site, interview a teacher and ask what tools he uses for assessing students. Ask why he selected the particular methods for assessment and whether he thinks the procedures are effective in identifying misconceptions or skill development. Compare his views with your own and record in your portfolio.
2. Place yourself in the role of the instructor for this course. If you were to assess college students on knowledge of assessment, what form(s) of assessment would you use? Indicate sample test items or authentic procedures. Compare with those of other students in the class and record your findings in your portfolio.

3. The rapid expansion in the use of computers and the Internet has brought with it the idea of electronic portfolios. Find out what technological resources are available to assist you in developing student portfolios. Share your findings in your portfolio.
4. Using a World Wide Web search protocol, find one or two sites that include assessment information. You may want to refer to the book *Science on the Internet: A Resource for K–12 Teachers* (2nd ed) (Ebenezer & Lau, 2002). How are the sites designed? How could you adapt what you found to your classroom? Check *http://www.prenhall.com/peters* for additional links. Record findings in your portfolio.

References

Aardema, V. (1992). *Bringing the rain to Kapiti Plain*. New York: Dial Press.
American Association for the Advancement of Science (AAAS). (1993). *Benchmarks for science literacy*. New York: Oxford University Press.
American Association for the Advancement of Science (AAAS). (1998). *Blueprints for reform*. New York: Oxford University Press.
American Forest Foundation. (1996). *Project learning tree* (4th ed.). Washington, DC: Author.

Carter, G., & Berenson, S. B. (1996). Authentic assessment: Vehicle for reform. In J. Rhoton & P. Bowers (Eds.), *Issues in science education* (pp. 96–106). Arlington, VA: National Science Teachers Association and the National Science Education Leadership Association.

Collins, A. (1991). Portfolios for assessing student learning. In G. Kulm & S. M. Malcom (Eds.), *Science assessment in the service of reform* (pp. 291–300). Washington, DC: American Association for the Advancement of Science.

Ebenezer, J. V., & Lau, E. (2002). *Science on the Internet: A resource for K–12 teachers (2nd ed).* Upper Saddle River, NJ: Merrill/Prentice Hall.

Gonzalez, V., Brusca-Vega, R., & Yawkey, T. (1997). *Assessment and instruction of culturally and linguistically diverse students with or at-risk of learning problems: From research to practice.* Boston: Allyn & Bacon.

Karlins, M. (1995). *Mendel's ladder.* New York: Simon & Schuster.

Kobella, T. R. (1989). *Research matters—to the science teacher: Changing and measuring attitudes in the science classroom.* Columbia, MO: National Association for Research in Science Teaching. Retrieved December 23, 2004, from *www.educ.sfu.ca/narstsite/publications/research/attitude.htm*

Krajcik, J., Czerniak, C., & Berger, C. (1999). *Teaching children science: A project-based approach.* New York: McGraw-Hill.

Lawrence Hall of Science. (1989). *River cutters* (Rev. ed.). Berkeley: University of California.

Locker, T. (1997). *Water dance.* Orlando, FL: Harcourt Brace.

Markle, S. (1993). *A rainy day.* New York: Orchard Books.

Mason, C. L. (1992). Concept mapping: A tool to develop reflective science instruction. *Science Education, 76*(1), 51–63.

Mason, C. L., Kahle, J. B., & Gardner, A. L. (1991). Draw-a-scientist test: Future implications. *School Science and Mathematics, 91*(5), 193–198.

McMillan, J. H. (1997). *Classroom assessment: Principles and practice for effective instruction.* Boston: Allyn & Bacon.

National Assessment of Educational Progress. (2003). *The nation's report card: Science 2000.* Washington, DC: National Center for Education Statistics. Retrieved December 23, 2004, from *http://nces.ed.gov/pubsearch/pubsinfo.asp?pubid=2003453*

National Board for Professional Teaching Standards. (1997). *What teachers should know and be able to do.* Washington, DC: Author.

National Research Council (NRC). (1996). *National science education standards.* Washington, DC: National Academy Press.

National Research Council (NRC). (2001). *Classroom assessment and the national science education standards.* Washington, DC: National Academy Press. Retrieved December 23, 2004, from *http://books.nap.edu/catalog/9847.html*

National Science Resources Center, National Academy of Sciences, Smithsonian Institution. (1997). *Science for all children: A guide to improving elementary science education in your school district.* Washington, DC: National Academy Press.

National Science Teachers Association (NSTA). (2001). *Assessment. A position statement.* Washington, DC: Author. Retrieved October 1, 2004, from *www.nsta.org/positionstatement&psid=40*

Novak, J. D., & Gowin, D. B. (1984). *Learning how to learn.* New York: Cambridge University Press.

Ochs, V. D. (1996). Assessing habits of mind through performance-based assessment in science. In J. Rhoton & P. Bowers (Eds.), *Issues in science education* (pp. 114–122). Arlington, VA: National Science Teachers Association and the National Science Education Leadership Association.

Resnick, L. B., & Resnick, D. P. (1989). Tests as standards of achievement in schools. In *Proceedings of the 1989 ETS Invitational Conference* (pp. 63–80). Princeton, NJ: Educational Testing Service.

Roth, W. M., & Bowen, M. (1993). The unfolding vee. *Science Scope, 16*(5), 28–32.

Roth, W. M., & Verechaka, G. (1993). Plotting a course with vee maps. *Science and Children, 30*(4), 24–27.

Rubba, P., Miller, E., Schmalz, R., Rosenfeld, L., & Shyamal, K. (1991). Science education in the United States: Editors' reflection. In S. Majumdar, L. Rosenfeld, P. Rubba, E. Miller, & R. Schmalz (Eds.), *Science education in the United States: Issues, crisis, and priorities* (pp. 532–537). Easton, PA: Pennsylvania Academy of Science.

Spier, P. (1997). *Peter Spier's rain.* Garden City, NY: Doubleday.

Stanley, S. (1993). *The rains are coming.* New York: Greenwillow Books.

Wick, W. (1997). *A drop of water: A book of science and wonder.* New York: Scholastic Press.

Williams, J. (2000). Implementing portfolios and student-led conferences. *enc focus, 7*(2), 21–23.

Suggested Readings

Agler, L. (1986). *Liquid explorations.* Berkeley: University of California, Lawrence Hall of Science. (a Great Explorations in Math and Science [GEMS] guide to additional water activities and assessments)

Anderson, R. D., & Pratt, H. (1995). *Local leadership for science education reform.* Dubuque, IA: Kendall/Hunt. (how changing teaching and assessment practices will assist in the reform process)

Brandt, R. S. (Ed.). (1992). Using performance assessment. *Educational Leadership, 49*(8). (special issue on performance assessment)

Brandt, R. S. (Ed.). (1994). Reporting what students are learning. *Educational Leadership, 52*(2). (special issue on assessment practices)

Hein, G., & Price, S. (1994). *Active assessment for active science: A guide for elementary school teachers.* Portsmouth, NH: Heinemann. (a practical guide on the rationale for active assessment; useful in enabling classroom teachers to develop, interpret, and score their own assessments)

Herman, J. L., Aschbacher, P. R., & Winters, L. (1992). *A practical guide to alternative assessment.* Alexandria, VA: Association for Supervision and Curriculum Development. (creation and use of alternative assessment procedures)

Linn, R. L., & Gronlund, N. E. (2000). *Measurement and assessment in teaching* (8th ed.). Upper Saddle River, NJ: Merrill/Prentice Hall. (a comprehensive text on assessment of learning)

McShane, J. B. (Ed.). (1994). Assessment issue. *Science and Children, 32*(2), 13–51. (a collection of relevant articles on assessment)

Raizen, S. A., Baron, J. B., Champagne, A. B., Mullis, I. V. S., & Oakes, J. (1989). *Assessment in elementary school science education.* Washington, DC: National Center for Improving Science Education. (a synthesis of reports and recommendations on assessment)

CHAPTER 6

SCIENCE EXPERIENCES FOR ALL STUDENTS

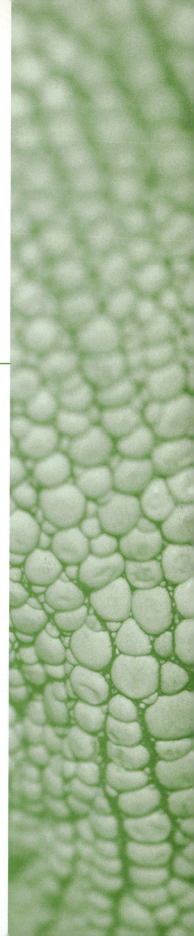

FOCUS QUESTIONS

- What is meant by "science for all students"?
- What is a science learning center and how can it support your science program?
- How could a science project promote a student's construction of knowledge?
- How could you incorporate science fairs into your curriculum?
- What are some strategies for working with students who are disabled, have limited English proficiency, or are gifted?

Focus on Inquiry

Women in Science

Katherine (Kata) McCarville,
South Dakota School of Mines and Technology

My daughter is now 9 years old. She and her friends are about the same age I was when I first read about Marie Curie. Marie Curie, winner of two Nobel Prizes, is one of my personal role models. I would encourage you and your students to discover her inspiring story and those of the many other phenomenal women of science. Look in libraries and on the Web for scientists like geophysicist Inge Lehmann, astronomer Maria Mitchell, physicist Lise Meitner, computer scientist Grace Murray Hopper, and biologist Barbara McClintock.

Knowing several 9-year-olds, however, I suspect that to many elementary school students today—and perhaps even to you—these women may seem quaint and distant, even irrelevant. But on "Crazy Career Day" at her school last year, my daughter chose to dress as her mom. So instead, let me tell you about a contemporary working geoscientist.

I began my professional career in 1978 as a uranium miner in Wyoming and then became a computer programmer and analyst for an engineering firm. In 1986, I moved to a position in academic computing services at the Colorado School of Mines, a college of engineering. Next, I worked as Director of Information Technology Services at the South Dakota School of Mines and Technology, in charge of all the university's computing and networking facilities.

I am now the Associate Director of a research institute focused in the atmospheric and earth sciences. We study weather, severe storms, hydrology, greenhouse gases, and cycling of elements like carbon, using observations made from towers, balloons, and aircraft. As a research scientist, I am beginning my own research career in paleoclimatology to improve our understanding of natural climate changes. I also teach in the academic program, mentor and advise students, write grant proposals to support research projects, and manage the institute's funds of about $2 million per year.

While working in highly technical jobs and moving into management, I became active in science education through volunteer activities. I developed a personal interest in paleontology over many years through continuing education opportunities. Starting with a bachelor's degree in geology and later earning a master's degree in geology and a doctoral degree in paleontology, I am engaged in applying computing techniques, imaging technologies, and scientific visualization to the study of fossils, paleoclimatology of continental interiors, and avian paleontology.

My career path may seem odd or unusual to many people, but my story illustrates many features of today's job markets and career opportunities. The pace of change in today's workplace is accelerating. New jobs are being created that have never existed before. An increasing number of jobs, even those that have been traditionally less rigorous, now require mathematical background, experience with computer technology, and the ability to apply logical reasoning or scientific methods to investigate situations and solve problems. Nearly all positions require communications skills—speaking, reading, and writing. Added to these factors is the growing participation of women and ethnic minorities in the workforce.

What does all that have to do with geosciences and careers for women? And how can you, as a teacher, possibly be expected to prepare every one of your students for future jobs and careers that do not even exist today?

First and most important, your students need to see that you are endlessly curious about the world, always learning something new, and willing to take risks in exploring the unknown. Each student must find and develop one or more areas of interest that provide personal motivation. The earth sciences integrate all the basic sciences and mathematics, with the earth, ocean, and sky as a free laboratory available to everyone for observation, description, and explanation.

My own story illustrates how the geosciences can serve as the foundation for a varied, engaging, and successful career. Geology is my "first love"; the ongoing scientific investigation of the geologic past holds a fascination for me like nothing else. During college, that fascination gave me a reason to persevere through difficult courses in mathematics, physics, and chemistry. In the interdisciplinary breadth of geoscience, I could find a real-world example of nearly every equation and principle that was presented in the traditional disciplines. This provided a context within which I could integrate many details into a coherent body of knowledge. Geoscience gives me a unifying theme that lends stability to personal and professional relationships, while leaving ample room for career flexibility and providing a framework for lifelong learning.

Each of your students needs to meet and learn about people who are passionate about their work. It is especially meaningful if these people resemble the student in some way, so it is important to expose all students to scientists, mathematicians, and engineers, including people representing a wide diversity of backgrounds.

Invite parents and others from the community to participate in classroom or school activities. Try to arrange visits to workplaces in your area. Many professional organizations (see information elsewhere in this chapter, and use libraries and the Web to locate resources) sponsor teaching materials and teacher-education programs. Some groups provide guest speakers, science-fair judges, or sponsor mentoring programs to engage interested students with practicing professionals. Many of these programs now match partners via e-mail; the wide availability of e-mail makes this method extremely cost-effective.

Encourage all students who show an interest in science, regardless of gender. These will be the scientists of the future. The results of scientific inquiries are increasingly used in making decisions that directly affect our lives. It is important that people from a wide variety of backgrounds be involved in determining which factors are important and which are not, choosing the questions to be asked, and guiding the direction of investigations.

Geoscience encompasses everything from the purely theoretical contemplation of the origin of the cosmos to the practical application of selecting a safe site for a garbage landfill. Bring geoscience into your classroom as a cornerstone on which to build a comprehensive view of the direct relevance of mathematics and the basic sciences—with the added zing of current topics such as climate change, meteorite impacts, and dinosaurs. From the use of clay minerals in cosmetics to the exploration of the solar system, there is something for everyone in geoscience!

SCIENCE FOR ALL STUDENTS

Have you thought about promoting scientific careers for the girls you will teach as suggested in the Focus on Inquiry: Women in Science?
What are some other ways that you could motivate your students to become interested in science?

You may remember that the science standards and benchmarks have as a primary goal *science for all students*. But, should we limit scientific inquiry to activities that the entire class completes as scheduled? Do you see a need to provide a wider range of science experiences to meet the needs of all students? In this chapter, we present four ways to assist you in providing science experiences for all students: science learning centers, science projects, science fairs, and strategies for teaching students with special needs. To begin, let's visit Mrs. Snyder's classroom.

Mandy's Science Fair

Mandy is excited today. Her group will present their science fair project at the school science fair. Mandy's group developed a project in which they compared three types of grasses with respect to ability to reduce soil erosion. They planted a type of turf grass, ryegrass, and crabgrass to see which held sandy soil the best when they ran water on the grass-covered sand hills. Mandy's group developed the idea after participating in activities from the "Agent Erosion" lesson found in the AIMS book *Primarily Earth* (Hoover & Mercier, 1996).

> **Teaching Tips** For additional erosion activities, see the GEMS book *River Cutters* (Lawrence Hall of Science, 1989).

Mandy's teacher, Mrs. Snyder, also arranged for Mrs. Penton to visit her students' science fair projects. Mrs. Penton will talk to the class about a career as a sedimentologist and the importance of this type of work to protect the many farms in their area. They will also participate in the AIMS activity "What on Earth Can We Do?" from the book *Down to Earth* (Erickson, Gregg, Helling, King, & Starkweather, 1987). This activity will cause the students to think about the impact of humans' activities on the soil.

Think about the classroom in which you plan to teach. How will you promote science for all? If you are one to consider science class as "just the facts," then ask yourself the following question: Will you teach as you were taught in elementary and middle school? As you contemplate this question, consider how science education was viewed in the past.

The Chapter 6 Web Destinations on the Companion Website (*http://www.prenhall.com/peters*) lists addresses for the Association for Women Geoscientists, Women in Mining, Association for Women in Science, and other related links.

Historical Perspective

The authors of the A Program for Teaching Science: *Thirty-First Yearbook* of the National Society for the Study of Education (NSSE, 1932) recommended a continuous, integrated program for elementary science. Subsequently, the Science Education in American Schools: *Forty-Sixth Yearbook* authors advocated a similar program (NSSE, 1947). The Rethinking Science Education: *Fifty-Ninth Yearbook*, printed shortly after the launching of the Soviet *Sputnik* satellite (NSSE, 1960), was in response to the contest of the space race. This information again prompted educational professionals to look at the inadequate elementary science program. More recently, reports of research surrounding the National Research Council (NRC) *National Science Education Standards* (1996) and the American Association for the Advancement of Science (AAAS) *Benchmarks for Science Literacy* (1993) reflected the common theme of these past reports.

The general recommendation of all the above mentioned reports is a student-centered, activity-based instruction in science at every grade level and for all students. Fortunately, we find that there are teachers who see a need to complement the basic science program. They augment the standard curriculum with supplementary and individualized activities. They find that all children learn differently and adjust their teaching accordingly. One way they accommodate different learning styles is through the use of learning centers.

SCIENCE LEARNING CENTERS

A classroom learning center is a place where one or several students at a time can do activities independently, working through the materials and directions found there. A learning center is arranged so that children may choose the activities they can do or are interested in and work at a pace that is right for each child. Some teachers also permit children to select the times they go to a center and partners to work with in a cooperative manner.

Refer to the Chapter 6 Web Destinations on the Companion Website (*http://www.prenhall. com/peters*) for links related to the weather learning center.

An example of a science learning center on weather for an elementary class is shown in Figure 6–1. The center allows children to explore an area of high interest independently and to develop a background that they may use in a variety of ways. About four children can use this center satisfactorily at one time. Notice the activity sheets on the bulletin board. Children use these to write down data or make drawings. Completed sheets are placed in a basket on the teacher's desk for later examination.

Figure 6–1   **A science learning center.**

Observe other features of this center. Children's literature is available for reading either individually or in a peer-tutoring situation. A weather radio is available for listening to the weather service and noting data such as temperatures and rainfall. Individual students can listen to a tape of pertinent weather information. Notice the materials for the students' interaction at the center: alcohol-filled thermometers for measuring temperatures, a wind gauge, and a tornado simulation bottle. A "weather book" contains blank pages on which students can draw and color the weather each day.

To construct this center, the teacher considered the following matters:

- Purpose and objectives
- Activity cards and worksheets
- Materials and their resupply
- Recordkeeping and evaluation
- The physical setup

Will you use learning centers? How will you begin your own learning center?

Refer to the Chapter 6 Web Destinations on the Companion Website (*http://www.prenhall.com/peters*) for links related to the use of children's literature in science.

Deciding the Purpose of a Learning Center

The first task in making a science learning center is to decide its purpose. Do you want it for general enrichment? Although this is the most common purpose, centers may also be used to complement an instructional unit or to present an entire unit when you only have a few materials.

Teaching Tips If materials are in short supply, then try sharing a learning center with other teachers.

One example of a learning center activity originated when Mandy's teacher, Mrs. Snyder, wanted to have students play the "Inside the Earth" game from the book *Thematic Unit: Geology* (Gosnell, 1994). Because Mrs. Snyder only made a few games, she used a center to facilitate this learning activity.

As a rule, avoid activities whose outcomes take more time to happen than the time you assign students to be at the center. Children generally want things to happen now, although activities, like the following are exceptions.

As an extension to the erosion activities, Mrs. Snyder started a "Things that Change" learning center (see Figure 6–2). Mrs. Snyder got the idea for the center from studying changes that occur with the earth's soil after reading *How to Dig a Hole to the Other Side of the World* (McNulty, 1979) and completing activities related to a story from the book *Thematic Unit: Rocks and Soil* (Hale, 1992). Mandy's classmates Paul and Billy began a "changes" jar. In the jar, they put materials that they thought would deteriorate. Over the course of a month or longer, they will view these slow changes.

Developing Activity Cards and Record Sheets

How can you communicate activities in the most understandable and appealing ways? The directions on activity cards must be simple so that independent work is possible. Use short sentences and easy words (see Figure 6–3).

Despite your best efforts, some children may not be able to read your directions. Keeping in mind the scaffolding approach, you may want to pair poor readers with good readers who will help. In some schools, the policy is to have multiage grouping for classes. In other schools, parents, a teacher aide, or a cross-age tutoring program assists students. Teachers at the primary level usually find that they must

Teaching Tips Draw pictures beside key words if the cards are intended for less able readers.
  For future use, cover the activity cards with transparent contact paper or laminate them.

Figure 6–2 A "changes" jar begun at a center allows children to continually observe slow changes away from the center.

#1

Make a "changes" jar!

Rubber band   Baby food jar   Plastic wrap

1. Put anything you want to watch in the jar.

Apple slice   Bread

2. Cover the jar with the plastic wrap. Put on a rubber band.

3. Label and date your jar.

Lisa-potato
Nov. 5

4. Choose where to put your jar.

Figure 6–3 An activity card and its accompanying record sheet.

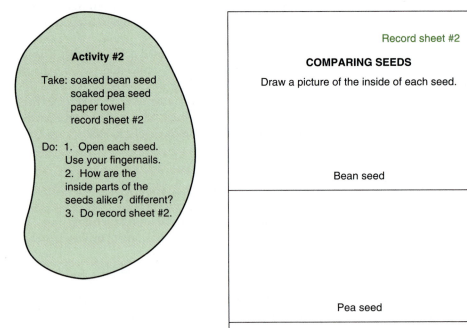

Activity #2

Take: soaked bean seed
soaked pea seed
paper towel
record sheet #2

Do: 1. Open each seed.
Use your fingernails.
2. How are the
inside parts of the
seeds alike? different?
3. Do record sheet #2.

Record sheet #2

COMPARING SEEDS

Draw a picture of the inside of each seed.

Bean seed

Pea seed

Scientist _____

briefly introduce each new activity to the entire class before most children can do the activity independently.

Try to make the design of your activity cards appealing and different for each topic. To do this, you might design the cards to go with the topic. For example, with the topic "volcanoes," make each card look like a cinder cone, shield, or composite volcano. For the rocks and minerals theme, make cards in various crystal shapes. Above all, make the cards as childproof as possible. Cut them from heavy paper or tagboard. Avoid having thin, easily bendable parts. Include as many open-ended activities as you can that have possibilities for process-skill development; these make it possible for children to suggest additional activities, which they enjoy doing.

A few teachers find that recording directions on a tape recorder works satisfactorily for nonreaders.

Record sheets are a convenient way to know what the child has done, if you cannot directly observe the child at work. A record sheet may be simply a plain sheet of paper on which the child has made a drawing or recorded some data after an activity card suggestion.

Some teachers like to have a record sheet for every activity. Other teachers reserve record sheets only for activities in which data recording is necessary for the activity to make sense—graphing temperature or other changes, keeping track of results from testing different materials, or drawing a conclusion from a series of facts. Record sheets can also be called skill sheets, laboratory sheets, or data sheets. Figure 6–3 shows an activity card and its accompanying record sheet.

Materials

Kitchen science activities that can be done with common materials are perfect for science centers. The children themselves may be able to bring in most of what is needed. This is a good way to dispel the idea that science is a strange enterprise conducted with expensive and mysterious objects. You can also place in your center printed and audiovisual materials or items lent by local colleges or museums.

Many ordinary learning center materials can be obtained as donations from local retail businesses.

Recordkeeping and Evaluation

Observing children in action is the best way to learn what they need help with and what they can do. Yet, if many activities are going on, it's difficult to keep track of everything each child has tried.

One way to record progress is to have a master list of all the center's activities or objectives with the children's names written to one side. If each activity has a record sheet, the child can file these. Use a folder at the center to collect sheets. Check the record sheet against your master list. The record sheet will show what activity was performed. Develop your own code system for recording the quality of the work, indicating what is incomplete and denoting what should be done over.

Try allowing the children to develop their own assessment system for center activities.

Sometimes it may be better to have a record system in which the child refers only to her own work. To do this, some teachers give each child who uses a center a record sheet containing only activity numbers (see Figure 6–4). At the top of the sheet, the child writes the title of the center in the space provided, and draws a line under the last number that equals the center's total activities. On completing an activity, the child circles the activity number on her sheet. The child keeps the record sheet handy for the teacher to review during informal or scheduled conferences. To save time, only the more important objectives

Figure 6–4   A record system in which each child refers only to her own work prevents all children from making critical comparisons of each other.

Record Sheet
Science Learning Center

on ___Magnets___

Circle activity finished:

(1)   8   15

2   9   16

3   (10) LM   17

(4) LM   11   18

(5)   (12)   19

6   13   20

7   14   21

Scientist ___Melinda___

---

may be sampled. The record sheet remains in the child's science folder, with worksheets and other work products.

Monitor student progress to be sure that center activities are meeting your objectives and maintaining the students' interest. What about the activities appeals to the students and gets the job done? Why are the students avoiding or doing poorly with other activities? Ask the students to give their views as well. Together you can continually improve the quality of your center's learning opportunities.

To learn more about each child's accomplishments, periodically schedule individual conferences. Can the child profit from further study in the form of an independent project? Such a project can be particularly valuable with the able and older child. This may be the time to set up an education "contract" between you and the child. This is a negotiated agreement between you and the child. This is a negotiated agreement between a teacher and student that generally addresses needs, expectations, roles, and content. In some cases, the child may make a preliminary study before deciding with you on the exact topic, time, and goals for the contract.

Arranging the Physical Setup

Where is the best place to put a science learning center? How should it look? What are some ways to cut down the work in setting up new centers? These are some questions worth thinking about.

Can children work inside the classroom without interfering with others? Do activity outcomes happen at the center during the allotted times? Locate the center where it will not interfere with other activi-

Teaching Tips

You can purchase a preconstructed backboard for your center or make one yourself with donated wood or heavy cardboard.

ties and where it is visible to you at all times. Will wall space be needed? Take this into account as you locate the center in your classroom.

You can draw enlarged background pictures by making transparencies of pictures and then projecting the transparencies with an overhead projector. With these, you can enliven your center's background with familiar characters for child appeal. It's also interesting to use mystery, surprise, oddities, contrast, and drama in captions or pictures.

Managing the Science Learning Center

How can you schedule, introduce the center to children, and keep things running smoothly? It's difficult to say precisely what will be useful in every situation, because schools and individual classrooms vary so much.

If you have never worked with learning centers, start out with a familiar topic. Investigations can be made into learning centers (see Figure 6–5). Always use clear directions and check to see that the students understand the procedure. Demonstrate an activity to get their interest and model appropriate behavior with materials. Finally, keep in mind that the noise level in the classroom may increase slightly. Allow yourself plenty of time at first to ensure a successful learning experience.

Use a prearranged signal, such as flashing the lights or raising your hand and loudly counting to three, if things get too noisy at the center.

Chances are your experience with science learning centers will be rewarding. If so, consider increasing the use of centers through a more flexible arrangement involving several subjects. Some teachers reserve mornings for the three R's and unit teaching. Afternoons are for individualized enrichment and skill-building activities at different learning centers, such as the following:

- Science
- Social studies/multicultural center

Figure 6–5   A sample learning center.

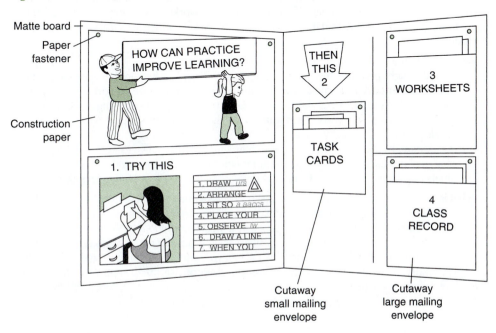

- Fine arts center
- Hobby center
- Literature center
- Writing center
- Speaking and listening center
- Math center

Work at the centers may be either assigned or optional. This choice allows you freedom to vary time and other considerations and to assist and confer with individuals. You and each child can cooperatively decide on ways to pursue interests, knowledge, and skills. The best learning usually happens when children themselves take an active part in planning their learning.

Live Animal Centers

Refer to Appendix D and *http://www. prenhall.com/peters* for animal care tips.

The use of living creatures such as mealworms, hermit crabs, lizards, fish, mice, hamsters, and rabbits is an excellent way to develop your students' observational skills and responsibility. When using animals, first refer to the school or district policy to determine which animals are acceptable for classrooms. The best policy is to have a veterinarian become your "partner in education" and ensure that the animals in your classroom are safe for student interaction.

Visit an Inquiry Classroom
The Role of Animals in the Classroom

View the *Moral Dimensions* video in the "Nature of Science" section of the Companion CD. Mr. McKnight discusses with his students the ethics of working with animals during a scientific study. They indicate that it would not be right to kill earthworms as part of scientific study.

Review the video and ask yourself the following:
- Mr. McKnight provides the following quote in his perspective on this video segment: "I think it's important to make the kids aware of their role as being sort of a guardian or steward of the earth in a way that they need to treat other living things with respect." How can having live plants and animals in the classroom support Mr. McKnight's goals provided in this statement?
- Mr. McKnight discusses the use of the Internet as an alternative to finding out specific things about earthworms. What are other ways to use the Internet to learn about animals or promote the idea of students being the "guardians or stewards of the earth"?

What is your opinion on the use of animals in the classroom? The American Society for the Prevention of Cruelty to Animals provides the website, Animals in the Classroom: Should You or Shouldn't You? at *http://www.aspca.org/site/PageServer? pagename= petsinclass*. Based on what this site provides, do you agree or disagree with the use of animals in the classroom? Explain your answer. Record your ideas and the answers to these questions in your portfolio or use the Companion Website to share your ideas.

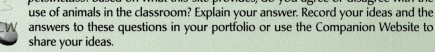

Care for the animals should be primarily the students' responsibility; however, you should monitor the cleaning, feeding, and exercise. Help out only when the students cannot provide effective care.

Ideas for animal centers include having the students observe life cycles, compare growth rates, or observe eating patterns. It is a good idea to provide a daily observation log for the students to complete if they are observing animals.

SCIENCE PROJECTS

As professional educators, we have seen withdrawn or listless girls and boys who did not come to life until they began to create science projects. Mandy and her group partners really became involved in science when given the opportunity to complete their project for the science fair. Because they were so interested in geology, Mandy's classmates Shauna and Danielle also completed an informal project on collecting rocks and minerals. The project began at the learning center where her group read *Everybody Needs a Rock* (Baylor, 1985), *Exploring Earth's Treasures* (Olson, 1996), and *The Magic School Bus Inside the Earth* (Cole, 1987). Later, they used *Rocks and Minerals: Mind-Boggling Experiments You Can Turn into Science Fair Projects* (VanCleave, 1995) in deciding on a particular project. The group spent many hours collecting and identifying rocks and minerals.

What specifically is a project, and how does it differ from other science activities? A *project* is an organized search, construction, or task directed toward a specific purpose. One person or a small team of two or three persons ordinarily completes a project with minimal guidance from the teacher. A project is generally less formal than a "science fair project" and may clarify, extend, or apply a concept. Working on projects causes children to use science processes and develop thinking strategies. Most projects require much independent effort, so they are less appropriate for early-elementary children, who usually lack the skills and perseverance needed to operate independently.

The need for projects most often arises during a regular instructional unit; but projects may also begin with interests expressed by the students. The teacher's job is to provide some realistic project choices, give deadlines for completing the projects, tell how they will be presented, indicate the credit that will be received for projects, and check at times for progress.

Using Investigations and Activities for Projects

Investigations that you might use with the whole class or in learning centers often present one or two extra open-ended opportunities to go beyond the basic investigation. Exploration of these questions can be an enriching activity when completed as a project.

> **Teaching Tips** | Project questions can originate from an informal query such as "What caused the Grand Canyon?"

Project activities can be short-range, straightforward demonstrations of concepts or procedures. Projects like these allow children to extend their interest by applying interviewing and reference skills to answer real needs.

Curriculum Projects

Project WILD (by the Council for Environmental Education) is a national program that promotes interdisciplinary, supplementary environmental and conservation activities for all grade levels. Teachers who attend Project WILD workshops are trained to facilitate numerous projects and activities that can be found in the guide provided to participants. The activities are grouped to take elementary or middle school students from the *awareness* of environmental concerns to the *action* of conservation and remediation.

Project WILD Aquatic (also by the Council for Environmental Education) is the companion series to Project WILD and is based on water environments. It contains many aquatic-based activities and extensions to terrestrial WILD activities.

Project Learning Tree (by the American Forest Foundation), similar to WILD, is an environmental education project that has trees as its theme. Teachers who attend these certification workshops are shown how to facilitate integrated projects and activities based on diversity, interrelationships, systems, scale, and patterns of change.

Refer to the Web Destinations for Chapter 6 on the Companion Website (*http://www.prenhall.com/peters*) for more information on Project WILD, Aquatic WILD, or Project Learning Tree.

Science Fairs

Mandy's classmates Lucinda and Raquel are displaying the books *Volcanoes* (Branley, 1985), *The Magic School Bus Blows Its Top* (Cole, 1996), *How Mountains Are Made* (Zoehfeld, 1995), *Volcanoes: Fire from Below* (Wood, 1991), and *Discovering Earthquakes and Volcanoes* (Damon, 1990) at their science fair table. They are also exhibiting charts, graphs, and pictures related to volcanoes. Together, they prepared a science fair project that explains volcanoes. They searched the Internet for ideas and found the Volcano World site where they gathered information and developed their project.

You may want to consider having a science fair to encourage inquiry and display successful projects. The "investigatory aspect of science fairs" supports reform efforts such as the National Science Education Standards and the Benchmarks for Science Literacy (Balas, 1998, p. 1). Science fairs are also exciting for students, as you found out with Mandy's project cited earlier in the chapter. Science fairs are also good public relations tools to promote your science program at school. A well-planned science fair will involve all students because they have more options available than with regular instructional periods.

Refer to the Web Destinations for Chapter 6 on the Companion Website (*http://www.prenhall.com/peters*) for sample volcano projects and links.

General Guidelines for Science Fairs

When beginning to consider a science fair, start small. A single classroom display at an open house is a good way to begin. Then, as you develop confidence, you may want to work with a fellow teacher for a combined event or even organize a schoolwide fair. Either way, allow plenty of time for the students to complete their projects. We suggest at least 6 weeks, as follows:

- *First Week* Hand out an information sheet and announce the science fair. Allow plenty of time for students to generate ideas and form groups if they are going to work on group projects.
- *Second Week* Students turn in preliminary proposals for their projects by the end of the week. Remind students that you will review the proposals with them for quality of the inquiry, completeness of the proposal, and their ability to complete the project.
- *Third Week* Hold individual meetings with students and their teacher to discuss proposals and refine projects.
- *Fourth Week* Students or groups begin setting up inquiry activities, gathering data, and beginning reports.

Teaching Tips

A certificate of completion or multiple prizes can formally recognize everyone's efforts, but downplay individual comparisons, which elementary or middle school students find hard to handle.

- **Fifth Week** Students continue to work on projects and begin work on presentations and displays.
- **Sixth Week** Students refine displays and presentations, complete reports, and present projects by the end of the week. Displaying projects on Friday afternoon and Saturday morning may increase parent participation.

Invention Conventions

As part of the trend to teach science that children can apply to their lives, some science programs today recommend "invention conventions," as well as typical science fairs. Because technology is science applied to solve practical problems, the idea is to give students chances to develop solutions to their everyday problems and interests:

> How can I tell how fast the wind is blowing? (A homemade wind gauge, fashioned from cardboard and wood, could fill the bill.)
>
> I'd like to make a weird toy that rolls uphill by itself. (Try a hidden rubber band inside a coffee can.)
>
> I've heard you can make a stool from newspaper that's so strong you can sit on it safely. (Rolled-up newspaper makes surprisingly sturdy columns.)

For a variety of fun-filled ideas and ways to stimulate inventiveness in your students, see the following resources:

- Caney, S. (1985). *Steven Caney's invention book*. New York: Workman.
- Eichelberger, B., & Larson, C. (1993). *Constructions for children: Projects in design technology*. Menlo Park, CA: Dale Seymour.
- McCormack, A. J. (1981). *Inventor's workshop*. Belmont, CA: David S. Lake.

If you are interested in a competitive awards program for projects, check the National Science Teachers Association's website. There you will find listed current national and regional science competitions.

> Refer to the Web Destinations for Chapter 6 on the Companion Website (*http://www.prenhall.com/peters*) for links to the National Science Teachers Association and other awards programs. **CW**

TEACHING STUDENTS WITH EXCEPTIONALITIES

After listening to *Caves and Caverns* (Gibbons, 1993) being read to the class, Tamika became very excited about speleology. She wanted to know more about stalactites, stalagmites, helictites, speleothems, flowstone, and dripstone. She thought that a career as a speleologist would be perfect because her physical disability would not interfere with spelunking. Fortunately, she is in an inclusive classroom where the teacher recognizes her interest as an opportunity and will support her curiosity. This situation is in keeping with McCann's (1998) statement, "Science classes provide special needs students with opportunities they may not get anywhere else" (p. 1).

Inclusive Classrooms

Inclusion is a concept that is becoming the standard in most K–12 classrooms. An inclusive classroom has a mix of physical and mental developmental levels of students, accommodating those identified as disabled in some way. According to the U.S. Department of Education (USDOE), nearly 12% of students were identified as disabled during the period 1991–1994 (USDOE, 1994). The Office of Special Education Programs reports that the number of students with disabilities served under the Individuals with Disabilities Education Act (IDEA)

> **Inclusion** is education in the least restrictive environment and means that students would, to the extent possible, be educated with their peers.

Science experiences provide students with exceptionalities with opportunities not found in other content areas.

continues to increase at a rate higher than both the general population and school enrollment (USDOE, 1999). IDEA guarantees a free, appropriate education in the least restrictive environment for students with disabilities. Obviously, science instruction is a part of this "appropriate education."

Science instruction for students with disabilities does involve some problems, however. A study by Stefanich and Norman (1996) includes the following information:

- Students with mild disabilities received only 1 minute of science instruction for every 200 minutes of reading instruction.
- Elementary science teachers have little training or experience in teaching students with disabilities.
- Most teachers agree that students with disabilities benefit from hands-on instruction, yet the reality is that they are generally taught from the textbook.

Elementary and middle school teachers need to understand that the special education teacher may not take primary responsibility for science instruction, because the students will probably be in regular classrooms for science class. If you are an elementary teacher, you

Visit an Inquiry Classroom
Special Needs Adaptations

View the *Special Needs Adaptations* video in the "Planning and Management" section of the Companion CD. Mr. McKnight's students are working on an earthworm activity.

Review the video and ask yourself the following:
• Can you identify any students with special needs in the video?
• According to Mr. McKnight's perspective: "Children with learning disabilities who really struggled to gain new information by reading it in a book I think, have the best opportunity to participate and learn on an equal footing with other kids when they're able to manipulate the materials themselves and participate directly in finding that information in the same process as everybody else." Support this viewpoint with specific examples that you have seen in a classroom (your own or a field placement site).

In *The Inclusive Classroom. Mathematics and Science Instruction for Students with Learning Disabilities: It's Just Good Teaching* (1999), Jarrett states that "today's classrooms are increasingly diverse. Students can have great differences in their abilities, life experiences, cultural backgrounds, and home languages. The general education teacher will want to use instructional strategies that respect and build on these differences while helping all students to learn important concepts and skills in mathematics and science." What instructional strategies have you seen in your field experiences that help the general education teacher reach to teach the student with exceptionalities? Record your ideas and the answers to these questions in your portfolio or use the Companion Website to share your ideas.

will have to seek out opportunities during college and through in-service to gain a better understanding of children who have disabilities. Likewise, if you are a special education teacher, you will need college and in-service opportunities related to elementary or middle school science. The following sections are designed as a first step in assisting you with this.

Assisting Students with Disabilities

Mainstreaming presents both opportunities and challenges to people in schools. Children who are mainstreamed learn to live and work in settings that are more likely to develop their potentials to the fullest. The other children profit from a heightened sensitivity and a greater capacity to live and work with individual differences.

The challenges largely come from the diversity of handicaps found in special populations. As an elementary teacher, everyone who comes to your classroom has been identified as a teachable child. To help ensure this, you should share in the placement decision. Students with disabilities who probably require the most change in the science curriculum are those who are totally blind or deaf (American Foundation for the Blind, 2004). For most students with disabilities, a solid hands-on program gives the multisensory experiences they need to learn science well.

Also, realize that an individualized education plan (IEP) is developed for each child by a team of persons. Included on the team is at least one person qualified in special education. By working with a team, you are able to draw on more skills, information, and ideas than by working alone. The team shares responsibility for the child's progress. In many

Refer to the Chapter 6 Web Destinations on the Companion Website (http://www. prenhall.com/peters) for links related to Individuals with Disabilities Education Act (IDEA).

states, the IEP is also accompanied by whatever special instructional media and materials the team believes are essential to meet objectives. What are some characteristics of students with disabilities you are likely to teach? How can you generally help them? What resources can you draw on that apply specifically to science? The following sections review students who are visually impaired, hearing impaired, and orthopedically impaired, and those who are mentally disabled.

Teaching Tips
Reauthorization of IDEA 2004 again calls for "not less than 1 regular education teacher" to participate on an IEP team.

Visually Impaired

The problems of students who are visually impaired may range from poor eyesight to total blindness. Most mainstreamed students will have at least some functional vision, although they frequently lack firsthand experience with many objects as reflected in their language. Vocabulary and descriptive capacity, therefore, need considerable strengthening. Keep in mind the following points with students who are visually impaired:

- Use concrete, multisensory experiences to build a greater store of needed percepts.
- Give plenty of time to explore and encourage the use of descriptive language during explorations.
- Encourage communication with the students throughout activity periods.
- Use tactile cues with materials, such as a knotted string for measuring.
    - Walk the students through spaces to demonstrate barriers and tactile clues.
    - Encourage the use of any remaining vision.
    - Encourage other students to be sensitive about their use of phrases such as "over there," "like that one," or any other descriptions that require vision.
    - Be tolerant of, and prepared for, spilled or scattered material.
    - Use oral language or a recorder for instructions and information.
- Pair each student with a tactful sighted partner who can assist in the scaffolding process.

Teaching Tips
The American Printing House for the Blind produces several current elementary science series in large print and Braille. Illustrations and graphs are often in the form of touchable raised-line drawings.

Hearing Impaired

Students with impaired hearing may range from mildly impaired to totally deaf. Most wear hearing aids and have partial hearing. Communication is easier when the child can read lips and certain facial movements and when sign language is used. Delayed language development is common. When teaching science to students who are hearing impaired, remember the following:

- Use concrete objects—pictures, sketches, signs, and the like—to get across ideas.
- Seat the students close to you or to the sound source.
- Give clear directions and face the students as you speak.
- Speak with usual volume and speed.
- Model, rather than correct, pronunciations for the students who are partially deaf.
- Allow longer periods of wait time.
- Make sure you have the students' attention; use direct eye contact.
- Use gestures and body language, but don't exaggerate these.
- Avoid speaking for the students or having classmates speak for the students.
- Talk with the students frequently about what they are doing.
- Maintain good lighting in the classroom.

Visit an Inquiry Classroom
Private Speech

View the *Private Speech* video in the "Constructivist Pedagogy" section of the Companion CD. Near the end of the video segment, students talk to themselves as a way to make sense of the activity in their own mind. As a teacher, this "private speech" is valuable in checking for understanding.

Review the video and ask yourself the following:

- When Mr. McKnight is interacting with the students, do you think they have a full understanding of what is being discussed? If not, how would private speech assist in understanding the concepts? If you do think they understand, what are specific things they say to show understanding?
- What are other ways that a teacher can informally check for understanding if a student is hearing impaired or has another disability that limits speech?

 What examples of private speech have you observed in your field placements? Explain the nature and result of the private speech. Record your ideas and the answers to these questions in your portfolio or use the Companion Website to share your ideas.

Orthopedically Impaired

Students who are orthopedically impaired typically have gross- or fine-motor malfunctions that cause problems in locomotion, coordination, balance, and dexterity. One of the most common impairments is cerebral palsy. Students who are orthopedically disabled may use walkers, wheelchairs, crutches, braces, or other aids. Keep in mind the following when teaching students who are orthopedically impaired:

- Encourage participation in all possible activities.
- Modify activities as much as possible to avoid frustrations.
- Encourage the use of limbs to the fullest ability.
- Find alternative ways to manipulate objects.
- Allow alternative methods for the students to respond.
- Keep traffic lanes clear in the classroom.
- Acknowledge and deal openly with feelings of frustration.
- Have other students assist these students in moving to the next activity if needed.
- Promote the students' confidence and independence when possible.
- Use activities that foster problem solving and growth in thinking skills.
- Present materials and activities at a comfortable height for individuals in wheelchairs.

Mentally Disabled

Students who are mentally disabled are significantly below average in the abilities of cognitive tasks and often in motor development. They are likely to have problems in learning, remembering, problem solving, and life skills. Other frequent characteristics are short attention span, poor selective attention, and limited ability to make choices. Often, the child with a mental disability will require shorter work periods, more concrete tasks, more direct and structured instruction, and more frequent reinforcement, because of a short attention span. Keep in mind the following points when teaching science to students who are mentally disabled:

- Use a variety of hands-on teaching methods and materials.
- Be sure you have the students' attention before you give directions, and frequently ask them to repeat directions back to you.
- Demonstrate and model as you give simple, clear directions.
- Review new concepts and vocabulary.
- Break tasks down to simple, step-by-step parts if necessary.
- Use the least complex language possible when giving instructions.
- Outline expectations clearly for the students before work begins.
- Review and summarize ideas and procedures frequently. Have the students recapitulate experiences.
- Give positive reinforcement immediately after each small success.
   - Give responsibility within the students' limits, and let the students observe and assist in a role before giving them responsibility.
   - Apply previously constructed concepts to everyday experiences.
   - Begin instruction with what the students know and build on those concepts.

Teaching Tips

Remember that children who are victims of alcoholic or drug-abusing parents may exhibit conditions similar to those of children who are mentally disabled.

Refer to the Web Destinations for Chapter 6 on the Companion Website (*http://www.prenhall. com/peters*) for a link to documents that were developed by the ERIC Clearinghouse on Disabilities and Gifted Education.

CW

Children with Disabilities

Children who are disabled are much more likely to have a poor self-concept than other children. Many adults realize this, but they overprotect children with disabilities in order to compensate. Unfortunately, this overprotection inhibits development and confidence. Children with disabilities, in turn, often learn and accept overdependence, so a cycle develops that feeds on itself. Keep the following in mind when teaching students who are disabled:

- Consider whether help is necessary, rather than convenient.
- Except for obvious needs, get consent from the students before giving help.
- Do not persist if the students decline help; let the students discover whether help is needed.
- Provide prompts instead of answers.
- Allow peers to help or offer help matter of factly.

Children with Special Needs

Many other kinds of disabilities are found in mainstreamed classrooms, including children who are learning disabled, speech/language impaired, health impaired, and those with multiple handicaps. Be aware that entire books are devoted to each one of these and the previously described handicaps. Fortunately, you do not have to become an expert in special education to help a specific mainstreamed child. Although it is nice to have some general knowledge about a handicap, it is far more important to know how that handicap affects a particular child and what the child's individual instructional needs are. You learn this by working with the child.

Resources for Science Teaching

Several sources offer programs and information to better teach students with disabilities in the regular classroom. An excellent and well-tested program is the Full Option Science System (FOSS). Designed for students with and without disabilities in grades K–6, FOSS was developed at the Lawrence Hall of Science. It is an outgrowth of earlier projects to improve science education for students who are visually impaired and physically disabled.

Visit an Inquiry Classroom
Team Formation

View the *Team Formation* video in the "Model Inquiry Unit" section of the Companion CD. This video shows Mr. McKnight forming investigative teams first by similar topics and then later by homeroom.

Review the video and ask yourself the following:

- How will Mr. McKnight ensure that his students with exceptionalities are included on the teams?
- What are some alternative ways that Mr. McKnight could form teams that would also include students with exceptionalities?

In the "Professional Literature" tab of the *Team Formation* video segment, there is reference to forming students into cooperative learning group teams as a way to shift the burden of learning from the teacher to the student. Explain the ramifications of this on the student with a disability who would be participating as a member of a team. Record your ideas and the answers to these questions in your portfolio or use the Companion Website to share your ideas.

Several modules at each grade level include lesson plans in the earth, life, and physical sciences. Extension activities include work in language, computer, and mathematics applications. The developers worked hard to match activities with students' ability to think at different ages. Further work was done to make the program easy to instruct and manage. The commercial distributor of FOSS is

Encyclopaedia Britannica Educational Corporation

310 South Michigan Avenue

Chicago, IL 60604

Further sources that can help you plan lessons for children with different disabilities are:

Alexander Graham Bell Association for the Deaf

3417 Volta Place, N. W.

Washington, DC 20007

American Printing House for the Blind

P.O. Box 6085

Louisville, KY 40206

Center for Multisensory Learning

Lawrence Hall of Science University of California

Berkeley, CA 94720

ERIC Clearinghouse on Handicapped and Gifted Children

1920 Association Drive

Reston, VA 22091

National Center on Educational Media and Materials for the Handicapped

The Ohio State University

154 West 12th Avenue

Columbus, OH 43210

Refer to the Web Destinations for Chapter 6 on the Companion Website (*http://www.prenhall. com/peters*) for links to FOSS and other resources.

Working with Students Who Are English Learners

Not long ago, only a few cities in the United States contained significant numbers of school-children whose native language was not English. Today, they are present in nearly every school. In some schools, foreign-born students who do not speak English may be placed in bilingual classrooms and taught by someone who is proficient in both English and the foreign language. As the students acquire some English proficiency, they are mainstreamed for larger parts of the school day. In other schools, they are taught in all-English classrooms. As a regular classroom teacher, expect to have English language learners in your classroom.

Many students who are English learners experience some culture shock because what they observe now may differ radically from their earlier environment. They may be reluctant to speak because they are afraid to make mistakes. Your warm acceptance and frequent praise will boost their confidence. Whatever you can do to reduce anxiety, increase meaning of content studied, model good English, and increase chances to interact informally with English speakers will benefit them. Students who are becoming proficient in English require some extra time and attention, but they can also enrich the curriculum by bringing multicultural knowledge and perspectives to what is studied. Following are some things that may work for you:

- Use a listening–speaking–reading–writing sequence in teaching when possible. Listening lays the foundation for the other language skills. It's easier to speak what we have first heard, read what we have spoken, and write what we have read.
- Use multisensory, hands-on teaching methods when possible. Concrete materials, investigations, demonstrations, audiovisual media, graphs, and diagrams are more likely to foster meaningful learning. One great advantage of hands-on science over most other subjects is that the actual doing demands little verbal ability.
- Pair English learners with bilingual partners or in cooperative learning groups to increase the scaffolding effect.
- Speak slowly, use short sentences, and rephrase what you say if a student seems unsure, rather than repeat what you have said. Use body language, props, pictures, and sketches to clarify your words.
- Check more specifically whether a student understands by asking yes-or-no questions or by having the student do something you can observe, such as pointing to an object.
- Avoid idiomatic expressions; they can be confusing when taken literally: "It's as easy as pie."
- Make whatever you refer to as concrete as possible—what you know the students have done or observed in the past. Give observable examples in the present as well: "The handle of this pencil sharpener is also a lever."
- To help the students build schemata, write key concepts and vocabulary used during a lesson on the chalkboard. Often make a concept map to outline what is to come in a lesson or to summarize the content of a lesson.
- Emphasize and repeat key words of the lesson as you teach. This cues the students about what to remember and how the words sound.
- For the easiest and most meaningful reading, make language experience charts.

 **Teaching Tips** | Try interactive reading with English learners.

Sixteen regional resource centers for bilingual education in the United States offer training and technical support services for schools. For the center nearest you, call or write the following:

National Clearinghouse for English Language Acquisition and Language Instruction Educational Programs

George Washington University
2121 K Street
Washington, DC 20037
(800)321–6223 *http://www.ncela.gwu.edu*

The following references from the National Clearinghouse for Bilingual Education can also further your work with English learners:

- Hamayan, E., & Perlman, R. (1990). *Helping language minority students after they exit from bilingual/ESL programs: A handbook for teachers*. Washington, DC: National Clearinghouse for English Language Acquisition and Language Instruction Educational Programs.
- Short, D. J. (1991). *Integrating language and content instruction: Strategies and techniques*. Washington, DC: National Clearinghouse for English Language Acquisition and Language Instruction Educational Programs.

Working with Students Who Are Gifted

What can you expect from mainstreamed students classified as gifted by your district? Children who are gifted display many of the same developmental qualities as most other children. The difference is in the greater degree to which, and the speed with which, these qualities develop. In kindergarten, for example, students who are gifted may perform like second graders. By their senior year in high school, they typically outperform average college seniors on academic tests.

What are some of their attributes? Compared with other students, the gifted child is much more likely to do the following:

- Tolerate ambiguity and complexity
- Have a longer attention span
- Be a highly curious and sharp-eyed observer
- Be a top-notch reader who retains what is read
- Have a well-developed speaking and listening vocabulary
- Have learned the basic skills well
- Understand complex directions the first time around
- Be imaginative and receptive to new ideas
- Be interested in broad concepts and issues
- Have one or more hobbies that require thinking

Gifted students who show all or most of these attributes are often placed in a full-time special class or a pull-out program during part of the school day. But many are totally mainstreamed. How can we challenge these children?

A common problem with having gifted children in regular classrooms is that the curriculum is restrictive and unchallenging for them. They soon become bored and often will seek attention in disruptive ways. One way to keep this problem from blossoming is to use many open-ended investigations and activities. Such a program stimulates the kind of creative, divergent thinking gifted students need to grow toward their potential. Fortunately for us as teachers, our experiences described here also work well for most nongifted students.

In-depth investigations of rocks and minerals can become an extension activity for gifted students.

A second important way to help mainstreamed gifted students is to encourage them to build a large knowledge base. This is usually easy because of their broad curiosity, strong ability to locate and understand information, and ability to retain information. A wide variety of open-ended science investigations stimulates them to try multiple observations and experiments and to read for background. Gifted children readily sense how a broad array of knowledge feeds their creative and problem-solving abilities; this motivates them to learn even more.

A third way to help gifted students is to let them manage their own learning through individual and small-group projects, including those done for school science fairs. Independent study also is fostered when we show students how to locate and use references, trade books, and other instructional materials in the school library.

A fourth way to help gifted students is to expose them to persons in science and other professions who can serve as information sources and future role models. This is particularly important for students who come from economically disadvantaged backgrounds. Gifted children have the interest and quickly develop the capacity to correspond with knowledgeable adults, interview them by telephone or in person, and understand much of what they see and hear.

We can also help gifted students by attending to their social skills as they interact with other children. Some of these students may be advanced academically but be average in

Teaching Tips | Inquiry activities can be valuable in motivating gifted students.

social and personal skills. These skills are needed not only for success in many professions but also for personal happiness. A central objective for mainstreaming the gifted is to help them communicate and get along with persons of all ability levels. Remember that gifted students may not necessarily be gifted in mathematics and science. Monitor your expectations to make sure you are not expecting too much from a child who may be gifted only in language, art, music, or another area.

Refer to the Chapter 6 Web Destinations on the Companion Website (*http://www. prenhall.com/peters*) for resources you can use when working with gifted students.

Summary

- The science standards and benchmarks have as a primary goal science for all students.
- A classroom learning center is a place where one or several students at a time can conduct activities independently using materials and directions found at the center. The center may be organized so that the students can choose at least some of the activities and work at their own pace and learning level. Open-ended experiences usually serve best for these purposes.
- A science project is an organized search, construction, or task directed toward a specific purpose and ordinarily carried out by one to three students. The need for projects often arises in instructional units through interests expressed by students.
- Science fairs and invention conventions will help you encourage inquiry. They are exciting for students and can be good public relations tools to promote your science program at school.
- The Individuals with Disabilities Education Act (IDEA) guarantees a free, appropriate education in the least restrictive environment for students with disabilities. Science instruction is a part of this appropriate education.

Reflection

Companion CD

1. Look at "The Digestive System" lesson linked to the *Paradigm Shifts* video on the Companion CD. How would you modify this lesson for students with visual or hearing impairments?
2. Look at "The Circulatory System" lesson linked to the *Active Learning* video on the Companion CD.

   How would you modify this lesson for use with English learners?
3. Look at "The Respiratory System" lesson linked to the *Social Learning* video on the Companion CD. How would you enhance this lesson for use with students who are gifted?

Portfolio Ideas

1. The policy in some schools is to not allow any type of live animal. In this case, you can search the Internet for sites that have permanently mounted cameras for your students to make "live" observations. What other types of environments can you find on the Internet? What other ways can you replace the use of classroom pets? Share ideas in your portfolio.
2. If you were to arrange a science competition in your classroom, what local community resources or industries could help out? Try contacting one or two and see what types of resources are available to you as a classroom teacher. Record findings in your portfolio.
3. Attend an individualized education program (IEP) meeting for a student. What is expected of the parents, the regular teacher, the special education teacher, and the child? Make an entry in your portfolio on what you found out about IEPs.

References

American Association for the Advancement of Science (AAAS). (1993). *Benchmarks for science literacy*. New York: Oxford University Press.

American Forest Foundation. (1993). *Project learning tree environmental education preK–8 activity guide*. Washington: DC, Author.

American Foundation for the Blind. (2004). *Educating blind and visually impaired students: Policy guidance from OSERS*. New York: Author. Retrieved December 23, 2004, from *www.afb.org/Section.asp?SectionID=3&TopicID=138&DocumentID=720&Mode=Print*

Balas, A. (1998). *Science fairs in the elementary school*. Columbus, OH: ERIC Digest.

Baylor, B. (1985). *Everybody needs a rock*. New York: Atheneum.

Branley, F. (1985). *Volcanoes*. New York: HarperCollins.

Cole, J. (1987). *The magic school bus inside the earth*. New York: Scholastic.

Cole, J. (1996). *The magic school bus blows its top*. New York: Scholastic.

Damon, L. (1990). *Discovering earthquakes and volcanoes*. New York: Troll Associates.

Erickson, S., Gregg, D., Helling, F., King, M., & Starkweather, J. (1987). *Down to earth*. Fresno, CA: AIMS Education Foundation.

Gibbons, G. (1993). *Caves and caverns*. New York: Voyager Books.

Gosnell, K. (1994). *Thematic unit: Geology*. Huntington Beach, CA: Teacher Created Materials.

Hale, J. (1992). *Thematic unit: Rocks and soil*. Huntington Beach, CA: Teacher Created Materials.

Hoover, E., & Mercier, S. (1996). *Primarily earth: AIMS activities grades K–3*. Fresno, CA: AIMS Education Foundation.

Jarrett, D. (1999). *The inclusive classroom. Mathematics and science instruction for students with learning disabilities: It's just good teaching*. Portland, OR: Northwest Regional Educational Laboratory. Retrieved December 23, 2004, from *www.nwrel.org/msec/images/resources/justgood/09.99.pdf*

Lawrence Hall of Science. (1989). *River cutters* (Rev. ed.). Berkeley: University of California.

McCann, W. (1998). *Science classrooms for students with special needs*. Columbus, OH: ERIC Digest. Available at *www.ericse.org/digests/dse98-5.html*

McNulty, F. (1979). *How to dig a hole to the other side of the world*. New York: Harper & Row.

National Research Council (NRC). (1996). *National science education standards*. Washington, DC: National Academy Press.

National Society for the Study of Education (NSSE). (1932). *A program for teaching science: Thirty-First Yearbook of the National Society for the Study of Education*. Chicago: University of Chicago Press.

National Society for the Study of Education (NSSE). (1947). *Science education in American schools: Forty-Sixth Yearbook of the National Society for the Study of Education*. Chicago: University of Chicago Press.

National Society for the Study of Education (NSSE). (1960). *Rethinking science education: Fifty-Ninth Yearbook of the National Society for the Study of Education*. Chicago: University of Chicago Press.

Olson, D. (1996). *Exploring earth's treasures*. Chicago: Kidsbooks.

Stefanich, G., & Norman, K. (1996). *Teaching science to students with disabilities: Experiences and perceptions of classroom teachers and science educators*. A special publication of the Association for the Education of Teachers in Science (AETS). (Available from AETS, Dr. Jon Pedersen, University of Oklahoma, 820 Van Vleet Oval, ECH 114, Norman, OK 73019)

U.S. Department of Education (USDOE). (1994). *Mini-digest of educational statistics: 1994*. Washington, DC: Author.

U.S. Department of Education (USDOE). (1999). *Twenty-first annual report to Congress on the implementation of Individuals with Disabilities Education Act*. Washington, DC: Author. Available at *www.ed.gov/offices/OSERS/OSEP/OSEP99AnlRpt/*

VanCleave, J. (1995). *Rocks and minerals: Mind-boggling experiments you can turn into science fair projects*. New York: John Wiley.

Wood, J. (1991). *Volcanoes: Fire from below*. Milwaukee, WI: Gareth Stevens.

Zoehfeld, K. (1995). *How mountains are made*. New York: HarperCollins.

Suggested Readings

Blume, S. (1991). *Science fair handbook*. New York: Macmillan/McGraw-Hill. (a resource for teachers, principals, and science fair coordinators)

Bochinski, J. (1991). *The complete handbook of science fair projects*. New York: John Wiley. (how to complete a project plus 50 award-winning examples)

Carratello, J., & Carratello, P. (1989). *All about science fairs*. Huntington Beach, CA: Teacher Created Materials. (a practical guide to help students and teachers with science fairs)

Council For Environmental Education. (2002). *Project WILD aquatic: K–12 curriculum and activity guide*. Houston, TX: Author.

DeBruin, J. (1991). *Science fairs with style*. Carthage, IL: Good Apple. (a comprehensive guide for upper-grade projects)

Fredericks, A., & Asimov, I. (1990). *The complete science fair handbook*. Glenview, IL: Good Year Books. (a good guide to conducting science fairs)

Hampton, C. H., Hampton, C. D., & Kramer, D. C. (1994). *Classroom creature culture: Algae to anoles* (Rev. ed.). Arlington, VA: National Science Teachers Association. (guidelines for setting up live animal centers in the classroom; also available as an ERIC microfiche, ERIC Document Reproduction Service No. ED 370 797)

National Science Teachers Association (NSTA). (1988). *Science fairs and projects: Grades K–8*. Washington, DC: Author. (a resource book from NSTA)

National Science Teachers Association (NSTA). (1990). *Science and math events*. Arlington, VA: Author. (a resource book on science and math events from NSTA)

Poppe, C. A., & VanMatre, N. A. (1985). *Science learning centers for the primary grades*. West Nyack, NY: Center for Applied Research in Education. (a comprehensive book for those interested in setting up centers)

Project WILD: K–12 Curriculum and Activity guide. Council for Environmental Education. (2002a). Houston, TX: Author.

Shubkagel, J. F. (1993). *Show me how to write an experimental science fair paper: A fill-in-the-blank handbook.* Independence, MO: Show Me How. (a step-by-step guide for teachers, parents, and students in upper-elementary grades)

Stone, G. K. (1981). *More science projects you can do.* Upper Saddle River, NJ: Prentice Hall. (a paperback book of many interesting projects for upper-elementary students)

Tocci, S. (1986). *How to do a science fair project.* New York: Watts. (a useful guide to science fair projects)

VanCleave, J. (1997). *Guide to the best science fair projects.* New York: John Wiley. (complete rules, display tips, and experiments on 50 topics)

CHAPTER 7

CONSTRUCTING TECHNOLOGICAL UNDERSTANDINGS

- What is the difference between educational technology and technology education?
- What are some ways to use computers in the elementary or middle school science classroom?
- What does science, technology, and society (STS) refer to as related to elementary or middle school science?
- What are some of the areas of technology education and how could you apply this information in your classroom?

Focus on Inquiry

Where the Wildflowers Are

Dr. Charlotte Boling and Dr. Pam Northrup
University of West Florida

To plan the upcoming fourth-grade unit on native wildflowers, Ms. Heubach uses STEPS (Support for Teachers Enhancing Performance in Schools), an online tool designed to assist in planning using a standards-driven model (*http://www.ibinder.uwf.edu/steps/*). The STEPS site contains a Lesson Architect that helps Ms. Heubach organize her lesson online. She will be able to store the lesson in her personal online folder and even e-mail it to her principal. Resources such as links to websites, best practices, and other model units help her in planning the lesson on wildflowers. Tutorial links are especially useful because Ms. Heubach is trying out some new technologies in her lesson. The tutorials within STEPS will guide her in how to use technology in the classroom. Using this online tool, she designed a unit that will last for several weeks.

On the first day of the unit, Ms. Heubach greets her fourth-grade students at the door and hands each a card with the words "Where the Wildflowers Are." Once everyone is seated, Ms. Heubach explains that the class will be embarking on a new unit about wildflowers. She then discusses the strategies the students will be following by using a PowerPoint presentation loaded with pictures and graphics taken from the Internet. The students will be researching wildflowers, learning about where they grow, and actually growing some in their classroom. At the end of the unit, the fourth-grade students will sell their wildflowers. Ms. Heubach then poses this question: "As a scientist, how would you go about gathering information, making initial hypotheses, testing the hypotheses, and reporting?" Using Inspiration concept mapping software shown through an LCD projector, Ms. Heubach notes the students' brainstorming answers to the question. Ms. Heubach organizes students into cooperative learning groups, and they begin.

Rashid, Sherry, Xuemin, and Cherian immediately embark on a virtual field trip to the desert, to the Pitcher Plant Prairie, and to the local garden store's website. (All pertinent websites had been bookmarked earlier by Ms. Heubach to save time.) The students take notes, copy interesting pictures to their group folder on the computer, and begin comparing and contrasting types of wildflowers. Rashid finally suggests that they begin looking at wildflowers that will grow locally. After a bit of problem solving, the students notice a link to the Global Temperature Cam and to Weather Underground. They are on their way!

Alla, Laszlo, Sharon, and Seth begin their investigation by using the CD-ROM Explorapedia. They look up wildflowers, gardening, and seeds to begin their search. They also jot down notes on their palm computers, save pictures to their computer folders, and even print some information for later use. Klaus, Zhiyong, Stuart, and Swarna's approach is to go online to the site Ask a Scientist and to study the Biomes projects. They think that the information they gain in other ways will help them better understand wildflowers. They e-mail a scientist who guarantees a 24-hour response. They also go to Global Schoolhouse to see whether other classes are studying the same topic and, they hope, to collaborate with students in other parts of the country.

After the information gathering is complete, the students create HyperStudio stacks to share with each other, with other students, and with new online partners. The stacks include projections of which types of flowers should be grown in their classroom, the soil that should be used, and the type of pot that would work best.

Kristina, Sherman, Theodore, and Barbara establish a relationship with a classroom in another part of the country. The two classrooms decide that they will plant wildflowers at the same time while predicting, observing, and recording plant data. To make the relationship as visual as possible, Ms. Heubach and Chandra create a simple website containing both classes' selection of wildflowers to grow, the type of soil selected, the HyperStudio lessons that were created, and a simple database for student groups to update weekly and monitor growth. To keep the website current, the students take digital pictures each week and load them on the website. Both classrooms download NetMeeting and begin daily conversations through their inexpensive Quick Cam camera. The students also create and share pictures of their plants with their new pen pals across the country.

While the plants mature, students establish marketing techniques. The fourth-grade students brainstorm the best approaches to marketing their wildflowers. Some engage in traditional marketing by creating posters to hang in the school. Others decide to create a bookmark by using a simple desktop publishing program and to distribute it to all they meet: *"Bookmark it! Wildflowers for Sale . . . "* along with the URL of the class website is their message. Another group believes that a video is a good approach. Using the resources that have been gathered during the past several weeks, the students go to the ITV room and create a short commercial to be played on the school's ITV network.

The plants are finally ready for sale! The students must keep track of the expenses they incurred while growing the plants (soil, pots, advertising, fertilizer) and make sure they sell the plants at a price that will allow them to make their money back and still have some left over for a class celebration. The students use a spreadsheet to keep up with the expenses and the profits.

"Step right up! This is where the wildflowers are" could be heard and seen on the school ITV system on the day of the sale!

EDUCATIONAL TECHNOLOGY, TECHNOLOGY EDUCATION, AND SCIENCE

With the possibility of exploring online resources as the students did in the Focus on Inquiry: Where the Wildflowers Are, children and their teachers have a new world of exciting possibilities open to them in today's classrooms. The students in the opening scenario constructed new knowledge about technology and science. They were excited about using their technologically enhanced learning environment and discovering new things about wildflowers as they developed inquiry skills through the use of educational technology.

What do you think of when you hear the words *technology* and *education?* If you are like most people, your response would include educational technology, or the use of computers in education. This is just one small part of technology, however. Technology education also includes the designed world (Rutherford & Ahlgren, 1990).

By including the **designed world,** we mean *technology education*, which includes areas such as the following:

- Agricultural technology such as precision farming with GPS devices, grafting, and hydroponics
- Materials technology such as ceramics, plastics, and composites
- Manufacturing technology such as a continuous-production automated assembly lines, welding robots, and computer-aided manufacturing
- Energy technology such as fossil fuels, solar energy, and wind power
- Communication technology such as cell phones, laser barcode scanners, and computers
- Health technology such as biotechnology and genetics to develop new drugs, artificial limbs, and nuclear magnetic resonance
- Construction technology such as building new skyscrapers, suspension bridges, and dams
- Transportation technology such as high-speed magnetic rails, hypersonic aircraft, and hybrid electric/gas cars

Designed world refers to the applications of science in the form of technology.

In the first part of this chapter, we look at educational technology, or using computers, laser discs, CDs, DVDs, and similar tools in the classroom. We then explore the science technology society (STS) movement. In the last part of the chapter, we explore the growing field of technology education in the elementary and middle school classroom.

USING EDUCATIONAL TECHNOLOGY IN THE SCIENCE CLASSROOM

A revolution occurred in education soon after the printing press was invented. The printed book became the tool of its time and has since been noted by many groups as the greatest invention of the past millennium. Today, computer technology is the educational tool of the times. Historians tell us of the resistance to books in the 15th century. As people relied more on the printed word for educational opportunity, however, this technological advancement became commonplace. Similarly, resistance to using computers and other technology in the classroom is rapidly changing today.

Not that long ago, a single computer for a school was rare. This is no longer the case. Computers of all sizes are located in media centers, labs, and individual classrooms. Computing capacity is now at the point where the average home video game has the computing ability of the most powerful computers manufactured just a few years ago. The automobile you buy today has a greater ability to process data than any computer you may have used in school. What does this mean for you as a teacher? *You will be challenged to use the technology as a learning tool rather than learning about the tool of technology.* A recent Net-Day Survey (2004) included the following information:

- Approximately 94% of teachers said they are comfortable using computers and 87% of them are comfortable using the Internet. Geographically, urban teachers are more comfortable using computers—65% are very comfortable compared to 54% of suburban and 54% of rural teachers. The majority of teachers believe that the Internet has become important to teaching in the past 2 years—48% feel that it has become very important.

- Three fourths of teachers agree that the Internet is a tool to use to conduct research for standards-based instruction and 84% of the teachers say it improves the quality of education—nearly half say it has improved the quality a lot. Another 77% of teachers believe that their peers without Internet access are at a disadvantage and an overwhelming 64% disagree that the Internet takes away from other important educational skills.

- Despite the high comfort levels and strong positive attitudes, 67% of the teachers acknowledge that the Internet is not well integrated into their classroom.

This last point was reinforced by other studies in which researchers found that, although significant advances have been made in instructional technology, actual practice in the classroom is status quo (Kozma & Shank, 1998; Means, 1994). This is not because of unwillingness on the child's part. A recent survey found the following to be true of children ages 8 to 18 in 2003–2004:

- 96% went online
- 74% have Internet access at home
- 61% use the Internet daily (Henry J. Kaiser Family Foundation, 2004)

See the Web Destination for Chapter 7 on the Companion Website (*http://www. prenhall.com/peters*) for links to other programs emphasizing the use of computers in the classroom.

Similarly, the estimated $16.9 billion video game industry indicates that 92% of children and adolescents age 2 to 17 years play video games (Henry J. Kaiser Family Foundation, 2002). In sum, the uses of advanced technologies *in the classroom* have not kept pace with advances in the community. If this is still the case for you, how can you change this practice? Will your classroom look like the one in Focus on Inquiry: Where the Wildflowers Are?

Standards Link

Science Program Resource Standard

The K–12 science program must give students access to appropriate and sufficient resources, including quality teachers, time, materials and equipment, adequate and safe space, and the community.

- **The most important resource is professional teachers.**

- **Time is a major resource in a science program.**

- **Conducting scientific inquiry requires that students have easy, equitable, and frequent opportunities to use a wide range of equipment, materials, supplies, and other resources for experimentation and direct investigation of phenomena.**

- **Collaborative inquiry requires adequate and safe space.**

- **Good science programs require access to the world beyond the classroom.**

(Program Standard D, National Research Council, 1996, p. 218.)

The Science Program Resource Standard is included here so that you can refer to it and see the need for educational technology. As noted, inquiry requires the right equipment. Computers can provide access to data and scientists beyond the classroom. The authors of the *National Science Education Standards* (National Research Council [NRC], 1996) suggest that your students can access scientific information as well as collect, store, analyze, and display data. Think about how students in the Focus on Inquiry: Where the Wildflowers Are used technology as a learning tool. Does it seem natural for them to use computers? Do students in the chapter-opening photograph show how commonplace computers have become in the elementary and middle school classroom?

Computer Advantages, Disadvantages, and Resources

You probably already have seen some ways that computer-assisted instruction can benefit you and your students in both learning centers and larger settings. Let's look at several more advantages and then address a few concerns.

It takes only a brief experience with computers to see how much children delight in this medium. The immediate feedback to their responses prompts them to learn more quickly and confidently. Slow or fast learners may progress at their own developmentally appropriate rates. When they respond incorrectly, a good program branches them into a remedial sequence that reteaches the material in simpler steps. When they respond correctly, a good program moves them quickly into more advanced material. Computers make individualized instruction more accessible.

One of the best uses of the computer in science education is with simulations. The computer-controlled videodisc, CD-ROM, and other resources offer all kinds of opportunities for making decisions and solving problems in realistic settings. Any airline pilot can tell you that what's seen through the cockpit windshield of a flight simulator just after a right or wrong move comes uncannily close to the real thing. Now the chances for children to encounter simulated experiences are increasing.

One problem with computers is that software can be a major part of a school budget. Fortunately, a growing supply of software is available on the Internet, and much of it is available to teachers for free or for a minimal registration fee. One type of software is the web-based application software called JAVA. Accessing this type of web page sends applets, or small programs, to your computer. Once loaded, applet programs provide specific applications.

Another drawback of some elementary and middle school science software is a lack of accompanying hands-on experiences. This is more likely with older and stand-alone materials. The software integrated into today's comprehensive multimedia science programs usually provides for concrete activity.

Nearly everyone needs some extra guidance and practice to apply this remarkable tool creatively. If you are new to computing, it's easy to feel overwhelmed by the sheer quantity of unfamiliar technology and methods employed. The good news is that plenty of help is available through user groups and schoolwide or districtwide technology coordinators. Both in-service workshops and informal, person-to-person arrangements are common. Don't be surprised to meet students with considerable expertise at computing. By the sixth grade, some children have had several thousand hours of experience with computers at home and at school. They can be invaluable aides to other students and to you. Employ them in cooperative situations as much as possible.

See the Web Destinations for Chapter 7 on the Companion Website (*http://www. prenhall.com/peters*) for sample science-related JAVA applets.

Teaching Tips
If you are new to a school, ask colleagues and the media specialist what devices and help are available at the school and district levels.

Software Sources and Reviews

How can you learn what is currently available and worthwhile? The supply of usable science software continues to grow. Software publishers are producing more materials that reflect the best thinking in constructivist psychology and science education. Science textbook publishers are integrating software titles into text units and chapters. In fact, now these publishers are more accurately called multimedia science program publishers. Some also develop their own software for that purpose.

If you are unsure about a software program, keep in mind that the National Science Teachers Association (NSTA, 1992) presents the following guidelines on the use of computers in science education:

- Computers should enhance, not replace, hands-on activities.
- Tutorial software should engage students in meaningful interactive dialogue.
- Simulation software should provide opportunities to explore concepts and models not readily available.
- Computer-based labs should permit students to collect and analyze data like scientists.
- Networking should permit students to emulate the way scientists work and reduce classroom isolation.

The Uses of Computers

School computers initially served for drill and practice in mathematics and language. Now, they are also being used to teach broader applications through simulations, computer-based laboratories, project-based science, multimedia, spreadsheets, databases, and learning activities related to the Internet. With more machines available, there are improved chances for us to apply them in science activities and in whole-class teaching. You will find that some schools pool their computer resources into laboratories, some distribute their computer resources into classrooms, and some use a combination of these methods. In most cases, you will have at least one machine to allow you to create a center in your classroom.

Setting up a computer center for science raises some of the same practical questions as learning centers for other disciplines:

- What do you want to accomplish with the center?
- Are other means of instruction better?
- What kinds of compatible hardware and software are available?
- Who will use the center and when?
  - What will the users need to know?
  - How can I best scaffold the learning environment for my students?

Check the NSTA site at *http://www.nsta.org/* for other suggestions on the use of technology in the classroom.

Often, the software available to you will dictate your use of the computer. What types of software are available? Consider the kinds of software programs you are now likely to see in your school.

Multimedia Tutorials and Skill-Building Games

Tutorials and skill-building games are used to teach vocabulary, facts, topical information, or skills. Let's look at the example of CHEM4Kids. Here, students can learn about matter, elements, atoms, and related topics. These tutorials are presented in a fun and interactive manner and include accompanying activities and resources.

Another example is Butterflies 2000—On the Wings of Freedom. Children can learn about the anatomy of butterflies, the travel patterns and other behaviors, and the reproductive cycle. There is also the ability to play associated games and share butterfly-related stories.

An example of a skill-building tool is Tracking a Moving Shadow, where students investigate questions about shadows and moving bodies to make indirect observations of the earth's rotation. Students construct an 18-centimeter gnomon to answer questions as they hypothesize and take measurements of the earth's movements. Tutorial programs can be useful in developing new concepts and skills, the language of science, or in the remediation of misconceptions.

See the Web Destinations for Chapter 7 on the Companion Website (http://www. prenhall.com/peters) for links to multimedia tutorials and skill-building sample websites.

Developing Individual Multimedia

Do you want your students to try to create their own media? HyperStudio (Roger Wagner Publishing) is an example of software that allows students to make their own multimedia presentations. With multimedia, each screen image is considered a card, and a collection of these cards is called a stack. When making stacks, students can type in text, import clip art from other disks, scan in their own pictures, record sounds, control a laser disc/CD player, or link their cards to other programs and Internet resources.

| **T**eaching **T**ips | If you are considering the purchase of a computer for your classroom, you may want to include a DVD drive to be able to play the growing number of titles becoming available for classroom use. |

Macromedia's Flash software provides a more advanced format for multimedia but will be too advanced for most elementary students. The advantages to using hypermedia are as follows:

- The students can research topics and make their own information stacks to share with others at their school or through the Internet.
- Classroom or school collections of hypermedia stacks provide information on a variety of topics from multiple perspectives.
- The students feel good about themselves when they are able to create a simple stack and share it with others.

You may want to try out HyperStudio or a similar program. Often, they are available free on a trial basis. How can you use such a program in your classroom? Here's an example: Have your students develop a classification of some common objects in the schoolyard, such as the rocks they can find. Use HyperStudio (Roger Wagner Publishing) to create a stack of cards based on the students' classification system.

Simulations

Simulation software is available in PC or Macintosh format and on CD-ROM or floppy disk. In simulations, students play roles in situations where they can explore scientific phenomena or approximate real events. For example, the Magic School Bus series (Scholastic/Microsoft)

See the Web Destinations for Chapter 7 on the Companion Website (*http://www. prenhall.com/peters*) for the links to sample simulation websites.

allows students to explore things like the human body, the solar system, and the ocean. Dangerous Creatures (Microsoft) allows students to explore the world of wildlife. Other programs develop early science skills through the help of an online friend such as Sammy's Science House (Edmark). Space Station Simulator (Maris) allows students to construct and view a space station. Other simulations such as PERIL (University of Guelph) allow players to decide what to do when given certain data. You can use PERIL with your upper-elementary and middle school students. They are presented information on health and safety, make appropriate choices, and identify misconceptions related to health risks.

Simulations are an excellent way to present science phenomena that are otherwise too remote, dangerous, complex, costly, or time consuming. The computer instantly feeds back information as the simulations assist students in constructing knowledge and making real-life decisions without facing real-life consequences.

One exceptional simulation is the Virtual Frog Dissection. Students can explore the frog as if they were actually dissecting it themselves. In this simulation, there is a great amount of detail without the familiar Formalin smell.

Internet Access

See Web Destinations for Chapter 7, on the Companion Website (*http://www.prenhall. com/peters*) for links to a variety of Internet resources related to zoos, science centers, and museums. You can also find the current addresses to science celebrities at this site or a variety of web search tools such a Google.

What is out there in cyberspace? A steadily growing number of people use an electronic mail address with the Internet. These are in the user@location format. Schools, Internet providers, or free services provide the mail addresses. Your students can send e-mail to people, asking for specific information related to the science topics your class is investigating. There are also millions of websites on the Internet to connect to, including zoos, science centers, museums, schools, research centers, and government agencies.

Before you explore the Internet with your students, be cautious to promote safe "surfing." Inform your students not to give out their names or personal information or assume that people they meet on the Internet are who they say they are. Monitor student browsing, check the browser's history file frequently, and complete a child/parent agreement

Visit an Inquiry Classroom
Safety

View the *Safety* video in the "Planning and Management" section of the Companion CD. Mr. McKnight's students investigate an earthworm's movement. They probe the earthworm with a pencil eraser to see its reaction and movement.

Review the video and ask yourself the following:
- Could science simulations such as the Virtual Frog Dissection offer viable alternatives to experimentation when safety is an issue? Why or why not?
- What other ways can computers be used to comply with safety issues of an elementary or middle school classroom?

The Council of State Science Supervisors provides a checklist of safety concerns in K–12 science laboratories at the *http://csss.enc.org/safety.htm* weblink. One item states, "Live animals and students are protected from one another." Explain how Mr. McKnight ensures that this guideline is being met. Record your ideas and the answers to these questions in your portfolio or use the Companion Website to share your ideas.

The use of the Internet provides powerful learning tools in the science classroom.

form (Haag, 1996). Your school or district may have specific software or regulations concerning the Internet, so make it a point to check into this.

Your students can find information or explore many science-related sites for free, once a local Internet connection to your classroom is established. Science celebrities such as Mr. Wizard, Bill Nye the Science Guy, and Beakman's World have Internet addresses.

Perhaps your school already has a *home page*, which is a globally accessible file of information on the Internet. Chances are that the college or university you are attending or your practicum site is on the web. Check with a computer support person to find out the address and how you can access these sites if you do not already know.

Can elementary or middle school students build web pages? Not only can your students access the web, but they can also become a part of the information superhighway. Students enjoy creating web pages based on science topics. Teachers also find it to be a fun activity and are delighted by the creativity of the students. The easiest way to develop a file for the web is to use a web page software tool such as FrontPage (Microsoft). This program works like a word-processing program but saves files in a format called hypertext markup language (HTML). Using HTML, any computer with browser software on the Internet can be used to access a file accurately.

Building web pages helps students develop the scientific skill of communication if they are sharing the procedure and results of an experiment. For example, Mr. McKnight's students on the Companion CD could share with other elementary and middle school classrooms the procedures and results related to the types of habitats the earthworms prefer. Other classes could repeat the activities and see if they have similar results. This models the scientific process.

Science activities are abundant on the Internet. We will begin by referring you to *Science on the Internet: A Resource for K–12 Teachers* (Ebenezer & Lau, 2003). Another good

See Web Destinations for Chapter 7, on the Companion Website (*http://www. prenhall.com/peters*) for links to creating and sharing web pages.

reference is *Internet Activities Using Scientific Data* (Froseth & Poppe, 1995), available from the National Oceanic and Atmospheric Administration (NOAA) (*http://www.noaa.gov/*). It has Internet activities involving real-time data. This guide, developed for teachers, takes you on a journey through the Internet. Your students can learn the basics of the Internet and explore possibilities for science learning.

The chapter "Science and Social Studies" in *Integrating Telecommunications into Education* (Roberts, Blakeslee, Brown, & Lenk, 1990) includes some exemplary programs, such as the National Geographic Kids Network. This project allows students to share their information with others through the Internet. Students in various schools gather data, transmit the data to a central computer, and share findings with other schools. In one unit, students in schools from around the nation measure the acidity of rain in their local area. They send the data to a scientist collaborating with the program. The data are then pooled through a central computer, organized on charts and maps, and sent back to the students. Electronic collaboration can also be a powerful way for you to improve your own classroom practice in the future (Koufman-Frederick, Lillie, Pattison-Gordon, Watt, & Carter, 1999).

> **Teaching Tips**
> Classroom Connect (*http://www.classroom.net/*) is another resource for well-written Internet-based activities. It produces the *lessonplan.net* series with thematic topics such as Catastrophe (Classroom Connect, 1998), which includes activities on earthquakes, hurricanes, El Niño, floods, and other disasters.

Data Management Tools

Data management tools, like spreadsheets and databases, provide essential support to science activities. They are useful in collecting and analyzing data and preparing charts and graphs.

Spreadsheets

Spreadsheets allow you to arrange and automatically compute data. The use of a spreadsheet for a gradebook is a typical example. As new grades are entered, students' final grades based on the input are automatically calculated.

> See Web Destinations for Chapter 7 on the Companion Website (*http://www.prenhall.com/peters*) for links to sample data-managment tool websites.

Excel (Microsoft) and ClarisWorks (Claris) are common tools for developing spreadsheets. The book *ClarisWorks 2.0 in the Classroom* (Claris, 1993) provides examples on how to use spreadsheets to determine the best factors for racing cars, to compare body measurements, or to find the best formulas for bubble mixtures. Spreadsheets can also be used to predict data. If information on plant growth is collected for a period of time, a spreadsheet can determine future trends. A spreadsheet can also be used to determine how long it would take a student to travel to another planet, given the speed of the spacecraft and the distance of the planets. Spreadsheet software such as Microsoft Excel also automatically produces charts and graphs.

Databases

A *database* is a way to create, categorize, sort, and view specific records. For example, a collection of records on Animals A–Z (Claris, 1993) may contain information like the type of animal, size, skin type, habitats, and number of legs. A database can be used to sort the information and display only records that match certain criteria. For instance, by selecting number of legs as a criterion, the database program will automatically sort the records and list those animals that have two legs.

> **Teaching Tips**
> You can use databases to categorize information on rocks and minerals, weather, and volcano records.

Trash Stats is an example of a spreadsheet to manage data. Students can use this program to monitor the number of pounds of trash they produce each day according to predetermined categories. Summary data are automatically calculated.

NASA's Planetary Photojournal database can show the advantage of a database while revealing outstanding images and information related to the solar system. Space missions, planetary satellite images and data, as well as information on people, facilities, and related technology are included.

Word Processing

Probably the most-used types of programs are the *word-processing* programs that students use to format text and correct spelling errors. This software is an excellent tool for creating science journals, writing science poetry, or creating science pal files to share over the Internet. Word processing can be promoted through selected Internet chats, instant message exchanges, and other online activities.

Research Tools

How do scientists use computers? Are children able to use computers in similar ways? Science educators and computer specialists are exploring both questions. The software and other materials coming from their efforts get children into the heart of science: gathering, organizing, and sharing real data.

Several software programs for students have accompanying hardware called *probes*. These are sensing devices connected through a cable to the computer. When used with the proper software, probes can measure temperature, light, sound, heart rate, acidity, motion, force, pressure, and other properties of matter. Several probe-type lab programs, called *computer-based labs*, have had much use in schools from about grade 3 through college.

Bank Street Laboratory (Sunburst) gives students chances to record and analyze graphs of temperature, light, and sound data. Science Toolkit (Broderbund) has rugged, easy-to-use probes for measuring light, temperature, time, and distance. Data are organized into tables, charts, and graphs. Probe labs make it easy to gather a lot of data over short or long periods and then instantly convert the data into analyzable forms.

If you do not have access to real equipment, data can be collected through numerous online sources. For example, temperature, wind speed, and other weather data are commonly found on the Internet. Tide and sea level data are another example of real-time data available through the Internet.

Software Evaluation

Finding good software for use with elementary or middle school students may be a difficult task, given the explosion of software writers and distributors. Because budgets are generally limited for software purchases, it is a good idea to complete a thorough review of the program before purchase.

A software checklist may be a helpful tool to assist you in selecting software appropriate for your students. It is important to prioritize your software purchases on the basis of the philosophy and needs of your program (Beaty, 1990). Some considerations are provided in the checklist in Figure 7–1.

Computer Accessories

If you want your students to use your classroom computer center for word processing science reports and the like, consider attaching a scanner to the computer. An inexpensive LED scanner can be purchased for under $50, and many schools and districts have small

See Web Destinations for Chapter 7 on the Companion Website (*http://www. prenhall.com/peters*) for the links to research tool–related websites.

See Web Destinations for Chapter 7 on the Companion Website (*http://www. prenhall.com/peters*) for other resources related to software examination and use.

See Web Destinations for Chapter 7 on the Companion Website (*http://www. prenhall.com/peters*) for links to available grants and grant assistance for purchasing items for your classroom.

Figure 7–1   Software checklist.

Y/N	Program: Distributor(s) and Price(s): Checklist:
	Is this program developmentally appropriate for children?
	Is the reading level of the program appropriate?
	Does this program meet your specific curricular needs?
	Can the child navigate through the program without adult assistance?
	Will the program hold the child's interest?
	Does the program contain positive reinforcement for children?
	Can you pilot this program to see whether it is compatible with your children?
	Does this software avoid culturally biased language or examples?
	Does this software avoid gender-biased language or examples?
	Will this program be compatible with your existing hardware?
	Will the RAM be sufficient to run the program?
	Will you have enough hard drive space for the program?
	Are any special input or input devices needed with this program?
	Will your monitor support the graphics in this program?
	Is the level of quality of this program sufficient for classroom use?
	Was this program rated by any external reviewers?
	Are there any technical problems that will make using this program difficult?
	Will other teachers be using this program, and can they help you if needed?
	Is the price of the program compatible with your budget?
	Is an educational discount available for this program?
	Are lab packs available if this program will be used on multiple machines?
	Can you make backup copies of the program for your protection?
	Is any special licensing required for this program?

grant programs to assist with this type of purchase. Like a photocopier, a scanner allows the user to incorporate photographs or drawings directly into a written report, multimedia presentation, or Internet web page.

A digital camera can be purchased for under $200 and works like a regular camera but saves the image on computer memory instead of film. The pictures can be transferred to a computer and used in other programs, like scanned pictures. The disadvantage of these cameras is that the less expensive models can only store a limited number of pictures at one time before the pictures need to be downloaded to a computer.

Computer video projectors can now be purchased for under $1,000, making them affordable for elementary and middle schools. These connect to classroom computers and project the image on a screen. The advantage of a video projector over an LCD panel is that the pictures are generally of a much better quality because they have higher resolu-

CDs and DVDs contain extensive science information and activities for children.

tions and are not subjected to the heat of an overhead projector. Most models now work in normal lighting, so students can take notes while viewing.

Other Technological Devices

The CD-ROM (compact disc, read-only memory) is a way to bring a vast amount of computer-controlled audiovisual material into your classroom. The CD-ROM is inserted into a CD-ROM drive connected to a computer. The material is accessed through the keyboard and viewed on the computer screen. The CD-ROM is simply a variation of the familiar audio compact disc. Today, almost every computer is sold with a CD-ROM drive. A CD can currently hold about 5 billion bits of information (the equivalent of 100 books), and technological advances will increase the amount to more than 50 billion bits.

DVD (digital videodisc or digital versatile disc) is a newer form of optical disk storage technology. DVD technology allows video, audio, and computer data to be encoded onto a compact disc. DVD can store greater amounts of data than a common CD. A DVD player is needed to read digital videodiscs. This player is sold as a self-contained, stand-alone device or as an accessory to a computer. Digital videodisc technology may soon replace laser disc, CD-ROM, and audio CDs.

SCIENCE TECHNOLOGY SOCIETY

The growing awareness of how *science, technology,* and *society (STS)* interrelate is evident in the STS movement in science education. The NSTA adopted the *Science-Technology-Society: Science Education for the 1980s* position statement in 1982. Ten years later, the International Council of Associations for Science Education (ICASE) developed an *STS Yearbook* (Yager, 1992). The following year, the NSTA developed another STS document for teachers (Yager, 1993), indicating the continued importance of STS in schools. NSTA continues to advocate this important topic, stating that teacher preparation programs need to cause students to consider the applications of science in society and the relationship of science to engineering (NSTA, 2004). Their shared view is that persons educated

Science and Technology Standard

As a result of the activities in grades K–4, all students should develop

- **Abilities of technological design**

- **Understanding about science and technology**

- **Abilities to distinguish between natural objects and objects made by humans**

(Content Standard E, National Research Council, 1996, pp. 135, 161.)

in the ideas and processes of science and technology can solve several of the problems we face today.

Included in the National Science Education Standards is a Science and Technology Standard (see Standards Link), which shows the relationship between the two entities. Scientific and technological literacy is essential for living, working, and decision making (NSTA, 1982). STS is seen as the teaching and learning of science in the context of human experiences. The NSTA advocates that science should be real to students. An indication of this is providing scientific problems for students to solve that are based on issues of genuine interest to them.

STS in the Classroom

The Science and Technology Standard outlines ways for students to consider such issues as the need to burn coal to produce electricity against the resulting acid rain, thermal pollution, and greenhouse effect. Elementary or middle school students try to answer questions such as the energy and the environment question, follow up by testing their answers to the questions, and then take action based on their findings. Another example of an STS question is, "What is the effect on natural resources if the world's population surpasses 14 billion people in the next century versus the religious and other aspects of controlling human growth?" The STS issue investigation and action instruction model (Rubba, Wiesenmayer, Rye, & Ditty, 1996) is a good example of this teaching strategy because of its four critical factors:

- Foundations
- Awareness
- Investigations
- Action phases (p. 25)

See Web Destinations for Chapter 7 on the Companion Website (*http://www. prenhall.com/peters*) for other resources related to STS.

The model begins with the *foundations* phase as the teacher assists students in understanding the nature of science and technology and their interactions. In the electricity example, for instance, the teacher guides students to finding out that electricity production is a result of scientific research. Generating electricity has trade-offs, such as gaseous emissions, that are balanced against society's need for electricity.

The teacher then discusses and guides students in understanding the concepts and issues related to the topic during the *awareness* phase. The issue would be studied from every aspect, including the scientific and social science points of view. What are the gases emitted? Are other pollutants produced? What are the alternatives to coal-fired plants? What laws and other regulations relate to the topic? What processes are used in generating electricity?

Students then experiment and investigate the STS issue during the *investigations* phase. They visit a plant to see the generation process. Students experiment with making electricity on their own or investigate the effects of production.

Green energy is energy that comes from renewable resources such as that produced by wind turbines, solar cells, and biofuels.

During the *action* phase, students develop ways to take action on the issue. Can **green energy** be purchased in their community? If not, what steps can be done to change this? Can energy be conserved to help reduce any negative effects on the environment?

In keeping with current reform efforts, science educators who advocate STS agree that the overall goal for science education is to develop scientifically literate graduates who can apply science to everyday life. These citizens will be able to understand the issues, take responsibility for the issues, and make informed decisions on these issues. These goals are further reflected in the science education benchmarks and standards.

Benchmarks, Standards, and Technology

According to authors of the *Benchmarks for Science Literacy* (American Association for the Advancement of Science [AAAS], 1993) and *Blueprints for Reform* (AAAS, 1998), educational research on what students know about technology is insufficient. We need to know more about how technology relates to science, or the structures and functions of the designed world. Because of the lack of research, the author groups suggest that technology is generally ignored in schools.

Technology can, nevertheless, be useful in developing scientific inquiry skills. Authors of the standards include science and technology in the content standards for students at every grade level (see the Science and Technology Standard on page 178).

See Web Destinations for Chapter 7 on the Companion Website (*http://www. prenhall.com/peters*) for technology education standards and information.

Students and Technology

You may have witnessed a child taking apart an old appliance, nailing together some old boards, building a bridge for toy cars in a sandbox, or otherwise interacting with

Visit an Inquiry Classroom
Science Technology and Society

View the *Science Technology and Society* video in the "Nature of Science" section of the Companion CD. Mr. McKnight and his students discuss earthworm reproduction and gender.

Review the video and ask yourself the following:
- What societal implications could be associated with what is being discussed in the video segment?
- What technological implications could be associated with what is being discussed in the video segment?

In the story *Alien Earthworms Changing Ecology of Northeast Forests* (McLeish, 2003), scientists Josef Görres and José Amador's research into the possible impact earthworms may have on the environment is discussed as follows:

> The researchers are also trying to determine whether the worms are increasing the amount of carbon dioxide and methane going into the atmosphere. "The leaf litter and duff layers consist almost entirely of stored carbon, so when the worms eat and process the litter and duff, they release carbon dioxide and possibly methane in their burrows," Amador said. "We're not predicting catastrophe, of course, since the total amount of the gases they release is small. But it's a previously unaccounted potential source of greenhouse gases entering the atmosphere."

Slater (2003) also found that "earthworms appear to be stripping some North American forests of their most essential feature: the decomposing leaves and other forest litter called duff, which provides nutrients and sanctuary to new generations of trees, plants and animals." What other STS impact could there be related to native and nonnative species of earthworms invading an area? Record your ideas and the answers to these questions in your portfolio or use the Companion Website to share your ideas.

technology. You will find that children are, without a doubt, curious about technology and the designed world.

As elementry and middle school students begin explorations of technology, they understand what is human-made and what is natural. Their designs are less elaborate or functional, and they cannot easily distinguish between science and technology. By the end of the elementary years, however, students will use scientific inquiry skills to assist them in a design that will solve a problem. They will also begin to see the important relationship between science and technology. Science is the quest for answers to questions about the universe. *Science relies on technology to assist us in discovering the universe. Technology is the application of science.* Technology supports science, helps us satisfy our wants and needs, and extends our capabilities to do those things.

As you read the Focus on Inquiry: Experiencing Technology Education, determine if the children are simply playing or if there is an objective in mind with this activity. Would you consider this lesson carefully structured to promote technological literacy? Should elementary or middle school students even be involved in design activities?

Focus on Inquiry

Experiencing Technology Education

A group of six- and seven-year-olds had completed some grouping and sorting of materials (fabrics, plastics, glass, wood, paper products, and so on) and an exploration of "connectors" (glues, brass fasteners, string, clips, nails, and so forth). They had learned how to use saws, drills, and hammers. They were given a twelve- by eighteen-inch sheet of paper and asked to design something they would like and be able to build that moved in some way. They were told they could use materials from their classroom recycling center such as cartons, containers of all sorts, fabric, dowels, cardboard, wheels, and centimeter wood strips. They could also use materials brought from home. The connectors they had explored were available.

Drawing was not new to these children. They had drawn from nature in their science studies, they had illustrated stories, and drawing materials were always an option for art or classroom choice times. They had built three-dimensional constructions in the block corner and in the classroom recycling center. However, they had never been asked to draw something to be constructed in the future and then to build from their drawings. The processes of moving from two to three dimensions and of committing themselves to a plan (as opposed to planning and creating as they went along) were new experiences for these children.

Ben, a six-year-old, drew a rather conventional house with a chimney on the roof and smoke coming out of the chimney. Looking over the materials, he passed by the rectangular boxes and selected a one-liter soda bottle as the basic structure for his house. He cut out freehand a door and some windows from construction paper and taped them to the bottle. Then he chose a dowel, taped a curvy piece of black construction paper to the end and showed his teacher where he wanted the two holes for the dowel to pass through the bottle. He inserted the dowel and proceeded to push and pull it up and down, making the "smoke" extend and retreat from the chimney. He was not bothered at all by the fact that the house looked nothing at all like his drawing. What counted was that the smoke moved in and out of the chimney. With construction successfully completed, his teacher asked him to evaluate his product. Did it come out the way he had planned it? Was there something that moved? A huge smile of satisfaction spread over his face. Yes, this was exactly what he had in mind, he said; the smoke moved out of the chimney (and back in), and he wondered if he could take it home and show his parents what he had made.

Across the room, two eight-year-olds were constructing boats they wanted to move by rubber-band-powered paddle wheels. They had completed their planning and construction and were now ready to test the boats. A small plastic wading pool was filled with water, the paddle wheels were wound up, and the boats were launched. As the boats moved forward, their structures began to come apart; the children realized to their dismay that the glue must be dissolving in the water.

"We should have used a glue gun."

Their teacher watched as they reassembled the boats, connecting the wooden frames with a glue gun, a time-consuming process; they tried them again in the water, and once again watched as they fell apart. The teacher debated whether or not to suggest that they test connecting materials in the water on just a few pieces of wood rather than take the time to reassemble the entire boat. She decided to let them do it their way, and hoped they would come to this realization themselves. If not, she would bring the subject up.

"We'll have to nail them together. Can we have some small nails?"

On the third try, the boat held together and paddled across the classroom pond. Delighted and relieved that their hard work and tenacity had paid off, the boat builders were not at all ready to think about shortcuts to finding the right materials to connect wood for use in water. For these students, this lesson would have to wait for another time. For their teacher, there still remained the issue of how much to tell students ahead of time and how much to let them discover, or not discover, for themselves.

The boys' classmate Kylie eyed the recycling center, spotted a shoe box, and decided to build a car that would carry her stuffed bear. She remembered her brother once built a rubber-band-powered car. Her drawing was a rectangle with small wheels. She selected four plastic wheels and found two dowels that fit through their centers. Using a ruler, she carefully planned where to punch holes in the shoe box so the axles would be parallel to the ends of the box. She attached the wheels to the outside of the box, front and back. She then began to puzzle out how to wind up a rubber band. Once she had an idea of how it might work, she asked her teacher if there was another box she could use to try out her ideas because she "didn't want to mess up my car." Unlike the boat builders, Kylie had discovered on her own the concept of building a prototype or model. Once she worked out a rubber band system, making her mistakes somewhere other than on her car, she was ready to complete her project.

Although the entire project was ultimately successful, asking the children to draw their desired object on paper as part of the design for the project may have been too ambitious. Children this age frequently find it difficult to conceptualize three-dimensional construction through two-dimensional drawing, and they become confused by the task. They may worry about their inability to transform their drawing into the object they imagined, and shy away from the task. For example, it is unclear how Ben's drawing helped him in the design of his project, which bore no relation to the picture he drew.

From Technology Education in the Classroom (*pp. 68–69*), *by S. A. Raizen, P. Sellwood, R. D. Todd, & M. Vickers, 1995, San Francisco: Jossey-Bass. Copyright © 1995 by Jossey-Bass. Reprinted by permission of John Wiley & Sons, Inc.*

TECHNOLOGY EDUCATION AND SCIENCE

Children's need to explore is a concrete reminder of our need throughout history to explore, understand, and survive in our environment (Dunn & Larson, 1990). Technology has been with us since the Stone Age when humans first began to modify their environment with the tools available to them. Throughout history, technology has played a significant role in the overall societal progress of humans, their struggle for freedom, and their advances in scientific knowledge. With technology being so prominent to everyday life, why is it so neglected in our schools?

> **Teaching Tips**   The study of technological advances is a good topic for social studies and science integration.

The term *technopeasants* refers to the common people who are left feeling that they are the victims of technology as a result of their lack of technical literacy (Pucel, 1995). Similarly, educators are viewed as *techno-ostriches* if they hide their heads in the sand when it comes to implementing technologies to create changes in schools (Papert, 1996). Either terminology insinuates that *technology education must play a larger role in the curriculum.* As suggested by some educators, society will not have future technicians if we do not integrate the curriculum and include technology education in today's classrooms (Hall & Bannatyne, 1999).

Resnick, Bruckman, and Martin (1999) question the appropriateness of children learning to play the piano versus learning to play the stereo. They cite that they would rather children become "creators" and not just "consumers" (p. 150), because this allows for a deeper understanding of music. Likewise, we want our students to design rather than just use technology.

We see technology in the schools evolving from two viewpoints. In the science curriculum, technology is used to demonstrate theories of science and to help develop inquiry skills. Technology is also a core element of the less familiar *technology education.* What specifically is technology education? It is a K–12 academic discipline designed to integrate academic and career skills with an emphasis on problem solving and decision making. In short, technology education focuses on working collaboratively through the application of technology. Whereas science seeks understanding, technology seeks solutions to problems.

To illustrate, during the elementary years, students should study such areas as "materials and their properties and how they can be used; energy in a variety of forms; control, in the form of switches, catches, valves, and mechanisms; and information used for communication" (Raizen, Sellwood, Todd, & Vickers, 1995, p. 67). Technology education should be a part of your everyday curriculum.

How can you integrate more technology into the curriculum? What are some technological areas that can be explored? The general categories to explore with your students include energy, materials, manufacturing, communication, bio-related, construction, and transportation technology.

Energy Technology

Energy comes in many forms: chemical, electrical, mechanical, radiant, thermal, and nuclear. Energy is one of the most important science and technology issues. Energy conservation awareness allows most people to realize now that we must continue to move away from exploiting the environment and toward conserving or using it wisely. Not only are energy resources of the planet limited, but also almost every year we see a greater demand on these resources from all nations. The history of progress in nations closely parallels a

A student engaged in a "mining for energy" activity.

rise in energy use. As fuels disappear, more attention will be turned to tapping into relatively inexhaustible sources such as solar, wind, tidal, and geothermal energy. Material progress and swelling populations have also increased air, water, and land pollution, along with the growing problem of managing solid waste.

Working on energy-related activities will help students construct an understanding of the importance of energy. The candle-powered steam engine and the candle-powered steamboat are two design activities that upper-elementary and middle school students could explore. The candle-powered steamboat requires an old-fashioned oilcan, a candle, and a milk carton. The steam engine uses an oilcan, a candle, wire, and an aluminum turbine blade. (See McCormack, 1981, for the full lesson on candle-powered steam engines and steamboats.)

We know that the sun is our ultimate source of energy. To demonstrate to our students the power of the sun, try cooking marshmallows. Students can design a solar cooker to capture the sun's rays in the cooker (see Miller, 1998, for an example of a solar cooker).

Materials Technology

Materials are important to technology because there would be no technical objects without materials. Materials can be the fossil fuel hydrocarbons that are mined or drilled such as coal, oil, and natural

See Web Destinations for Chapter 7 on the Companion Website (*http://www. prenhall.com/peters*) for more information on energy teaching ideas and resources.

 See resources such as *Machine Shop* (Battcher et al., 1993), *Under Construction* (Gossett, 1997), and *Inventa Book of Mechanisms* (Catlin, n.d.) for technology project ideas.

 Remember that safety is a consideration with this solar activity. Be sure to warn the students not to look directly at the sun or to stay out in the sunlight for prolonged periods.

gas. Materials can be genetic materials harvested from farming, forestry, or husbandry such as wheat, wood, or wool. They can be minerals that are mined such as metal ores, nonmetallic minerals, precious gems, or ceramics and clays. The study of materials helps students develop their observational skills as they interact with various materials. Students explore physical properties and determine whether materials are artificial or natural. They begin to see the need for specific materials in some designs. They also find that some materials can be used in a variety of ways.

Discussions of materials can originate with the story of *Three Little Pigs* (Feasey, 1999). Students investigate properties of the items that the pigs used for their houses, as well as several other materials. Ask your students which materials would be best if they were designing a house or a roof. Now have your students make up newspaper headlines about the materials the pigs used or should have used.

The *anoraks* activity is a primary activity during which students explore the materials of an Eskimo parka or heavy jacket. They are challenged to design an anorak for a season. This activity is a good integration with social studies if you want to develop a thematic unit (see Stringer, 1996, for the full activity).

A rough-and-smooth-surface activity is a good way for students to investigate materials (Stringer, 1998). They can even design wooden ramps of various textures and experiment on the effects of friction. Distance traveled, speed of an object down a ramp, height of the ramp, and the relation to surface friction are some beginning variables to explore. Students can also examine the use and integrity of structures and compare such variables as strength, weight, and reinforcement (Tickle, Lancaster, Devereux, & Marshall, 1990).

Upper-elementary and middle school students can design an experiment to explore bike helmet materials in relation to safety (Stringer, 1996). They can look at various helmet types and which materials are better at protection of the cranium. This activity is a good lead into the skeletal system and the protection of bones. *Designs in Science: Materials* (Morgan & Morgan, 1994) provides background information on materials and activities to extend materials investigations.

Manufacturing Technology

Custom production is the making of products one at a time. Intermittent production is the making of a limited quantity of a product at one time.

Continuous production is a steady, assembly-line, mass production of items.

Manufacturing involves using materials to make parts, putting parts together for a finished product that has value, and supplying the products to meet a demand. Primary manufacturing processes involve converting raw materials into industrial materials; this may include changing natural gas into plastic sheets or pellets, wood into paper stock, bauxite into rolled aluminum, or wheat into flour. Secondary manufacturing processes include forming, casting, molding, separating, conditioning, assembling, or finishing the manufactured items. Production can also be **custom** or **continuous.**

Activities that model the manufacturing process are good problem-solving tasks for students. Cooperative groups of students can be assigned to design a conveyor belt made from common materials. The conveyer belt should be able to move products effectively from one location to another. Students could also design a robot that is able to pick up and move materials (Miller, 1998). These design challenges involve all the process skills of science. Robotics kits from Lego Dacta™ are one way to integrate the use of the computer in the design (*http://www.pitsco-legodacta.com/*).

 Teaching Tips | Making paper is one design activity in which elementary and middle school students enjoy learning about manufacturing. Making writing paper from toilet paper (Stringer, 1996) is generally less disappointing than making paper from recycled scrap paper.

Communication Technology

Communications include the transfer of information from one place to another. This information could be raw data from spacecraft exploring the solar system, organized data called information, or information that is used for a purpose called knowledge. Following are ways to transmit information, or communicate:

Have your students consider communication with people from other countries who do not speak English, along with communication with alien beings. The students can brainstorm what to communicate, how to communicate, and what materials may be needed to design a communications system.

- *Printed communications,* or images printed on a material such as paper
- *Telecommunications,* or telephone, computer networks, radio, and television
- *Photographic communications,* or digital and film pictures
- *Technical communications,* or blueprints, technical illustrations, and engineering drawings

In summary, communication technology is people, their information exchange skills, and the equipment or other tools that help send and receive messages.

What if we were to communicate with space aliens? An interesting design activity for students to consider is how we would communicate with beings from other worlds (Association for Science Education [ASE], 1995).

Students may discuss or make presentations on environmental issues as a way to develop their communications skills (Miller, 1998). Technology has both positive and negative effects on our planet. For this activity, group students on both sides of such issues as the ozone layer, the greenhouse effect, vehicle emissions, and the use of landfills. Have students prepare a debate of the issues to be argued in front of an audience.

Communications is a rapidly changing area of technology. Discuss with your students any changes that they may be aware of or changes that their parents or guardians at home may have talked about. You may want to use this activity to discuss a general timeline for telecommunications (Oxlade, 1997).

Bio-Related Technology

Bio-related technology includes the disciplines of agricultural technologies, health care technologies, and technologies related to living things such as genetics. From the food you eat, the water you drink, the clothes you wear, and the health care you receive, biotechnology touches all aspects of our lives.

Discuss how science and technology have changed current farming methods.

Technology is present in preserving and preparing foods. If the color or texture is not right, the food will not be pleasing to eat. Experimentation can be done to see the science behind food and what is appealing. Try arranging various foods for birds or other animals to eat to test which foods are most popular (Stringer, 1996). Does color make a difference? Try using M&Ms to design an experiment involving classmates. What are the variables? What are the results? Discuss genetic farming (Jefferis, 1999) and the history of past farming methods (Roden, 1996).

Designing an experiment that shows the technology used in producing hand soaps demonstrates biotechnology in action. Students can experiment with eliminating microbes by washing hands (International Council of Associations for Science Education [ICASE], 1988). Try using regular soaps versus antibacterial soaps, liquid soaps versus solid

Have students discuss whether cloned humans would have the same fingerprints on their fingers or the same DNA "fingerprint" in their cells.

soaps, or short washing periods versus longer washing periods as variables. Agar is a nutrient medium available from scientific suppliers. It is put on sterilized plates for this activity. Students touch the agar on the plates after various hand washes; the microorganism their hands left behind will then grow on the agar.

Students may also want to discuss how biotechnology is used in courtrooms. Rainis and Nassis (1998) discuss the use of DNA testing as a replacement for fingerprints. This is a good area to integrate STS issues.

Construction Technology

Construction is the process of producing structures for shelter or transportation such as houses, skyscrapers, or other buildings, stadiums, roads, tunnels, bridges, airports, or monuments. The four generally accepted types of construction are residential, commercial, public, and industrial. Technology plays a key role in helping the structures meet the personal and environmental needs of the construction project. Science is also involved in significant ways. The materials, such as plastics or alloys, used in many structures are the result of scientific research applied technologically. Geologic research on the foundations of structures is important for buildings such as skyscrapers.

A technological extension to animal and habitat study is to have students create a PowerPoint R or other slide show on the habitats of animals (Donato, 1998).

Elementary and middle school students can further develop observation and inference skills when they investigate natural structures. Looking at bird homes may result in inferences about why the birds construct the nests as they do or build them in the places they do. Adaptation to the environment is evidenced by how animals build their homes. Habitat study is a good scientific exploration for students.

Lasers are used in many construction projects. An electronic distance meter or laser transit saves time over less technical tools. Many students with access to laser pointers and mirrors can design experiments that will provide results similar to those obtained by the construction equipment.

Bridge activities are a popular technology activity. Designing a bridge that supports the most weight in relation to its own weight is a good upper-elementary or middle school activity. Bridges can be built with construction paper (Eichelberger & Larson, 1993) or toothpicks (Pollard, 1985).

Transportation Technology

Transportation technology includes air, rail, water, pipeline, space, and automobile or truck transportation. The connections between transportation and science are numerous. For instance, fuel types, the design of the vehicle to reduce friction, and alternative energy sources are examples for scientific discussion and research.

An activity that you can try with elementary and middle school students is to send e-mail to other countries and ask students there about their transportation systems. This activity provides a good contrast and comparison to different transportation systems and helps develop communication skills.

Observation and classification skills are sharpened if primary students cut transportation-related pictures from magazines and classify them in various ways. They can look at air versus water or land vehicles. Sizes of vehicles, the numbers of passengers, or energy use by the vehicle produce other classification schemes. Try to have the students develop their own classification system.

One design challenge that works with upper-elementary or middle school students is building mousetrap cars (Balmer, 1997). With the assistance of their parents, students build and race cars that are powered by mousetraps. The car that goes the farthest is the winner.

Rubber-band transportation can be explored with rubber-band-powered airplanes or vehicles (Eichelberger & Larson, 1993). Students use simple materials to design and build airplanes or other vehicles that work with the use of rubber bands. Experimentation skills are involved as students explore the effects of winding the rubber band too tight or not enough, reducing friction of the vehicle, placing weight, finding ways to make the vehicles track a straight line, or designing propellers. Balloon-powered cars (Miller, 1998) offer similar experimentation skill development for upper-elementary or middle school students.

Building model hovercraft is an interesting design activity related to transportation (ICASE, 1987). Balloons and wooden disks are all that are needed to make simple hovercraft.

Paper airplane design is another great transportation technology activity. Male pilots and astronauts are better known than female pilots and astronauts. Therefore, one way to initiate this design contest is to read about pilots in *Females First in Their Fields: Air and Space* (Buchanan, 1999). Have a challenge to see which team of girls can make the most paper airplanes fly over a 5-meter (20-foot) mark in 1 minute. Supply each team with a stack of copier paper and a marked off area to fly the planes. Holding group brainstorming and trial sessions beforehand will enhance flight distances.

As with other activities, adjust variables such as times and distances according to your students' developmental needs. It may be helpful to include the five-stage framework for technological design provided by the standards (NRC, 1996, pp. 137–138, 165–166):

1. Identify a simple problem.
2. Propose a solution.
3. Implement proposed solutions.
4. Evaluate a product or design.
5. Communicate a problem, design, and solution.

The process begins with students renaming the problem using their own words. Next, students form possible solutions—given time, costs, and materials. Then students work together to try solutions and see how their design solves the problem. Finally, students communicate how they solved the problem, including their design and evaluation.

Technology and Career Awareness

Technology is concerned with controlling or managing objects and events in improved ways. With the prevalence of technology in today's society, it is vital to prepare the future workforce for these occupations. Many career opportunities are related to technology (Schwartz & Wolfgang, 1996).

Research scientists, professional engineers, skilled technicians, and computer operators are required to have the scientific knowledge to plan and design useful inventions and creative solutions. Demand will continue to grow for workers qualified in the areas of environmental engineering, biological engineering and biotechnology, energy systems, telecommunications research and maintenance, and advanced transportation systems. Inventions and inventors are good topics to explore for promoting technology awareness and showing careers related to technology.

See *http://www.prenhall. com/peters* for references to books on invention topics.

Gender Issues and Technology

Technology topics lend themselves to opening up a new world for girls of all age levels because technology is a subject for everyone (Cross, 1998). We need to involve females in technological topics and activities when possible, not because the future workforce will rely on highly skilled, technologically literate women, but because we owe it to all our students to allow them the opportunity to be able to make good career choices later in life. These career choices will be possible because we have provided a solid scientific and technological background for males and females during the elementary and middle school years.

Look at your own practices in the classroom either now or in the future. Ask yourself these questions:

- Do my female students feel comfortable engaging in science and technology activities?
- Do my female students ask the same number of questions or provide a similar number of responses as my male students?
- Do I give equal amount of attention to both male and female students?
- Are female students embarrassed to take part in activities?

It may help to videotape yourself, or have another person observe you, and then complete a checklist to see whether you are being biased. Whether you are a male or female teacher, you may be biased toward boys when it comes to science and technology. Another tactic is to discuss careers and what future courses students should take or activities they should accomplish to be able to achieve their career goals. Also, make sure that you occasionally set up all-female learning groups, forcing girls to participate and not sit back and allow the boys to take control. Use books that focus on successful females in the sciences and technological areas. Make everyone in your class comfortable while learning or asking questions.

Teaching Tips

One good starting point is *Girls and Technology Idea Book* and *Girls and Technology Resource Guide.* These publications are available from the National Coalition of Girls' Schools, 228 Main Street, Concord, MA 01742 or *http://www.ncgs.org.*

Finally, begin now to collect resources that will assist you in your classroom.

Technology and the Curriculum

The following notions about teaching science still exist today:

> Even a new science textbook is dated by the time it's distributed.
> I can't teach science. Who has time to keep up with it?

Contrary to these views, the basic ideas and processes taught in the science curriculum last a long time. Scientific information and vocabulary do change, but this is expected when you consider the nature of science. This changeability is all the more reason to teach about the nature of science and STS. Discussing the application of science in new technologies helps show students how science theories can be modified. Consider the shift from copper telephone wires to fiber optics, the change in the precise measurement of the speed of light from 186,198 miles per second to 186,282 miles per second, or the discovery of new subatomic particles.

Basic concepts and generalizations in effective science programs are often linked to technological applications, aeronautics, telecommunications, electric circuitry, soil conservation, and food processing. Learning about these applications can change the way children view many of the useful inventions at home and in school. Understanding how systems operate develops a realistic perspective toward the mechanisms of everyday life. A well-constructed elementary curriculum will be rooted in the basic ideas and processes of science. Technological investigations, however, will enhance science understanding by providing concrete examples of science in action.

See Web Destinations for Chapter 7 on the Companion Website (*http://www. prenhall.com/peters*) for links to current science news.

CW

Visit an Inquiry Classroom
Technology Education in the Classroom

View the *Preparing Resources* video in the "Model Inquiry Unit" section of the Companion CD. Mr. McKnight and his students discuss some of the things that they have found out about earthworms.

Review the video and ask yourself the following:
- How is communication technology being used in the study of earthworms?
- What other forms of technology (e.g., energy, materials, manufacturing, communication, biotechnology, construction, or transportation) are being used, or could be used, in the study of earthworms?

Cornell entomologist John Losey and his colleagues sparked a worldwide controversy with the publication of a scientific paper in the journal *Nature* (1999) where he reported laboratory findings that Monarch butterfly larvae died after eating milkweed plants containing pollen from genetically modified corn. What effects could genetically modified crops have on earthworms? Research this topic and record your ideas and the answers to these questions in your portfolio or use the Companion Website to share your ideas.

Summary

- A computer center can be set up and run much like a regular learning center. Computer software can include such programs as tutorials and games, multimedia, simulations, Internet access tools, spreadsheets, databases, word processing, and research tools.
- Science technology society (STS) is the teaching and learning of science in the context of human experiences. Advocates of STS think that science should be real to students and that scientific problems provided for students to solve should be based on issues that are of genuine interest to students. The STS issue investigation and action instruction model has four crucial phases: foundations, awareness, investigations, and action phases.
- Technology use in the science classroom evolves from two viewpoints. One is from using technology to demonstrate theories of science and to help develop inquiry skills. The other is from the applied technology-based curriculum called technology education. Technology education is an academic discipline designed to integrate academic and career skills with an emphasis on problem solving and decision making.
- Areas of technology include energy, materials, manufacturing, communication, biotechnology, construction, and transportation.

Reflection

Companion CD

1. Look at the "The Nervous System" lesson linked to the *Zone of Proximal Development* video on the Companion CD. How could you modify this lesson so that students could incorporate individual multimedia projects?
2. Look at the "Environment Is Important to Living Things" lesson linked to the *Private Speech* video on the Companion CD. How could you modify this lesson plan so that students could incorporate Internet access tools?
3. Look at "The Earthworm and Soil" lesson linked to the *Scaffolding* video on the Companion CD. How could you modify this lesson plan so that students could incorporate spreadsheets or databases into the lesson?

Portfolio Ideas

1. You can learn *from* computers, *with* computers, and *about* computers. You can also learn to think with computers or use computers to manage learning. In your portfolio, list examples of how computers and software can be used for each of these categories.
2. Check with your field placement site and college or university to see whether it celebrates National Science and Technology Week (*http://www.nsf.gov/od/lpa/nstw/geninfo/brochure.htm*). How can you become involved with your future students? Write some sample ideas in your portfolio.
3. Look at the National Science Teachers Association (NSTA) website (*http://www.nsta.org/programs/*) for technology-related competitions that would involve your future elementary or middle school students. Which competitions are especially helpful in developing technological literacy? Enter ideas in your portfolio.
4. Read *The Trouble with Dad* (Cole, 2004) and *It Could Still Be a Robot* (Fowler, 1997). In your portfolio, share with your class about the use of robots in everyday life. Also discuss society's images of scientists and inventors.
5. Look at *Standards for Technological Literacy: Content for the Study of Technology* from the International Technology Education Association (*http://www.iteawww.org/*) and National Educational Technology Standards from the International Society for Technology in Education (*http://cnets.iste.org/*). In your portfolio, compare and contrast these standards and the National Science Education Standards from the NRC (*http://stills.nap.edu/html/nses/*).

References

American Association for the Advancement of Science (AAAS). (1993). *Benchmarks for science literacy*. New York: Oxford University Press.

American Association for the Advancement of Science (AAAS). (1998). *Blueprints for reform*. New York: Oxford University Press.

Association for Science Education (ASE). (1995). *Science in space*. Hatfield, Herts., UK: Author.

Balmer, A. (1997). *Mouse-trap cars: A teacher's guide*. Austin, TX: Doc Fizzix Comix.

Battcher, D., Martini, K., Shennan, W. B., Erickson, S., Rogers, C., & Wiebe, A. (1993). *Machine shop*. Fresno, CA: AIMS Education Foundation.

Beaty, J. J. (1990). *Computer as a paintbrush: Creative use for the PC in the preschool classroom*. Upper Saddle River, NJ: Merrill/Prentice Hall.

Buchanan, D. (1999). *Female firsts in their fields: Air and space*. Philadelphia: Chelsea House.

Catlin, D. (n.d.). *Inventa book of mechanisms*. London: Valiant Technology.

Claris. (1993). *ClarisWorks 2.0 in the classroom*. Santa Clara, CA: Author.

Classroom Connect. (1998). Catastrophe! *lessonplan.net, 2*(5), 1–48.

Cole, B. (2004). *The trouble with dad*. London, UK: Egmont Books.

Cross, A. (1998). *Coordinating design and technology across the primary school*. New York: Falmer Press.

Donato, D. (1998). *Integrating technology into the science curriculum*. Westminster, CA: Teacher Created Materials.

Dunn, S., & Larson, R. (1990). *Design technology: Children's engineering*. New York: Falmer Press.

Ebenezer, J. V., & Lau, E. (2003). *Science on the Internet: A resource for K–12 teachers*. Upper Saddle River, NJ: Merrill/Prentice Hall.

Eichelberger, B., & Larson, C. (1993). *Constructions for children: Projects in design technology*. Palo Alto, CA: Dale Seymour.

Feasey, R. (1999). *Primary science & literacy links*. Hatfield, Herts., UK: Association for Science Education.

Fowler, A. (1997) *It could still be a robot*. New York: Children's Press.

Froseth, S., & Poppe, B. (1995). *Internet activities using scientific data (National Oceanic and Atmospheric Administration)*. Washington, DC: Government Printing Office.

Gossett, C. (1997). *Under construction*. Fresno, CA: AIMS Education Foundation.

Haag, T. (1996). *Internet for kids*. Huntington Beach, CA: Teacher Created Materials.

Hall, R., & Bannatyne M. (1999). Technology education and the 21st century. *Connect, 24*(4), 1–3. *www.unesco.org/education/educprog/ste/index.html*

International Council of Associations for Science Education (ICASE). (1987). *Experiments and activities on the three laws of dynamics: A teacher resource book commemorating the 300th anniversary of Newton's Principia 1687–1987*. Hong Kong: Author.

International Council of Associations for Science Education (ICASE). (1988). *Pasteur and microbes: A teacher resource guide commemorating the 100th year of the Pasteur Institute 1888–1988*. Hong Kong: Author.

Jefferis, D. (1999). *Cloning: Frontiers of genetic engineering*. New York: Crabtree.

Henry J. Kaiser Family Foundation. (2002). *Key facts: Children and video games*. Menlo Park, CA: Author. Retrieved September 27, 2004, from *www.kff.org/entmedia/loader.cfm?url=/commonspot/security/getfile.cfm&pageID=14092*

Henry J. Kaiser Family Foundation. (2004). *Survey snapshot: The digital divide*. Menlo Park, CA: Author. Retrieved September 27, 2004, from *www.kff.org/entmedia/loader.cfm?url=/commonspot/security/getfile.cfm&PageID=46366*

Koufman-Frederick, A., Lillie, M., Pattison-Gordon, L., Watt, D. L., & Carter, R. (1999). *Electronic collaboration: A practical guide for educators*. Providence, RI: LAB at Brown University.

Kozma, R., & Shank, P. (1998). Connecting with the 21st century: Technology in support of educational reform. In C. Dede (Ed.),

1998 ASCD Yearbook: Learning with technology (pp. 3–27). Alexandria, VA: ASCD.

Losey, J. E., Rayor, L. S., & Carter, M. E. (1999). Transgenic pollen harms monarch larvae. *Nature, 399,* 214.

McCormack, A. J. (1981). *Inventors workshop.* Torrance, CA: Fearon Teacher Aids.

McLeish, T. (2003, September). Alien earthworms changing ecology of Northeast forests. *The University Pacer.* Kingston, RI: University of Rhode Island. Retrieved December 23, 2004, from *http://advance.uri.edu/pacer/september2003/story12.htm*

Means, B. (1994). Introduction: Using technology to advance educational goals. In B. Means (Ed.), *Technology and education reform* (pp. 1–21). San Francisco: Jossey-Bass.

Miller, L. (1998). *KidTech: Hands-on problem solving with design technology for grades 5–8.* Menlo Park, CA: Dale Seymour.

Morgan, S., & Morgan, A. (1994). *Designs in science: Materials.* New York: Facts on File.

National Research Council (NRC). (1996). *National science education standards.* Washington, DC: National Academy Press.

National Science Teachers Association (NSTA). (1982). *Science-technology-society: Science education for the 1980s. A position statement.* Washington, DC: Author.

National Science Teachers Association (NSTA). (1992). *The use of computers in science education* (NSTA position statement). *www.nsta.org/handbook/position.asp*

National Science Teacher Association (NSTA). (2004). *Science teacher preparation. A position statement.* Washington, DC: Author. Retrieved October 1, 2004, from *www.nsta.org/positionstatement&psid=42*

NetDay. (2004). *NetDay survey 2001.* Irvine, CA: Author. Retrieved September 27, 2004, from *www.netdaycompass.org/outside_frame.cfm?thispath=instance_id= 1701^category_id=5&thislink=http://www.netday.org/anniversary_ survey.htm&instance_id=3123*

Oxlade, C. (1997). *20th century inventions: Telecommunications.* Austin, TX: Raintree Steck-Vaughn.

Papert, S. (1996). *The connected family: Bridging the digital generation gap.* Marietta, GA: Longstreet Press.

Pollard, J. (1985). *Building toothpick bridges.* Palo Alto, CA: Dale Seymour.

Pucel, D. J. (1995). Developing technological literacy. *The Technology Teacher, 55*(3), 35–43.

Rainis, K. G., & Nassis, G. (1998). *Biotechnology projects for young scientists.* New York: Watts.

Raizen, S. A., Sellwood, P., Todd, R. D., & Vickers, M. (1995). *Technology education in the classroom.* San Francisco: Jossey-Bass.

Resnick, M., Bruckman, A., & Martin, F. (1999). Construction design: Creating new construction kits for kids. In A. Druin (Ed.), *The design of children's technology* (pp. 149–168). San Francisco: Morgan Kaufman.

Roberts, N., Blakeslee, G., Brown, M., & Lenk, C. (1990). *Integrating telecommunications into education.* Upper Saddle River, NJ: Prentice Hall.

Roden, K. (1996). *Then & now: Farming.* Brookfield, CT: Copper Beech Books.

Rubba, P. A., Wiesenmayer, R. L., Rye, J. A., & Ditty, T. (1996). The leadership institute in STS education: A collaborative teacher enhancement, curriculum development, and research project of Penn State and West Virginia University with rural middle/junior high school science teachers. *Journal of Science Teacher Education, 7*(1), 23–40.

Rutherford, F. J., & Ahlgren, A. (1990). *Science for all Americans.* New York: Oxford University Press.

Schwartz, L., & Wolfgang, T. (1996). *Children's occupational outlook handbook.* Auburn, CA: CFKR Career Materials.

Slater, E. (2003). *Earthworms show killer instinct.* Detroit: The Detroit News *detnews.com.* Downloaded December 23, 2004, from *www.detnews.com/2003/nation/0309/24/a08d-279359.htm*

Stringer, J. (Ed.). (1996). *Science & technology ideas for the under 85.* Hatfield, Herts., UK: Association for Science Education.

Stringer, J. (Ed.). (1998). *More science & technology ideas for the under 85.* Hatfield, Herts., UK: Association for Science Education.

Tickle, L., Lancaster, M., Devereux, M., & Marshall, E. (1990). Developing practical knowledge for teaching design and technology. In L. Tickle (Ed.), *Design and technology in primary school classrooms* (pp. 29–78). New York: Falmer Press.

Yager, R. E. (Ed.). (1992). *The status of science-technology-society reform efforts around the world.* Hong Kong: International Council of Associations for Science Education.

Yager, R. E. (Ed.). (1993). *What research says to the science teacher: The science technology society movement.* Arlington, VA: National Science Teachers Association.

Suggested Readings

Cross, G., & Szostak, R. (1995). *Technology and American society: A history.* Upper Saddle River, NJ: Prentice Hall. (a text about the history of invention and the interaction of technology and society)

Eggleston, J. (1996). *Teaching design and technology* (2nd ed.). Bristol, PA: Open University Press. (a text about design and technology and its role in the national curriculum of England)

Forcier, R. C., Descy, P.E. (1999). *The computer as an educational tool: Productivity and problem solving, 2005* (4th ed.). Upper Saddle River, NJ: Merrill/Prentice Hall. (a book on the application of computers in the curriculum to include problem solving)

Kimbell, R., Stables, K., & Green, R. (1996). *Understanding practice in design and technology.* Bristol, PA: Open University Press. (a research-based text on technology education in England)

Reynolds, K. E., & Barba, R. H. (1996). *Technology for the teaching and learning of science.* Boston: Allyn & Bacon. (a comprehensive resource on integrating technology into science education)

CHAPTER 8

SCIENCE LEARNING OPPORTUNITIES

- What types of out-of-school science learning opportunities could support your science curriculum?
- What science learning community resources are available to support your teaching?
- How can you develop individual partners in education?

Focus on Inquiry

Zoos as Science Education Resources

Dr. Sue Dale Tunnicliffe
University of London, England, and ICASE Presecondary Science Representative

Visits to live animal collections can provide excellent opportunities for science learning. This is especially true if the teachers taking the students are familiar with the pedagogy of such visits and what opportunities are available. The knowledge that teachers need for zoo visits (and for visits to other animal collections such as natural history museums) includes the following:

- The stages of a visit in terms of the attention of students during the visit to the animals
- The features of anatomy and behaviors of the animals that the students are likely to notice spontaneously
- The colloquial or everyday names the students will use and any scientific names the teacher wants to be used
- The ability to identify and understand the concepts that the teacher wants the students to acquire

It is also very important to communicate to the chaperones who accompany your students the aims and objectives in terms of education outcomes, as well as the "housekeeping" details. If this is not done, the experience that the students within the chaperoned groups receive is different from that experienced by the students with you. It is up to us, as teachers, to ensure that each student has equal access to an effective experience.

Stages of a Visit

Students do not focus on exhibits in the same manner throughout their visit. It is important to be aware of the different phases within a school visit and to plan activities for your students accordingly.

First, groups undergo an orientation phase, when they look around and find their way. You can shorten the length of this stage by providing orientation to the site beforehand. Show slides or a video, provide the groups with a timetable, discuss opportunities for visits

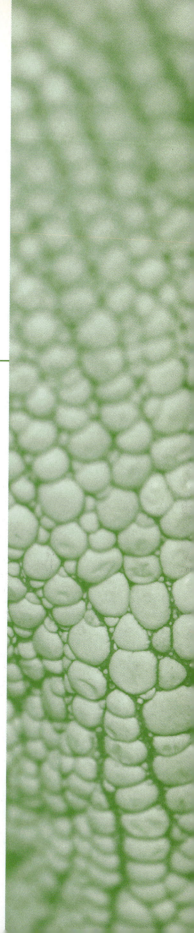

to the gift shop, tell when and where lunch is to be taken, and make other similar "house-keeping" arrangements.

Following orientation, the group embarks on the concentration phase: focusing on the tasks you have set, concentrating on exhibits, or participating in an educational activity provided by the zoo. It is unrealistic to expect the students to be involved in a focused task throughout the visit. After their concentration wanes, they move into the leisure-looking phase, during which their comments and observations are similar to those of "noneducation" visitors. Finally, during the leave-taking phase, the attention of the group is concerned with gathering together for the journey home.

Spontaneous Observations

Elementary students, their accompanying adults, and family groups follow a fundamental pattern when looking at animal exhibits. It is important to be aware of this so that you can plan your activities for young students and the questions the accompanying adults or the activity sheets will ask of them; these are the starting points for science observations. Children spontaneously notice certain phenomena, such as names, anatomical features, and animal behavior, so use these as the introduction to the topic you plan.

Names

Children spontaneously use everyday or colloquial names for the animals. Primary grade students often use the term *animal* to mean only mammals, the term *bird* to mean any bird other than very memorable ones such as ostrich, eagle, penguin, vulture, and parrot. Reptiles are never referred to as such by children, and fish are called *fish* by children except for sharks, piranhas, eels, and any particular species about which the visitor happens to have firsthand knowledge, such as chubb or perch. Young students, those under age 7, are unable to cope with two names for one animal; if they call a shark by that name, they deny that it is also a fish. Similarly, all insects and arachnids are "bugs" (in the everyday sense, not the zoological one) unless they know the name, such as ladybug. Spiders are just that unless they are a tarantula or black widow. You should use colloquial names but make it clear to everyone which scientific name(s) you want them to learn. This will allow you to develop zoological classification with the students during the visit or back in school.

Anatomical Features and Behavior

When looking at the structure of the animals, the students will spontaneously comment on the shape, size, color, any particularly unusual feature, such as horns, and parts that disrupt the body outline and/or move, such as legs and tails. If the animal is performing some behavior, the students will notice it. The position of the animal within the enclosure or display case is important to the students and school. Groups also refer in about half of all conversations to other aspects of the exhibit, such as rocks and trees or feeding bowls, often in referring to the location of the animal.

If the animal is doing nothing, the students will query whether it is real, a common question posed about crocodilians in zoos. In museums, the students will be interested in the authenticity of the specimens and how they were prepared for display. Thus, the meaning of the word *real* depends on the context in which it is used. Often, children use the word *real* to refer to whether the animal is alive or not.

The science learning opportunities in a zoo for elementary students are content (science facts), the process (science method and inquiry), and science language and communication skills.

The science content can be biological or physical. The biological content is either botanical (which highlights the role of plants in the food chain and forming the natural habitats of animals) or zoological.

Zoological studies can focus on taxonomic studies or on adaptations to the environment, including adaptations for feeding. Animal behaviors are used to establish the taxonomy of a specimen, as well as to study adaptation and forms. Behavior is thus another important area of study, in which students can make, record, and interpret their firsthand observations of the animals. Such studies require the students to observe salient features of animals, such as form, number of locomotory organs, and body covering.

Elementary students should be able to group animals into their major groups—mammals, reptiles, birds, fish, amphibians, arthropods, mollusks, and annelid worms. They should also be able to say why they make these categorizations. Students should be able to use **branching keys** and picture keys at grade 4, and by grade 6 they should be able to use and construct dichotomous keys. Students should develop an understanding of the needs of animals and the essential life processes and should be able to identify how individual specimens meet them. Natural history museums are often better equipped than zoos to provide realistic habitats, therefore providing a more satisfactory study of this feature.

Animal behavior studies can be frustrating if the students are looking for action, but action is just as important and should be used constructively. Find out before your visit which animals are likely to be active and visible within their enclosures. Ask about the pattern of the day of inactive and inaccessible animals so that the students can be given a time chart for these animals and can identify which part of their activity profile the animals are in when the students observe them. Ask the students to find the pattern of these animals' days so that the lack of activity is not a source of frustration, but an active learning experience.

Adaptation to the environment is a topic often well presented by zoo education programs. Decide which adaptations you wish your students to focus on. Very popular topics are birds' beaks (studying adaptations within this class of animals for different types of foods and, hence, different habitats), feet in mammals and birds, color of body coverings, and camouflage.

> **Branching key** lists a common category at the top of the sheet (e.g., Fish) and then branches down into secondary categories (e.g., one top fin; two top fins). These are further branched into tertiary categories (e.g., flat or round body; long and thin; or short and round) and so on until specific species are identified (e.g., catfish, grouper).

> See Chapter 8 Web Destinations on the Companion Website (*http://www. prenhall.com/peters*) for examples of picture keys available on the Internet.

Planning an Opportunity to Learn

Planning and delivering the opportunities for experiences that involve your students is essential. Instead of replying with a name when a student asks, "What is that animal?" ask the student to work out what it could be as far as she is able. Should a student identify an animal, ask him what features enabled him to make that identification.

Science is about communicating. If scientists don't communicate, no one else knows of their work. Encourage your students to share their observations and findings in a variety of ways: a science report, drama, art, journalist's report, or spoken address.

SCIENCE LEARNING OPPORTUNITIES

As you may infer from the Focus on Inquiry: Zoos as Science Education Resources, trips to the zoo are an important science education **opportunity to learn.** Together with other forms of learning opportunities in the community, trips to a zoo will round out students' science experiences and help them construct understandings of biodiversity and conservation.

> **Opportunity to learn** refers to quality of the instruction and curricular program provided for students.

Mrs. Blackwelder's Class Trip

Mrs. Blackwelder and her third-grade class are excited today. They are planning a trip to the state park. Ranger Kellison will be discussing the wolf population and the recovery of a young wolf that was recently shot. She is glad to see the students' interest in learning about wolves.

> **Teaching Tips**
>
> The wolf theme is a good topic for integrated activities. Check the Companion Website (*http://www.prenhall.com/peters*) for ideas related to this topic.

The idea for this trip began 2 weeks ago as a social studies experience when the class read variations of the story of Little Red Riding Hood. Everyone became interested in comparing and contrasting accounts of this fable. Each story group read a different version. Will's group began with the traditional story *Little Red Riding Hood* (Schmidt, 1986). Erica's group read *Little Red Riding Hood: A Newfangled Prairie Tale* (Ernst, 1995), in which Grandma turns out to be the one surprising the wolf. Katelyn's group read *Red Riding Hood* (Marshall, 1987), a modern retelling of the tale. Tyler's group read a version from *Yo, Hungry Wolf!: A Nursery Rap* (Vozar, 1993), which is a retelling of three wolf-related stories in rap form.

After discussing accounts of these tales, the class investigated versions of the Three Little Pigs story. This time, Alex read the traditional *Three Little Pigs* (Gay, 1997) tale. Celeste read *The True Story of the Three Little Pigs* (Scieszka, 1989), as told by "A. Wolf." Emerald read *The Three Little Wolves and the Big Bad Pig* (Trivizas, 1993), which is a role-reversal account of the allegory. Again, the class discussed the versions.

See Chapter 8 Web Destinations on the Companion Website (*http://www.prenhall.com/peters*) for links related to wolves and the International Wolf Center.

CW

Following up on the stories, Mrs. Blackwelder asked her students what they really knew about wolves. The students had many misconceptions about wolves, mostly from the children's stories they read and others like *It's So Nice to Have a Wolf Around the House* (Allard, 1997) and *Lon Po Po: A Red-Riding Hood Story from China* (Young, 1989). Television cartoons also provided misinformation. To provide an opportunity for her students to identify their misconceptions and develop a true understanding of the wolf, Mrs. Blackwelder encouraged the students to read more about wolves. She arranged a science center with wolves as the theme, made the Internet available, and bookmarked the International Wolf Center. Here, the students could see pictures of wolves and follow their migratory paths online.

Mrs. Blackwelder also provided a selection of other print resources on wolves. These included *Julie of the Wolves* (George, 1972), *The Call of the Wild* (London, 1993), *Baby Wolf* (Batten, 1998), *Look to the North: A Wolf Pup Diary* (George, 1998), *The Land of the Grey Wolf* (Locker, 1996), *Gray Wolf, Red Wolf* (Patent, 1990), *The Eyes of Gray Wolf* (London, 1993), *Wild, Wild Wolves* (Milton, 1992), and other reference books.

See Chapter 8 Web Destinations on the Companion Website (*http://www.prenhall.com/peters*) for links related to "Journey North."

CW

Mrs. Blackwelder began reading the book *Wolf Stalker* (Skurzynski & Ferguson, 1997) to discuss wolf restoration projects. This, of course, led to the students wanting to visit the wolf sanctuary at the state park and Ranger Kellison.

Later, Mrs. Blackwelder encouraged other science learning opportunities with her students. Some of her students will participate in "Journey North." This Annenberg/CPB Internet-based learning activity engages students in a global study of wildlife migration. Other students will visit the local natural history museum or engage in similar out-of-class experiences to develop an understanding of wolves and their habitats.

Science Learning Opportunities and the Formal Curriculum

We are familiar with the formal learning that takes place in the school, but if you look at Mrs. Blackwelder's activities, you will notice that she strives to go beyond the traditional teacher–student classroom setting. Her curriculum planning includes endeavors to integrate other learning opportunities as part of her students' knowledge construction about wolves and their environments.

Science learning takes place outside the classroom. One viewpoint is that these learning activities are voluntary and not developed primarily for school use or an ongoing school curriculum (Crane, 1994). Others see experiences outside the classroom as supportive of the existing curriculum (Landis, 1996; Tunnicliffe, 1992).

Science learning opportunities can be in the schoolyard, at home, or in any other social setting. They can also be brought into the classroom when traditional activities are suspended. The class trip to the state park is an example of science learning in support of Mrs. Blackwelder's curricular objectives. This learning is encouraged because it can be motivating for students, can enhance social interaction, and generally provides a rich observational experience.

> **Teaching Tips** Although it takes more time for you to arrange, children generally experience meaningful learning with out-of-school science learning opportunities.

Science learning facilities outside the classroom are generally supportive and provide programs and resources for working with your students and even for your own professional development. They can be especially helpful to new teachers who are having difficulty preparing science lessons and organizing activities (Melber, 2000). Another important reason for using these learning resources is that activities can support gaps in formal education where resources are not available to the teacher. Even if learning experiences were redundant, the crucial overlap can increase the opportunity to learn important science skills and concepts (Honeyman, 1998).

The National Science Teachers Association (NSTA) "strongly supports and advocates" out-of-school science learning opportunities for children (1998, p. 1). Figure 8–1 is a summary of the association's views related to this issue.

See Chapter 8 Web Destinations on the Companion Website (*http://www. prenhall.com/peters*) for links to NSTA's position statements.

Do you think you need to go beyond the "traditional classroom" with your own science teaching? According to National Science Education Standards (National Research Council [NRC], 1996), "Good science programs require access to the world beyond the classroom" (p. 218). This idea is further reflected in the Inquiry Teaching Standard found in the Standards Link. The authors of this standard call for the identification and use of resources outside the school environment. They suggest that inquiry occurs as students engage in investigations, including those outside school. In this respect, the standards are used by teachers to bridge the gap between in-school and out-of-school experiences because they are common references for both types of learning (Hofstein, Bybee, & Legro, 1997; Katz & McGinnis, 1999).

The external resources offered generally require that you seek out community partners, parents, scientists, engineers, and business leaders in support of your goals for science education (National Research Council, 1998). This is exactly what Mrs. Blackwelder did with the wolf project and other thematic units throughout the year.

Standards Link

Inquiry Teaching Standard

Teachers of science design and manage learning environments that provide students with the time, space, and resources needed for learning science. In doing this, teachers

- **Structure the time available so that students are able to engage in extended investigations.**

- **Create a setting for student work that is flexible and supportive of science inquiry.**

- **Ensure a safe working environment.**

- **Make the available science tools, materials, media, and technological resources accessible to students.**

- **Identify and use resources outside the school.**

- **Engage students in designing the learning environment.**

(Teaching Standard D, National Research Council, 1996, p. 43.)

Figure 8–1   NSTA declarations on informal science education.

- Informal science education complements, supplements, deepens, and enhances classroom science studies. It increases the amount of time participants can be engaged in a project or topic. It can be the proving ground for curriculum materials.
- The impact of informal experiences extends to the affective, cognitive, and social realms by presenting the opportunity for mentors, professionals, and citizens to share time, friendship, effort, creativity, and expertise with youngsters and adult learners.
- Informal science education allows for different learning styles and multiple intelligences and offers supplementary alternatives to science study for nontraditional and second language learners. It offers unique opportunities through field trips, field studies, overnight experiences, and special programs.
- Informal science learning experiences offer teachers a powerful means to enhance both professional and personal development in science content knowledge and accessibility to unique resources.
- Informal science education institutions, through their exhibits and programs, provide an effective means for parents and other care providers to share moments of intellectual curiosity and time with their children.
- Informal science institutions give teachers and students direct access to scientists and other career role models in the sciences, as well as to opportunities for authentic science study.
- Informal science educators bring an emphasis on creativity and enrichment strategies to their teaching through the need to attract their noncompulsory audiences.
- NSTA advocates that local corporations, foundations, and institutions fund and support informal science education in their communities.
- Informal science education is often the only means for continuing science learning in the general public beyond the school years.

Source: National Science Teachers Association, 1998, Position Statements. Reprinted with permission.

When planning her activities, Mrs. Blackwelder generally begins with the selection of a theme that her students have generated an interest in learning about and that would also be supportive of her learning goals. Next, she makes a mental list of what resources may be available for that theme. As she continues to plan activities related to the theme, she incorporates out-of-class learning possibilities. Sometimes she brainstorms with a listing of possibilities such as those contained in Figure 8–2.

Keep in mind that the listing in Figure 8–2 should be considered a starting point for ideas. This guide is not meant to be comprehensive for every theme. The resources in your community will vary, depending on the topic under study. Other important considerations are student interest, available time in your own teaching schedule, time considerations of other professionals involved, general availability of community resources, and most important, the opportunity to learn that the resource will provide.

Figure 8–2   Areas of informal science education.

Museum and Science Center Resources	Museums of Science/Science Centers/Hands-on Science Centers/Equipment Lending Centers Natural History Museums Military Museums Other Types of Museums
Zoo Resources	Zoological Parks Aquariums Aviaries Specialized Zoos
Horticulture Resources	Plant Conservatories Herbariums Botanical Gardens County Extension Offices
Industrial Resources	Television/Cable Stations Radio Stations Public Utilities Malls, Stores, and Shops
Media Resources	Television Production Companies Film Production Companies Radio Broadcast Companies
Park Resources	National, State, and Local Parks Animal Refuges Geologic Sites Dendrology Exhibits Aquatic Sites Bird, Butterfly, or Insect Areas
College Resources	Biologic Displays and Groups Archeological Displays/Museums and Groups Astronomy Groups and Observatories Earth Science Displays and Groups
Community-Based Resources	Professionals in the Community Scientists High School Student Volunteers
Home-Based Resources	Parent Educators Science-Related Toys Science and Nature Magazines

SCIENCE LEARNING RESOURCES

Where can your students see science-related objects and events in their community? The many places to explore may include a zoo, wooded area, garden, nursery, greenhouse, pond, brook, bird refuge, observatory, natural history museum, road cut, construction site, waterworks, sewage treatment plant, dairy, airport, and weather bureau. Each of these places is a rewarding learning site for elementary school students to visit. Before you take a trip, however, some preparation will help make it worthwhile.

> **Teaching Tips**
>
> See how a zoo, museum, or related resource would fit into your curriculum before proceeding with specific arrangements.

A school district catalog of suggested places to visit in the community may be available. It can furnish the necessary details for educational trips. In general, however, you will want to keep the following points in mind:

- Be clear about the purpose for leaving the classroom.
- Check with the principal about policies such as student supervision.
- Visit the site yourself.
- Plan with the children what to look for on the trip.
- Develop behavior and safety standards to be remembered.
- At the site, make sure everyone can see and hear adequately.
- Develop a timetable of events and activities.
- Ask questions if desired.

> **Teaching Tips**
>
> After returning to the classroom, help your students evaluate the trip. Allow them to tell whether the trip was a meaningful educational experience.

Place special emphasis on the reason for the trip, as you consider the above points. Give your students an assignment during the trip so that they know the reason for the activity. This assignment does not have to be a written report; it should focus their observations and reduce behavioral problems. Be sure to select adults to help supervise students. These adult chaperones will need to be briefed to provide a better learning opportunity during the visit (Tunnicliffe, 1997). The following sections contain further explanation of some of the resources in Figure 8–2.

Museums and Science Centers

Mrs. Blackwelder began her investigation of wolves long before she guided her class into a unit on wolves. She read *Child of the Wolves* (Hall, 1996) and wanted to become more familiar with wolves and their travels. When she called a museum, she found out that she could work with a museum staff member to learn more about wolves. This situation is not uncommon.

In *Inquiry and the National Science Education Standards* (NRC, 2000), we find a story about a teacher named Joanna. She is participating in activities at a science museum. There, she finds that her own inquiry methods are enhanced as she participates in science as a learner. In cooperation with the museum staff, she is learning inquiry-based teaching methods such as the following:

- How both science subject matter and inquiry outcomes can be built into learning experiences
- How a deeper understanding of scientific concepts can promote discussion and the formulation of productive questions
- How the essential features of classroom inquiry can be woven into a learning experience

Wolves and children's misconceptions about wolves are good elementary and middle school science topics of study.

- What it feels like to learn this way, complete with frustrations and struggles
- The roles and behaviors instructors can use to promote and support learning (NRC, 2000, p. 101)

Joanna's experience represents a shift in the role of the museum as part of a **stakeholder** in science education as opposed to maintaining a curatorial function. Put another way, museums today are no longer static collections of human-made or natural history. Rather, they function to develop public understanding of scientific and technological concepts and provide an interface between these concepts and related societal issues. Where in the past, a staff scientist or curator provided the tour, today it is given by educational specialists or museum staff with special training in educational philosophy (Bitgood, Serrell, & Thompson, 1994). These professionals are better able to support state and national standards and science learning in general.

> **Stakeholders** are those individuals or groups that have a "shared interest" in science education and scientific literacy.

This philosophy provides another source of out-of-school education, such as museums, for your students as well as yourself. Another reason museums are a beneficial experience for students relates to the nature of out-of-school education itself. In-school education is a well-ordered system. Knowledge and instruction are continuous, sequential, often guided by textbooks or a specified curriculum, and explicitly assessed (Templeton, 1988). Out-of-school learning, contrarily, is often freely chosen. Exhibits at museums or similar facilities are specifically designed to attract the viewer's attention. Here, the instruction is planned to promote easy understanding. Knowledge is represented in things, not in textbooks. This representation often promotes deeper learning and can be very motivating for students and teachers alike.

Museums are also important proponents of constructive principles. A report of one such elementary-level partnership contained this quote: "If children learn best when

After reading Focus on Inquiry: Zoos as Science Education Resources, you should have begun to understand the rich opportunity to learn provided by the zoo animals, the environment, and the zoo staff.

constructing their own meaning from their experiences, then indeed informal learning such as that occurring in science museums is an important model to become immersed in while learning to teach" (Nagel, Ault, & Rice, 1995, p. 34).

In sum, whether you personally take an entire class to the museum for predetermined activities in support of your curriculum, plan and encourage individual learning experiences, or provide external rewards for students who make visits on their own time, your students will certainly benefit from the experience. An analogous resource with many of the same learning benefits of the museum is the zoo.

Zoos

Mrs. Blackwelder will provide enough time for her students to draw pictures and describe the animals that they find while on the visit. This will make the experience more meaningful.

Observing animals, inquiring about their behaviors and habitats, and communicating observations provide excellent opportunities for science learning. Zoo experiences can also provide students a conservation-minded value system as they begin to appreciate the animals that are a part of the ecosystem (Harvey & Erickson, 1988).

Mrs. Blackwelder's class will arrange a visit to a zoo as a culminating activity for the wolf unit. After reading about arctic wolves in the books *To the Top of the World* (Brandenburg, 1993) and *Journey of the Red Wolf* (Smith, 1996), her students are particularly interested in looking at the physical characteristics of wolves and similar animals. They want to know what helps the wolves travel in the way that is discussed.

For a trip to a zoo to be a beneficial learning experience and not just an "entertaining outing," planning is important (Prather, 1989). You may want to try visiting only one area or ecosystem on each trip. The first step in using a zoo as a resource is to visit the zoo and contact the zoo staff to see what is available for you or your students. Today's zoos offer broader experiences than just observing animals. The zoo staff offers interactive learning experiences for children (Rennie & McClafferty, 1995). Some may even display animatronics (Tunnicliffe, 1999) so that an animated animal and its behavior can be studied in detail. Many zoos offer group tours, special programs designed just for children, career presentations, gifted or challenged student programs, or outreach programs during which the zoo staff bring animals to a class that is not able to travel to the zoo facility.

As you begin your career as a teacher, contact local zoos, museums, and other facilities to see what professional development opportunities are available there.

Keep in mind that not only is a zoo a resource for your students, but, like museums, many zoos provide professional development opportunities for teachers. Whether a curriculum development project, a summer workshop, or a paid internship, you can benefit from the experience provided by zoo educational specialists.

Horticultural Resources

See Chapter 8 Web Destinations on the Companion Website (*http://www. prenhall.com/peters*) for links related to conservatories and arboretums.

Mrs. Blackwelder's class dialogue of what wolves eat from the book *Wolves* (Dudley, 1997) initiated a discussion of different types of edible mushrooms. Now, Mrs. Blackwelder is making arrangements for her class to talk with a horticulturalist. She will show interested students local varieties of mushrooms, including those that are edible and those that are poisonous.

Conservatories, herbariums, arboretums, and botanical gardens, like their animal counterparts, can be resources for indispensable science learning opportunities. These re-

Visit an Inquiry Classroom
Using Zoos, Science Centers, and Museums

View the *Scientific Method* video in the "Nature of Science" section of the Companion CD. In this video segment, Mr. McKnight works with students to develop new questions to explore about earthworms.

Review the video and ask yourself the following:
- How could Mr. McKnight use zoos, science centers, or museums to extend his students' study of earthworms?
- The students in the video engage in inquiry with earthworms. If you were using zoos, science centers, or museums local to your area, what other animals could you study? What resources could the zoos, science centers, or museums provide for your classroom?

Explore the Association of Science-Technology Centers's website (*http://www.astc.org/*). In the *ASTC Dimensions* (2004), George Hein makes the following statement:

> Effective museum education activities allow students to ask questions, interact with objects, and explore the processes that lead to a richer understanding of the world. In this era of standards-based curricula and high-stakes testing, it is worth reemphasizing the importance of keeping museum education focused in the direction of open, inquisitive use of material resources—not in the direction of the constrained, answer-driven minutiae of worksheets.

Explain what he means by this quote and describe your reaction to it. Record your ideas and the answers to these questions in your portfolio or use the Companion Website to share your ideas.

---

sources provide out-of-school learning education experiences such as schoolyard ecology programs for elementary and middle school students. Conservatories and arboretums also provide teacher education programs such as faculty development workshops. Examples of organizations that provide services or contact with experts are as follows:

- National Arbor Day Foundation
- North American Conservatories
- United States National Arboretum
- Ecological Society of America
- American Association of Botanical Gardens and Arboreta
- National Park Service
- Botanical Society of America
- National Association of State Foresters

As you can see, this is a diverse group of institutions and experts ready to assist you with your learning goals. When looking for local botanical resources, it may be helpful to begin with your county extension office. You may also want to refer to the document *Resources for Teaching Elementary School Science* (National Science Resources Center, National Academy of Sciences, Smithsonian Institution, 1996) for contacts in your area.

See Chapter 8 Web Destinations on the Companion Website (*http://www.prenhall.com/peters*) for links to county extensions.

Industrial-Based Resources

Alliances among business, industry, government, higher education, and the K–12 educational community are effective ways to supplement learning and bring the community together for science education improvement (American Association for the Advancement of Science [AAAS], 1998; International Council of Associations for Science Education [ICASE], 1990). Teachers who participate in industry-based work experiences report the following:

- Using new teaching strategies in their classrooms
- Introducing updated content into the curriculum
- Increasing the use of computers in the classrooms
- Seeking ways to work with other teachers and maintaining their connections to the businesses in which the teachers previously worked or had a summer internship
- Adding career information to the curriculum
- Gaining in self-esteem
- Affirming their decisions to become teachers

Alliances and business partners can also contribute to effective standards-based reform (Business Coalition for Education Reform, 1998; Rigden & McAdoo, 1995; Triangle Coalition for Science and Technology Education, 1996). They provide support to elementary and middle school classrooms through a variety of means such as summer internships, mini-grants to teachers or students, volunteers for tutoring, mentoring, guest lecturing, sponsoring clubs, judging contests, institutes for professional development, speaker bureaus, loans and donations of equipment, technical assistance, curriculum assistance, program development, public awareness campaigns, clearinghouses, databases, hotlines, projects for women and minorities, computer assistance, administrator training, and school restructuring (Triangle Coalition for Science and Technology Education, 1991).

See Chapter 8 Web Destinations on the Companion Website (*http://www. prenhall.com/peters*) for links related the U.S. Chamber of Commerce.

To get a better perspective on which businesses in your area are supporting education, contact the Triangle Coalition for Science and Technology Education, 1201 New York Avenue, NW, Suite 700, Washington, DC, 20005. This organization provides information on the Scientific Work Experiences for Teachers (SWEPT) program. You may also want to refer to the document *A Business Guide to Support Employee and Family Involvement in Education* (Otterbourg, 1997).

To see what other resources are available in your area, your first step should be contacting your local chamber of commerce. You can begin by viewing the U.S. Chamber of Commerce Chamber Mall.

Media Providers

See Chapter 8 Web Destinations on the Companion Website (*http://www. prenhall.com/peters*) for links to endangered species sites.

Mrs. Blackwelder encouraged her students to take a virtual tour of an endangered species site after reading the Ranger Rick book *Wolves for Kids* (Wolpert, 1990). This is one of many out-of-school learning resources available from the National Wildlife Federation. An ever-increasing supply of resources is available from media providers about wolves and many other elementary and middle school science topics. One place to begin looking for resources is with your local cable company.

The Cable in the Classroom program is a public service effort supported by the cable industry. Cable companies provide free cable connections to many classrooms in their area, as well as hundreds of hours of free programming to the schools. Videotaping of the shows is encouraged, allowing teachers flexibility in when they show the productions in their individual classrooms. Teachers can refer to Cable in the Classroom magazine, which lists the schedule and provides feature articles. The Cable in the Classroom program also provides a professional development institute that includes traveling and virtual workshops for teachers.

The Public Broadcasting System (PBS) has many science-related series, including *Nova, Scientific American Frontiers, Newton's Apple, Bill Nye,* and *PBS Online*. PBS includes resources such as an online *TeacherSource* guide and program listings. The *Nova* series covers a variety of science topics that are useful to teachers and students. Lesson ideas, past show resources, and online activities are available on the Internet. A printed teacher's guide is also available.

Scientific American Frontiers, produced in association with *Scientific American*, has a website that includes "Ask the Scientists," "In the Classroom," "Cool Science," and "Resource" sections.

Newton's Apple series is an excellent resource for science subjects. This is a family and classroom science show. Many "Science Try Its" are available on the related website, as are numerous activity guides for the past season's shows. New program guides are generally available a few weeks before the show, and a printed program guide is available for teachers.

Bill Nye's website is a gateway to episode guides for more than 100 shows. This site has "sounds of science" clips and home demonstrations of science phenomena.

One related but often overlooked resource for science is science fiction. It is a good beginning point for discussion of topics that are of student interest. Actual scientific principles used or misused in films and television can be better learned through the use of science fiction (Dubeck, Moshier, & Boss, 1988) because film or television series directors often use concrete ways to demonstrate abstract principles. Science fiction can be a tool for the elementary or middle school science teacher in identifying misconceptions.

See Chapter 8 Web Destinations on the Companion Website (*http://www.prenhall.com/peters*) for Cable in the Classroom links and for Discovery Channel School links. The Discovery Channel School lists programming previews, lesson plans to accompany shows, weblinks, and discussions. *Discovery's Educator Guide* is a free reference to the educational programming on Discovery Channel, The Learning Channel, Travel Channel, and Animal Planet. There are also links to Nickelodeon, PBS, *Nova, Scientific American Frontiers, Newton's Apple, Bill Nye,* and *PBS Online*.

See Chapter 8 Web Destinations on the Companion Website (*http://www.prenhall.com/peters*) for links to ICASE, NSTA, and science clubs.

Visit an Inquiry Classroom
Links Beyond Schooling

View the *Links Beyond Schooling* video in the "Constructivist Pedagogy" section of the Companion CD. This video segment displays some obvious and subtle instances of links beyond the classroom. Students engage in an Internet activity from Discovery Communications's Yuckiest Site. Mr. McKnight also has donated materials and supplies as well as posters on his classroom wall.

Review the video and ask yourself the following:
- Are there resource people or companies in your community that you could contact for classroom materials and supplies?
- Is there an agency, company, or other group close to your school that could become your partner in education?

 Look at the Education Community links on the National Science Foundation Division of Elementary, Secondary, and Informal Education's website (*http://www.ehr.nsf.gov/esie/resources/EdCommLinks.asp*). Identify resources that you could use. Record your ideas and the answers to these questions in your portfolio or use the Companion Website to share your ideas.

"Partners in education" can bring science into your classroom in special ways.

Other Resources

Resources such as state parks, local parks, colleges, community-based businesses, and home-based resources are also available to you as an elementary or middle school teacher. One specific example is the science club. Science clubs allow members to choose areas of study based on mutual interest as opposed to a specific curriculum (Tunnicliffe, 1998). For further information, see the International Association of Science Clubs, the International Council of Associations for Science Education (ICASE), or the National Science Teachers Association (NSTA) websites.

In planning to use resources, first identify your specific learning goals and then check for a local contact that will meet those needs. One way to begin is by contacting a curriculum specialist, elementary science specialist, or lead teacher within your local school or district. You can also try a general Internet search for resources in your area.

INDIVIDUAL PARTNERS IN EDUCATION

Teaching Tips Community resource individuals can be utility-based professionals; animal care technicians; earth, space, and weather experts; botanists and agriculture specialists; social science researchers; or scientists and engineers working in general industry.

The story *The Boy Who Cried "Wolf!"* (Schecter, 1994) begins with a boy earning a living as a shepherd in his village. The villagers come to help the boy when he cries out, "Wolf!" *Peter and the Wolf* (Lemieux, 1991) is a similar story of villagers coming to the rescue when a wolf is present. Although these stories contain misinformation about wolves, they do illustrate how community members are willing to help out in difficult situations. This maxim is still true today. Parents and other community leaders are willing to help you out with your elementary or middle school science program.

Figure 8–3   Individual partner examples.

Utility-Based Partners	Engineers
	Electricians
	Environmental Scientists
	Telecommunications Specialists
	Television/Radio Technicians
	Computer Systems Designers/Operators
Animal/Human Care Partners	Veterinarians
	Zoologists
	Entomologists
	County Health Department Employees
	Hospital-Based Professionals
Earth, Space, and Weather Partners	Weather Forecasters
	Pilots/Astronauts
	Geologists
	Surveyors
	Civil Engineers/Contractors
	Paleontologists
Botanists and Agricultural Partners	Forest/Park Rangers
	Farmers and Ranchers
	Horticulturists/Landscape Workers
	County Extension Employees
Social Science Partners	Psychiatrists
	Psychologists
	Sociologists
	Anthropologists
	Geographers
General Industry Partners	Chemists
	Biologists
	Physicists
	Geologists
	Inventers
	Architects
	Engineers

When it is impossible to arrange visits away from the school, resource persons from the community may be able to visit your classroom. Many districts compile lists of informed persons who are willing to volunteer. Like the science education resources discussed in the previous section, individual partnerships can be an excellent source of assistance, ideas, and materials to support your elementary or middle school science program. Figure 8–3 lists some contacts within these categories.

The following guidelines will help in the success of developing partnerships on an individual basis. First, contact the volunteer in advance and arrange your first meeting outside the classroom. This will allow plenty of time to answer questions, explain general class procedures, determine any specific materials or equipment needed, and discuss the objectives of the visit. As the time approaches, remind the volunteer of her visit and provide the

Teaching Tips

Do not forget to offer soft drinks, water, or coffee to visitors. Also show all visitors where the restrooms are located.

school's telephone number and your home telephone number for a return call. The schedules of many professionals change often, and mistakes can occur. You do not want to have a disappointed class or have future experiences jeopardized from a poor initial experience.

When the visitor arrives, have someone there to greet her and make her comfortable with the experience. You can do this personally while another teacher or an administrator watches your class. You could also have a teacher aide or the room parent greet the visitor and bring her to the classroom. Arrange for a name tag if possible, and introduce the speaker to the class.

After the visit, follow up with a thank-you card or telephone call. Let the principal know something about the volunteer and the outcomes of the visit. The principal or you may want to alert the news media about positive experiences. If volunteers will be visiting on a continuous basis, do not forget to provide them your schedule changes. Meet with them periodically to see whether the objectives of the visits are still being met and whether they have any further suggestions.

Scientists as Professional Development Partners

A partnership with a scientist is a strategy suggested for professional development of teachers who may need to build their content knowledge or confidence in teaching science (Loucks-Horsley et al., 1999). Scientists are good partners in education, especially from a "real" science or equity standpoint. Scientists can provide real-world applications of science as they mentor teachers. Teachers, in return, allow scientists to see firsthand the condition of school science programs. Scientists also benefit by enhancing their own teaching effectiveness as they learn new strategies from educational professionals.

Following are specific goals for having a scientist make a presentation or work with your class:

- To help students understand science
- To help students gain an understanding of the work scientists do
- To help students see scientists as real people
- To help scientists develop insight into today's schools and students (Shaw & Herminghaus, 1993)

Teaching Tips

If the scientist visiting your class is new to the educational field, it may be helpful to provide some initial suggestions, such as the elements of a successful presentation or things to do in the classroom.

As a classroom teacher, you should select a topic for the scientist to present. Call the scientist and explain your needs. Be sure to provide background information and how his presentation will support your learning goals. Make sure you discuss appropriate behavior with your students beforehand.

See the article "Scientists in the Classroom" (Shaw & Herminghaus, 1993) for ideas and a reproducible checklist of things the scientist should know and "do" as part of the presentation. This resource contains information that a teaching professional will understand but that a scientist may not be aware of before the presentation. A summary developed from the list is found in Figure 8–4. The book *Science Education Partnerships: Manual for Scientists and K–12 Teachers* (Sussman, 1993) is also a good resource for use in understanding how a scientist can support science learning in your classroom and how you can develop a partnership program in your school.

Figure 8–4 Do and because list for scientists.

Do	Because
Make eye contact with students	Students love personal contact
Have presentation materials organized	Students have a hard time waiting
Use student volunteers	Students love to feel important
Require students to raise their hands	Students will all want to talk at once
Make sure they understand the task	This avoids unnecessary questions
Face the students and move about	This will help maintain interest
Ask the teacher for help with discipline	The teacher will know how to help
Use wait time	The students need time to think
Praise good behavior	This will encourage more good behavior
Enjoy the students	They have a unique perspective

Source: From Shaw & Herminghaus, 1993, p. 119.

Visit an Inquiry Classroom
Partnerships with Scientists

View the *Paradigm Shifts* video in the "Nature of Science" section of the Companion CD. Mr. McKnight's students are cleaning up after an activity where they explored earthworms. They have answered the questions that they set out to explore.

Review the video and ask yourself the following:

• If you were to bring an agronomist (scientist who specializes in soil and crops), an ethologist (scientist who studies animal behavior), or an oligochaetologist (scientist that studies earthworms), into the classroom, how might this affect how the children study earthworms?

• If a scientist was overseeing the experiments that the students just completed, what changes in your classroom routine may be needed to make the activities more successful?

 Gordon Gates is a well-known oligochaetologist. Research his work on the Internet and identify some of his findings related to earthworms. Record your ideas and the answers to these questions in your portfolio or use the Companion Website to share your ideas.

Parents as Partners

Parents are essential to their children's success in school. Out-of-school time is an important opportunity for learning (Bergstrom, 1984). According to the NSTA Board of Directors, parents can help their children by

• *Seeing science everywhere* Parents can help their children feel the excitement of observation and discovery. They can also promote growth in thinking, further develop problem-solving abilities, and encourage positive attitudes toward science.

• *Doing science together* Parents can share experiences and demonstrate that science learning is enjoyable.

- *Developing a variety of skills*   Parents can assist their children in developing science process skills and comprehending scientific information.
- *Finding the appropriate level*   Parents can assess the developmental level of their children and seek out appropriate strategies and ideas to assist their children with scientific understandings. (NSTA, 1994)

Parents can achieve the NSTA goals by simply taking the time to listen to their child, building a resource collection, and co-investigating science at home and within the community on a daily basis. Parents should also become involved in the school to make sure that science-related experiences are ongoing.

Teachers can support parents by keeping 15 to 30 kits containing activities that the students can check out and take home. These kits can be stored in small plastic containers and are easy to prepare with help from a teacher aide or parents. Begin by looking through this text and other resources that may be available to you. Look for activities and investigations that might enrich your regular science program. Select any number of these activities and make one copy of each activity.

Bring these copies to Parents' Night or similar meetings early in the school year. Start by briefly introducing your science program. Next, discuss what topics your students will study and some of the materials they will work with throughout the year. Then, show your activity sheets and example kits and give their purpose. Hand out the duplicated activity sheets, have parents examine them, and then ask for volunteers to make the kits. Encourage the parent volunteers to do the activities with their children, discuss the results together, and return the completed kits.

Teaching Tips   Do not be afraid to ask parents to assist you in the classroom. Many are afraid to take the first step to ask you, but are willing to help out in any way they can.

Some teachers like to have parents experience firsthand a few children's activities across the curriculum. This puts the parents in better touch with their children's work. Parents who are involved with your program are typically willing to supplement your science supplies with discardable items from around the home. Some will volunteer to assist at science learning centers or will share their expertise in science or technology. But for these things to happen, parents need to hear details from you about what's needed.

Parents are usually more concerned about their children's progress in reading than in other subjects. Point out to them the value of parents reading aloud with their children, sharing books, and discussing concepts that come up in the reading. Show parents several kinds of science trade books available that correlate with upcoming units. The students may check out these books from several sources, including the school, district, or public library. If your school has a newer multimedia science program, check out the science-related literature books that typically accompany these programs.

Show parents examples of useful articles from a newspaper, news magazine, *National Geographic*, or other sources they might share with their children who, in turn, might share the information at school. Explain that this material is easier to understand and remember when it relates to topics and concepts being studied at school. Stress the need to discuss the articles with the children, because these are seldom written in an age-appropriate style. Mention, too, some titles of science periodicals for children. They contain excellent current material, are more age appropriate, and will help students learn what to look for when scanning newspapers and other publications.

Some parents and children will already have visited a local natural history museum, zoo, observatory, bird refuge, or botanical garden. Ask parents about these experiences and suggest additional places recommended by seasoned colleagues and school district publications. A school catalog will have descriptions and a listing of places for families to visit at different grade levels or for certain units of instruction; and if you intend to take your

Visit an Inquiry Classroom
Family Science

View the *Team Work* video in the "Planning and Management" section of the Companion CD. Groups of students watch videos of earthworms, including a heart video.

Review the video segment and ask yourself the following:
- How could you involve parents as part of your earthworm inquiry team?
- What could the students do to showcase their earthworm explorations during a science festival or parent night?

Newton-Hair (2004) discusses having a "Compost Carnival" or "a science fair with a carnival flair." What other parent-related activities can you think of with respect to earthworms? Record your ideas and the answers to these questions in your portfolio or use the Companion Website to share your ideas.

class on study trips to these places, a parents' meeting is a good time to solicit volunteers to accompany the class.

You probably realize that we have mentioned more things to inform parents about than you will have time for in one introductory meeting, especially if you discuss other subjects. Periodic newsletters, a classroom newspaper, individual conferences, and further parent–teacher meetings all present more chances to reach them. The content of your message is far more important than its forum. When you give parents specific ways to help their children study science and support your efforts, everyone gains.

Family Science Festivals

A family science festival is a recreational community event where families participate in science activities after school (MCCPTA-EPI Hands-On Science, 1985). They are not science fairs but community events where people can have fun while they increase their awareness of science. When planning and implementing a festival, keep the following five important considerations in mind:

A family science festival is a time when parents can share with their children without any fears of "failure," such as a low science grade.

1. *Project Leader* The project leader is the head of the committee and is in charge of areas such as recruitment of volunteers and keeping people on task.
2. *Volunteers* Volunteers make telephone calls and make arrangements for festival day such as reminder letters, name tags, and thank-you notes.
3. *Publicity* The publicity person develops the announcements or flyers to give to the graphics team, arranges photographic support, and seeks media coverage of the event.
4. *Graphics* The graphics people print the signs or flyers for the event, as well as any necessary table decorations or instructions needed for the event.
5. *Activities/Materials* The activities crew selects and makes arrangements for the activities, including arranging to have the necessary materials on hand to complete the events. (MCCPTA-EPI Hands-On Science, 1985, p. 4)

The important thing to remember about family science festivals is that they should be fun and indicative of your school or community. They should also be a positive support for science learning.

Summary

- Science learning opportunities that take place outside the classroom can support or supplement an ongoing school curriculum. This type of learning can be in the schoolyard, at home, or in any other social setting.
- Museums and science centers, zoos, horticulture exhibits and experts, industrial resources, and various forms of media all provide learning opportunities for students and professional development opportunities for preservice and in-service teachers.

- Utility-based partners; animal/human care partners; earth, space, and weather partners; botanists and agriculture partners; social science partners; and general industry partners are all available to support your elementary or middle school science program.
- Parents can be essential learning partners for your students. One type of event that can involve parents is a family science festival, where families participate in science activities after school.

Reflection

Companion CD

1. Look at the "Earthworm Longevity: It's an Earthworm's Life" lesson associated with the *Links Beyond Schooling* video on the Companion CD. Although students do not go to zoos and natural history museums to learn about earthworms, there are many other animals available for exploration. Choose a zoo animal and develop a lesson plan on "It's an [insert your animal's name here]'s Life."
2. Look at the "Invertebrate Versus Vertebrate: Which Animals Are Which" lesson associated with the

Invitation video on the Companion CD. Develop a lesson plan that you could use at a natural history museum that would have children learn about invertebrates versus vertebrates.
3. Look at the "What Is Anatomy: What Is Earthworm Anatomy" lesson associated with the *Science as Inquiry* video on the Companion CD. Brainstorm ways that a classroom science partner could present a lesson on the anatomy of another animal.

Portfolio Ideas

1. Look at Chapter 9 of *Resources for Teaching Elementary School Science* (National Science Resources Center, 1996) or *Science Fun in Chicagoland: A Guide for Parents and Teachers* (Stills, 1995). Enter into your portfolio some out-of-school science education resources located near your community.
2. Read through *Helping Your Child Learn Science* (Paulu, 1992). Would you recommend this reading to parents? Why or why not? What does it say to you as a future teacher? Did you get any new ideas from the "Activities in the Community" section? Record ideas in your portfolio.
3. Obtain a copy of *Science Education Partnerships: Manual for Scientists and K–12 Teachers* (Sussman, 1993) and identify in your portfolio ways to develop and fund partnerships. These could be with your

students or on an individual basis as a means to further your own scientific knowledge.
4. *Learning in Living Color: Using Literature to Incorporate Multicultural Education into the Primary Classroom* (Valdez, 1999, pp. 60–79) will help you to develop lessons to integrate the wolf theme with multicultural themes such as Native American history for inclusion in your portfolio. Also show the relationship between the nature of science (skepticism) and stereotyping. What facts are related to wolves, and what fiction has skewed our understanding of wolves?
5. Review the National PTA's National Standards for Parent/Family Involvement Programs at *http://www. pta.org/parentinvolvement/standards/index.asp*. In your portfolio, develop a presentation that you can use in the future to seek parental support for your science program.

References

Allard, H. (1997). *It's so nice to have a wolf around the house*. New York: Picture Yearling Books.

American Association for the Advancement of Science (AAAS). (1998). *Blueprints for reform*. New York: Oxford University Press.

Batten, M. (1998). *Baby wolf*. New York: Grosset & Dunlap.

Bergstrom, J. (1984). *School's out—now what? Creative choices for your child*. Berkeley, CA: Ten Speed Press.

Bitgood, S., Serrell, B., & Thompson, D. (1994). The impact of informal education on visitors to museums. In V. Crane, H. Nicholson, M. Chen, & S. Bitgood (Eds.), *Informal science learning: What the research says about television, science museums, and community-based projects* (pp. 61–106). Ephrata, PA: Science Press.

Brandenburg, J. (1993). *To the top of the world: Adventures with arctic wolves*. New York: Walker.

Business Coalition for Education Reform. (1998). *The formula for success: A business leader's guide to supporting math and science achievement*. Washington, DC: U.S. Department of Education.

Crane, V. (1994). An introduction to informal science learning and research. In V. Crane, H. Nicholson, M. Chen, & S. Bitgood (Eds.), *Informal science learning: What the research says about television, science museums, and community-based projects* (pp. 1–14). Ephrata, PA: Science Press.

Dubeck, L. W., Moshier, S. E., & Boss, J. E. (1988). *Science in cinema: Teaching science fact thorough science fiction films*. New York: Teachers College Press.

Dudley, K. (1997). *Wolves*. Austin, TX: Raintree Steck-Vaughn.

Ernst, L. C. (1995). *Little red riding hood: A newfangled prairie tale*. New York: Aladdin Paperbacks.

Gay, M. L. (1997). *The 3 little pigs*. Buffalo, NY: Groundwood Books.

George, J. C. (1972). *Julie of the wolves*. New York: HarperTrophy.

George, J. C. (1998). *Look to the north: A wolf pup diary*. New York: HarperTrophy.

Hall, E. (1996). *Child of the wolves*. New York: Bantam Doubleday Dell.

Harvey, P., & Erickson, D. (1988). Making the most of the zoo. In M. Druger (Ed.), *Science for the fun of it: A guide to informal science education* (pp. 78–82). Arlington, VA: National Science Teachers Association.

Hein, G. (2004, January/February). Museum-school bridges: A legacy of progressive education. *ASTC Dimensions*. Washington, DC: The Association of Science-Technology Centers.

Hofstein, A., Bybee, R., & Legro, P. (1997). Linking formal and informal science education through science education standards. *Science Education International, 8*(3), 31–37.

Honeyman, B. (1998). Non-formal and formal learning interactions: New directions for scientific and technological literacy. *Connect, 23*(1), 1–2.

International Council of Associations for Science Education (ICASE). (1990). *Industry–education liaison*. Hong Kong: Author.

Katz, P., & McGinnis, R. (1999). An informal elementary science education program's response to the national science education reform movement. *Journal of Elementary Science Education, 11*(1), 1–11.

Landis, C. (1996). *Teaching science in the field*. ERIC/CSMEE Digest, EDO-SE-96-7. Columbus, OH: ERIC/CSMEE.

Lemieux, M. (1991). *Peter and the wolf*. New York: Mulberry Paperbacks.

Locker, T. (1996). *The land of the gray wolf*. New York: Dial Books.

London, J. (1993). *The eyes of grey wolf*. San Francisco: Chronicle Books.

London, J. G. (1993). *The call of the wild*. New York: Scholastic Paperbacks.

Loucks-Horsley, S., Hewson, P. W., Love, N., Stiles, K. E., Dyasi, H. M., Friel, S. N., Mumme, J., Sneider, C. I., & Worth, K. L. (1999). Ideas that work: Summaries of 15 strategies for professional development. In A. Thorson (Ed.), *Ideas that work: Science professional development* (pp. 10–44). Columbus, OH: Eisenhower National Clearinghouse for Mathematics and Science Education.

Marshall, J. (1987). *Red riding hood*. New York: Dial Books.

MCCPTA-EPI Hands-On Science. (1985). *Putting together a family science festival*. (Available from author at 12118 Heritage Park Circle, Silver Spring, MD 20852)

Melber, L. (2000). Tap into informal science learning. *Science Scope, 23*(6), 28–31.

Milton, J. (1992). *Wild, wild wolves*. New York: Random House.

Nagel, N., Ault, C., & Rice, M. (1995). Learning to teach and the science museum. *Science Education International, 6*(2), 31–34.

National Research Council (NRC). (1996). *National science education standards*. Washington, DC: National Academy Press. http://books.nap.edu/html/nses/html/index.html

National Research Council (NRC). (1998). *Every child a scientist: Achieving scientific literacy for all*. Washington, DC: National Academy Press.

National Research Council (NRC). (2000). *Inquiry and the national science education standards*. Washington, DC: National Academy Press. http://books.nap.edu/html/inquiry_addendum/

National Science Resources Center, National Academy of Sciences, Smithsonian Institution. (1996). *Resources for teaching elementary school science*. Washington, DC: National Academy Press. http://stills.nap.edu/html/rtes/contents.html

National Science Teachers Association (NSTA). (1994). *An NSTA position statement: Parent involvement in science education*. Arlington, VA: Author. www.nsta.org/handbook/position.asp

National Science Teachers Association (NSTA). (1998). *An NSTA position statement: Informal science education*. Arlington, VA: Author. http://www.nsta.org/handbook/position.asp

Newton-Hair, D. (2004). *Bin bug bingo!* Grants Pass, OR: Worm Digest. Retrieved December 23, 2004, from www.wormdigest.org/binbugbingo.html

Otterbourg, S. (1997). *A business guide to support employee and family involvement in education*. New York: Conference Board. www.ed.gov/pubs/BusinessGuide/

Patent, D. H. (1990). *Gray wolf, red wolf*. New York: Clarion Books.

Paulo, N. (1992). *Helping your child learn science*. Washington, DC: U.S. Department of Education.

Prather, J. P. (1989). Review of the value of field trips in science instruction. *Journal of Elementary Science Education, 1*(1), 10–17.

Reiff, A. (n.d.). *Coming up worms*. Belleville, IL: St. Clair County Regional Schools. Retrieved December 23, 2004, from http://web.stclair.k12.il.us/splashd/wormsexp.htm

Rennie, L. R., & McClafferty, T. (1995). Using visits to interactive science and technology centers, museums, aquaria, and zoos to promote learning in science. *Journal of Science Teacher Education, 6*(4), 175–185.

Rigden, D., & McAdoo, M. (1995). *Supporting the national education goals: A guide for business leaders*. New York: Council for Aid to Education.

Schecter, E. (1994). *The boy who cried "wolf!"* New York: Bantam Book.

Schmidt, K. (1986). *Little red riding hood*. New York: Scholastic.

Scieszka, J. (1989). *The true story of the 3 little pigs!* New York: Puffin Books.

Shaw, D., & Herminghaus, T. (1993). Scientists in the classroom. In G. Madrazo & L. Motz (Eds.), *Sourcebook for science supervisors* (4th ed., pp. 117–121). Arlington, VA: National Science Teachers Association.

Sills, T. W. (1995). *Science fun in Chicagoland: A guide for parents and teachers*. Chicago: Dearborn Resources.

Skurzynski, G., & Ferguson, A. (1997). *Wolf stalker*. Washington, DC: National Geographic Society.

Smith, R. (1996). *Journey of the red wolf*. New York: Cobblehill Books.

Sussman, A. (1993). *Science education partnerships: Manual for scientists and K–12 teachers*. San Francisco: University of California.

Templeton, M. (1988). The science museum: Object lessons in informal education. In M. Druger (Ed.), *Science for the fun of it: A guide to informal science education* (pp. 83–88). Arlington, VA: National Science Teachers Association.

Triangle Coalition for Science and Technology Education. (1991). *A guide for building an alliance for science, mathematics, and technology*. College Park, MD: Author.

Triangle Coalition for Science and Technology Education. (1996). *A look at industry and community commitment to educational systematic reform*. College Park, MD: Author.

Trivizas, E. (1993). *The three little wolves and the big bad pig*. New York: Aladdin Paperbacks.

Tunnicliffe, S. D. (1992). The school visit as a science learning opportunity. In *Annual proceedings of the American Association of Zoological Parks and Aquariums* (pp. 342–349). Toronto: AAZPA/American Zoo and Aquarium Association.

Tunnicliffe, S. D. (1997). The effect of the presence of two adults—chaperones or teachers—on the content of conversations of primary school groups during school visits to a natural history museum. *Journal of Elementary Science Education, 9*(1), 49–65.

Tunnicliffe, S. D. (1998). Science clubs. *Science Education International, 9*(3), 36.

Tunnicliffe, S. D. (1999). Use with care: Animatronics in museums and zoos—a new type of exhibit. *Science Education International, 10*(3), 34–37.

Valdez, A. (1999). *Learning in living color: Using literature to incorporate multicultural education*. Needham Heights, MA: Allyn & Bacon.

Vozar, D. (1993). *Yo, hungry wolf!: A nursery rap*. New York: Doubleday.

Wolpert, T. (1990). *Wolves for kids*. Minnetonka, MN: NorthWord Press.

Young, E. (1989). *Lon Po Po: A red-riding hood story from China*. Ossining, NY: Paper Star.

Suggested Readings

Committee on Biology Teacher Inservice Programs, Board on Biology Commission on Life Sciences, National Research Council. (1996). *The role of scientists in the professional development of science teachers*. Washington, DC: National Academy Press. *http://stills.nap.edu/html/role/* (a comprehensive report and reading list on the topic of the use of scientists in teacher professional development)

Kubota, C. (1993). *Education-business partnerships: Scientific work experience programs*. ERIC/CSMEE Digest, EDO-SE-93-3. Columbus, OH: ERIC/CSMEE.

National Science Resources Center, National Academy of Sciences, Smithsonian Institution. (1997). *Science for all children: A guide to improving science education in your school district*. Washington, DC: National Academy Press. (provides examples of specific partnerships in support of elementary science education)

Paulu, N., & Martin, M. (1991). *Helping your child learn science*. Washington, DC: U.S. Department of Education, Office of Educational Research and Improvement. (how parents can increase their children's science interests through home activities; available at $3.25 from OERI Outreach Office, 555 New Jersey Ave., NW, Washington, DC 20208-5570)

Pearlman, S., & Pericak-Spector, K. (1992). Helping hands from home. *Science and Children, 29*(7), 12–14. (parent volunteers make active science more manageable)

PROFESSIONAL BIBLIOGRAPHY

GENERAL SOURCES OF ACTIVITIES

American Association for the Advancement of Science, & Walthall, B. (Ed.). (1995). *IdeAAAS: Sourcebook for science, mathematics, & technology education.* Washington, DC: Learning Team.

American Chemical Society. (2001). *The best of wonderscience* (Vol. 2). Belmont, CA: Wadsworth.

Cothron, J., Giese, R., & Rezba, R. (2002). *Science experiments by the hundreds* (2nd ed.). Dubuque, IA: Kendall/Hunt.

DeVito, A. *Creative sciencing.* Minneapolis, MN: Sagebrush Educational Resources.

Freidl, A., & Koontz, T. (2004). *Teaching science to children: An inquiry approach.* New York: McGraw-Hill Higher Education.

Sewall, S. (1990). *Hooked on science: Ready-to-use discovery activities for grades 4–8.* West Nyack, NY: Center for Applied Research in Education.

Stringer, J. (Ed.). (1996). *Science and technology ideas for the under 85.* Hatfield, Herts., UK: Association for Science Education.

Stringer, J. (Ed.). (1998). *More science and technology ideas for the under 85.* Hatfield, Herts., UK: Association for Science Education.

Strongin, H. (1991). *Science on a shoestring.* Reading, MA: Addison-Wesley.

Van Cleave, J. P. (1989–1999). *Science for every kid* (5 volumes: biology, chemistry, earth, astronomy, physics). New York: John Wiley.

OTHERS

Also visit the AIMS Education Foundation (*http://www.aimsedu.org/*), Great Explorations in Math and Science (*http://www.lhs.berkeley.edu/GEMS/ gems.html*), National Science Teachers Association (*www.nsta.org*), and the Association for Science Education (*http://www.ase.org.uk/*) for new activity books and ideas.

TEACHER PERIODICALS

Discover, 114 Fifth Ave., New York, NY 10011. (monthly; interesting, up-to-date information about developments in science; *http://www.discover.com/*)

Journal of Elementary Science Education, (*http://static.highbeam. com/j/journalofelementaryscience.education/*) (practical and theoretical articles related to elementary science teaching and learning)

Journal of Science Teacher Education, contact Jon Pederson, Association for the Education of Teachers in Science Executive Secretary, University of Oklahoma, Norman, OK 73070; *pedersenj@ou.edu.* (practical and scholarly articles related to teacher preservice, teacher in-service, and science teaching)

School Science and Mathematics, http://oreganstate.edu/ pubs/ssm/ (monthly; nine issues a year; includes articles on methods and research)

Science, American Association for the Advancement of Science. (accurate, up-to-date nontechnical information about developments in science; *http://www.scienceonline.org/*)

Science Activities, Heldref Publications, 1319 Eighteenth Street, NW, Washington, DC 20036-1802. (10 issues a year; useful activities for teachers of the upper grades and beyond; *http://www.heldref.org*)

Science and Children, National Science Teachers Association, 1840 Wilson Blvd., Arlington, VA 22201-3000. (monthly; eight issues a year; articles of interest and practical value to elementary school teachers; *www.nsta.org/*)

Science Education, John Wiley and Sons, Inc., 605 Third Ave., New York, NY 10158. For individual subscriptions contact Jon Pederson, Association for the Education of Teachers in Science Executive Secretary, University of Oklahoma, Norman, OK 73070; *pedersenj@ou.edu*. (reports of research and essays on the teaching of elementary and secondary school science)

Science News. (weekly; brief, easy-to-read reports on current findings of scientific research; *http://www.sciencenews.org/*)

CHILDREN'S PERIODICALS

National Geographic Kids Magazine, National Geographic Society, 1145 17th St. NW, Washington, DC 20036. (monthly; articles on environmental features of interest to children; *http://www.nationalgeographic.com/world/*)

Odyssey, Cobblestone Publishing Company, 30 Grove St., Suite C, Peterborough, NH 03458. (bimonthly; full-color astronomy and space magazine for children 7–13; *http://www.odysseymagazine.com/*)

Ranger Rick Nature Magazine, National Wildlife Federation, 11100 Wildlife Center Drive, Reston, VA 20190–5362. (monthly; for children of elementary school age; interesting stories and pictures on natural subjects, including ecology; *Your Big Backyard* is for preschool and primary-level children; *http://www.nwf.org/kidzone/*)

3–2–1 Contact, Sesame Workshop, P.O. Box 2933, Boulder, CO 80322. (10 issues a year; experiments, puzzles, projects, and articles for children 8–14; *http://www.sesameworkshop.org/*)

Wonderscience, American Chemical Society, 1155 16th St., NW, Washington, DC 20036. (science activities for children; also includes *Best of Wonderscience*; *http://www.chemistry.org/portal/a/c/s/1/acsdisplay.html?DOC= education%5curriculum%5cwondsci.html* and *http://www. chemistry.org/portal/a/c/s/1/wondernetdisplay.html?DOC= wondernet\topics_list\index.html*)

PROFESSIONAL TEXTS

Abruscato, J. (2004). *Teaching children science: A discovery approach* (6th ed.). Needham Heights, MA: Allyn & Bacon/Pearson Education. (methods, activities, and content for elementary school science)

Barba, R. H. (1998). *Science in the multicultural classroom: A guide to teaching and learning* (2nd ed.). Needham Heights, MA: Allyn & Bacon. (elementary science methods)

Carin, A., & Bass, J. (2005). *Teaching science as inquiry* (10th ed.). Upper Saddle River, NJ: Merrill/Prentice Hall. (methods and activities, with emphasis on discovery teaching)

Ebenezer, J., & Conner, S. (1998). *Learning to teach science: A model for the 21st century*. Upper Saddle River, NJ: Merrill/Prentice Hall. (methods and activities, with emphasis on discovery teaching)

Esler, W. K., & Esler, M. K. (2000). *Teaching elementary science* (8th ed.). Belmont, CA: Wadsworth. (methods and subject matter; exemplifies and applies three kinds of lessons)

Gabel, D. (1993). *Introductory science skills*. Prospect Heights, IL: Waveland Press. (a laboratory approach to learning science and mathematics skills and basic chemistry)

Harlan, J., & Rivkin, M. (2004). *Science experiences for the early childhood years: An integrated affective approach* (8th ed.). Upper Saddle River, NJ: Merrill/Prentice Hall. (everyday science activities for younger children)

Howe, A. C. (2002). *Engaging children in science* (3rd ed.). Upper Saddle River, NJ: Merrill/Prentice Hall. (elementary science methods)

Krajcik, J., Czerniak, C., & Berger, C. (1999). *Teaching children science: A project-based approach*. New York: McGraw-Hill.

Lind, K. K. (1999). *Exploring science in early childhood: A developmental approach* (3rd ed.). Albany, NY: Delmar. (elementary science methods)

Martin, D. J. (2003). *Elementary science methods: A constructivist approach* (3rd ed.). Albany, NY: Delmar. (elementary science methods)

Martin, R. E., Jr., Sexton, C., & Gerlovich, J. (2005). *Teaching science for all children: Inquiry lessons for constructing understanding* (3rd ed.). Needham Heights, MA: Allyn & Bacon. (methods and content of elementary school science)

Rezba, R., Sprague, C., Fiel, R. L., & Funk, H. J. (2002). *Learning and assessing science process skills* (4th ed.). Dubuque, IA: Kendall Hunt. (process skill development and assessment)

Tolman, M. N. (2001). *Discovering elementary science: Method, content, and problem-solving activities* (3rd ed.). Needham Heights, MA: Allyn & Bacon. (elementary science methods and content)

Victor, E., & Kellough, R. (2000). *Science K-8: An integrated approach* (10th ed.). Upper Saddle River, NJ: Merrill/Prentice Hall. (methods, content, and activities; features an extensive scope of subject matter in outline form)

AGENCIES AND SOCIETIES

The Association for Science Teacher Education (ASTE), contact Walter S. Smith and Caryl Kelley Smith, ASTE Executive Secretaries, Department of Biology, Ball State University, Muncie, IN 47306-0440, *wsmith@bsu.edu* (WSS) or *eelslake1@aol.com* (CKS and WSS) (*http://theASTE.org*).

Computer Learning Foundation, P.O. Box 60007, Palo Alto, CA 94306-0007 (*http://www.computerlearning.org/*).

Foundation for Science and Disability, E. C. Keller, Jr., Treasurer, 236 Grand St., Morgantown, WV 26506-6057 (*http://www.as.wvu.edu/~scidis/organizations/FSD_brochure.html*).

The Franklin Institute Science Museum, 222 North 20th Street, Philadelphia, PA 19103, (215) 448-1200 (*http://www.fi.edu/*).

International Council of Associations for Science Education (ICASE), Jack B. Holbrook, Executive Secretary, ICASE, P.O. Box 6138, Limassol, Cyprus.

National Audubon Society, 700 Broadway, New York, NY 10003, (212) 979-3000, fax (212) 979-3188 (*http://www.audubon.org/*).

National Energy Foundation, 3676 California Ave. Suite A117, Salt Lake City, UT 84104 (*http://www.nefl.org/*).

National Science Foundation, 4201 Wilson Blvd., Arlington, VA 22230 (*http://nsf.gov/*).

National Science Teachers Association, 1840 Wilson Boulevard, Arlington, VA 22201-3000, (703) 243-7100 (*http://www.nsta.org/*).

National Weather Service, 1325 East West Highway, Silver Spring, MD 20910 (*http://www.nws.noaa.gov/*).

Office of Indian Education Programs, Bureau of Indian Affairs (*http://oiep.bia.edu/*).

Society for Advancement of Chicanos and Native Americans in Science (SACNAS), P.O. Box 8526, Santa Cruz, CA 95061, (831) 459–0170 (*http://www.sacnas.org/*).

Technical Education Resource Center, 2067 Massachusetts Ave., Cambridge, MA 02140, (617) 547-0430, fax (617) 349-3535 (*http://www.terc.edu/*).

U.S. Environmental Protection Agency, Ariel Rios Bldg., 1200 Pennsylvania Ave. NW, Washington, DC 20460, (202) 272-0167 (*http://www.epa.gov/*).

U.S. Geological Survey, Information Services (*http://www.usgs.gov/*).

SCIENCE CURRICULUM PROJECTS

ACTIVITIES FOR INTEGRATING MATHEMATICS AND SCIENCE (AIMS)

Grades K–8. This program, developed at Fresno (California) Pacific College, was originally funded by the National Science Foundation to train a group of teachers in the rationale and methods for integrating science and mathematics in grades 5–8. The classroom testing of written materials produced such positive results that a full-fledged writing project was launched to develop additional teaching booklets. Materials are now available for K–8.

The rationale for AIMS includes these points: (a) Mathematics and science are integrated outside the classroom and so should also be integrated inside it; (b) as in the real world, a whole series of mathematics skills and science processes should be interwoven in a single activity to create a continuum of experience; (c) the materials should present questions that relate to the students' world and arouse their curiosity; (d) the materials should change students from observers to participants in the learning process; and (e) the investigations should be enjoyable because learning is more effective when the process is enjoyed.

For more information, write to AIMS Education Foundation, 1595 S. Chestnut Ave., Fresno, CA 93702-4706 (*http://www.aimsedu.org/*), 888-733-2467.

FULL OPTION SCIENCE SYSTEM (FOSS)

Grades K–6. The FOSS program is designed to serve both regular and most special education students in a wide cross section of schools. Developed at the Lawrence Hall of Science, in Berkeley, California, the program features several modules at each grade level that include science lesson plans in the earth, life, and physical sciences and extension activities in language, computer, and mathematics applications.

The laboratory equipment includes several package options, from complete kits to individual items. Materials assembly directions show how teacher and students can gather and construct equipment for many activities. A correlation table tells how to integrate activities with other programs and state department of education guidelines for science.

Much care is taken to have a suitable match between activities and students' ability to think at different ages. Further work has made the program easy to instruct and manage. Provisions for preparation time, ease of giving out and retrieving materials, cleanup, storage, and resupply have continually guided program developers.

The commercial distributor of FOSS is Delta Education, 80 Northwest Blvd., P.O. Box 3000, Nashua, NH 03061-3000, 800-258-1302 (*http://www.delta-ed.com/*, *http://www.lawrencehallofscience.org/foss/*).

GREAT EXPLORATIONS IN MATH AND SCIENCE (GEMS)

Grades Preschool–9. Gems is a growing resource for activity-based science and mathematics. Developed at the University of California at Berkeley's Lawrence Hall of Science and tested in thousands of classrooms nationwide, more than 50 GEMS teacher's guides and handbooks offer a wide spectrum of learning opportunities from preschool and kindergarten through 10th grade. GEMS guides can be integrated into your curriculum or stand on their own as a stimulating way to involve students. The GEMS series interweaves a number of educational ideas and goals. GEMS guides encompass important learning objectives, summarized on the front page of each guide, under the headings of skills, concepts, science themes, mathematics strands, and the nature of science and mathematics. Taken together, these headings help provide a summary of the unit objectives. These objectives can be directly and flexibly related to science and mathematics curricula, local and district guidelines, state frameworks, benchmarks, and the national standards. For more on flexible ways to build your own curricula using GEMS, contact the University of California, GEMS, Lawrence Hall of Science #5200, Berkeley, CA 94720-5200 (*http://lhsgems.org/gems.html*).

NATIONAL GEOGRAPHIC KIDS NETWORK

Grades 4–6. The National Geographic Kids Network is a program that has children gather data on real science problems and then use a computer network to share their data with a scientist and children in other locations. The developer is the Technical Education Resource Center (TERC) in partnership with the National Geographic Society, which publishes and distributes the program.

Each instructional unit is 6 weeks long and focuses on a central science problem. Children learn to ask questions and gather data in scientifically acceptable ways. The data are transmitted to an interested scientist who analyzes the data, answers children's questions, and then sends back an overview of all the collected information from cooperating schools. Curriculum materials include children's handbooks that have background information on the topic of study, teacher guides, and computer software. The software is made up of a word-processing program, data charts, and a computer map of North America, all of which are used to ready and transmit data. For details, write National Geographic Society, 1145 17th St. NW, Washington, DC 20036-4688 (*http://www. nationalgeographic.com/kids/*), 800-647-5463.

OUTDOOR BIOLOGY INSTRUCTIONAL STRATEGIES (OBIS)

Ages 10–15. Developed at the Lawrence Hall of Science, University of California (Berkeley), OBIS is designed for use with community youth organizations and schools that want to offer outdoor laboratory experiences. Four activity packets offer a broad selection of interesting, firsthand activities for studying ecological relationships in different environments: desert, seashore, forest, pond and stream, city lots, and local parks. Each activity card consists of background information for the leader, description of materials needed and any advance preparation required, a lesson plan, and several follow-up suggestions. Each activity can be used alone or as part of a developmental sequence. For more information see *http://www.lawrencehallofscience.org/OBIS/OBISpubs.html*, University of California, OBIS, Lawrence Hall of Science #5200, Berkeley, CA 94720-5200.

SCIENCE FOR LIFE AND LIVING

Grades K–6. The full name for this curriculum is "Teaching Relevant Activities for Concepts and Skills." The developer is the BSCS Group, a nonprofit foundation for science education.

After readiness activities at the kindergarten level, these concepts and skills form the main curriculum structure: order and organization (grade 1); change and measurement (grade 2); patterns and prediction (grade 3); systems and analysis (grade 4); energy and investigation (grade 5); and balance and decisions (grade 6). Children build their own understanding of an integrated world of science, technology, and health as they work through activities that bring out the concepts and skills.

Each complete lesson contains five consecutive phases: (a) An engagement activity begins the lesson. Children connect what they know to the current material and reveal their prior knowledge, including misconceptions. (b) Exploration follows, in which students explore the materials or environment and form a common base of experience. (c) An explanation phase gives students a chance to describe what they are learning and gives the teacher an opportunity to state the intended learning. (d) Elaboration then provides activities that extend understandings and give further chances to practice skills. (e) The last phase, evaluation, allows students and teacher to assess what has been learned.

Published materials are available from the Kendall/Hunt Publishing Company, 4050 Westmark Drive, P.O. Box 1840, Dubuque, IA 52004-1840 (*http://www. kendallhunt.com/*).

SCIENCE AND TECHNOLOGY FOR CHILDREN (STC)

Grades 1–6. The developer of the STC curriculum project is the National Science Resources Center, established in 1985 by the National Academy of Sciences and the Smithsonian Institution to improve the teaching of science and mathematics in the nation's schools. The project's mission is to increase significantly the number of schools that offer hands-on science programs to children and to interest more females and minority members in science.

Teaching units include such titles as Weather (grade K–1), The Life Cycle of Butterflies (grade 2), Plant Growth and Development (grade 3), Electric Circuits (grade 4), Microworlds (grade 5), and Magnets and Motors (grade 6). They are designed to focus on easy-to-use materials and integrate science with other areas of the curriculum. Each unit includes a teacher's guide; pupil activity booklet; description of needed materials; and annotated lists of recommended trade books, computer software, and audiovisual materials.

The developers sought to make the management of materials and activities as practical as possible. In the field testing of units, evaluation procedures monitored how well the units worked under a wide variety of classroom conditions.

For details, contact the National Science Resources Center, 901 D St. SW, Suite 704B, Washington, DC 20024 (*http://www.nsrconline.org/*).

SCIENCE CURRICULUM IMPROVEMENT STUDY (SCIS)

Grades K–6. SCIS is organized on a base of powerful and modern science concepts. Each of 12 instructional units features a central concept, with supporting subconcepts and process skills integrated into the activities.

Lessons have three parts: exploration, invention, and discovery. In the exploratory part, children are given objects to observe or manipulate. At times, these observations are guided by the teacher; otherwise, the children observe and manipulate the objects as they wish.

Explorations allow firsthand contact with the material under study and provide a basis for children to use language. At the same time, the need arises for an explanation to make sense out of what has been observed. This is taken up in the second part of the lesson sequence. After discussion, the teacher gives a definition and a word for the new concept.

This "invention" of a concept sets up the third part of the lesson. Now, children are given a variety of further experiences within which they discover many applications of the concept. These extend and reinforce their knowledge and skills.

An updated version of this program, SCIS3, is available from Delta Education, 80 Northwest Blvd., P.O. Box 3000, Nashua, NH 03061-3000 (*http://www.delta-ed.com/*).

SCIENCE IN A NUTSHELL

Grades K–8. Real fun with real science. Discover how exciting real science can be with Delta's Science in a Nutshell mini-kit series. Introduce or enhance specific science content areas in the classroom, at home, in a resource room, or in an after-school program. Clearly written, hands-on activities challenge young scientists aged 6–12 to investigate their world. Mini-kits are suitable for use with individuals or with small groups of two to three. Contact Delta Education, 80 Northwest Blvd., P.O. Box 3000, Nashua, NH 03061-3000 (*http://www.delta-ed.com/*).

WONDERSCIENCE

Wonderscience offers hands-on science activities for elementary school teachers and students. The *Best of WonderScience* was developed as a joint effort of the American Chemical Society (ACS), and the American Institute of Physics. The ACS is at toll-free 1-800-227-5558 (*http://www.chemistry.org/portal/a/c/s/1/acsdisplay.html? DOC=education%5curriculum%5cwondsci.html*).

COMMERCIAL SCIENCE SUPPLIERS

The following classifications of suppliers may not be entirely accurate, because suppliers often change offerings with business conditions. A current catalog should reveal the full scope of materials for sale in each case. Use school stationery when requesting free elementary-level catalogs. An annual, comprehensive listing of suppliers accompanies each January issue of *Science and Children*.

GENERAL SUPPLIES

Wisconsin Fast Plants Program, University of Wisconsin-Madison, Science House, 1630 Linden Drive, Madison, WI 53706, 1-800-462-7417 (*http://www.fastplants.org/_home_flash.html*), *info@fastplants.org*.

Carolina Biological Supply Company, 2700 York Road, Burlington, NC 27215 (*http://www.carolina.com/*, carolina@carolina.com, 800-334-3551.

Delta Education, 80 Northwest Blvd., P.O. Box 3000, Nashua, NH 03061-3000 (*http://www.delta-ed.com/*).

Edmund Scientific Company, 60 Pearce Ave, Tonawanda, NY 14150, 1-800-728-6999 (*http://www.edsci.com/*).

Frey Scientific Company, P.O. Box 8101, 100 Paragon Parkway, Mansfield, OH 44903, 1-800-225-3739 (*http://www.freyscientific.com/*).

Ward's Natural Science Establishment, 5100 West Henrietta Road, P.O. Box 92912, Rochester, NY 14692-9012, 800-962-2660, (*http://www.wardsci.com/*).

BALANCES

Ohaus Scale Corporation, 19A Chapin Road, P.O. Box 2033, Pine Brook, NJ 07058, 800-672-7722 ext. 7804 (*http://www.ohaus.com/*).

MICROSCOPES AND MICROPROJECTORS

Brock Optical, 1959 Barber Road, Sarasota, FL 34240, 941-342-7727 (*http://www.magiscope.com/*).

Leica Microsystems, Inc., 90 Boroline Rd., Allendale, NJ 07401, 201-236-5900 (*http://www.discovermicroscopy.com/website/sc_ead1.nsf*).

Ken-A-Vision Manufacturing Company, 5615 Raytown Road, Raytown, MO 64133 (*http://www.ken-a-vision.com/*) 800-501-7366, *info@ken-a-vision.com*.

Swift Optics, 1190 North 4th St., San Jose, CA 95112, 800-523-4544 (*http://www.swift-optics.com/*).

AQUARIA, TERRARIA, CAGES

Carolina Biological Supply Company, 2700 York Road, Burlington, NC 27215 (*http://www.carolina.com/*), carolina@carolina.com, 800-334-3551.

Delta Education, 80 Northwest Blvd., P.O. Box 3000, Nashua, NH 03061-3000 (*http://www.delta-ed.com/*).

Frey Scientific Company, P.O. Box 8101, 100 Paragon Parkway, Mansfield, OH 44903, 1-800-225-3739 (*http://www.freyscientific.com/*).

KITS AND MODELS

Delta Education, 80 Northwest Blvd., P.O. Box 3000, Nashua, NH 03061-3000 (*http://www.delta-ed.com/*).

SOFTWARE

Scholastic Software & Multimedia, 2931 East McCarty Street, Jefferson City, MO 65101, 1-800-724-6527 (*http://scholastic.com/*).

Sunburst Technology, Inc., 1550 Executive Drive, Elgin, IL 60123, 1-800-321-7511 (*http://store.sunburst.com/*).

Environments and Nutrition for Classroom Animals

Animal[1]	Environment	Nutrition[2]
Ants	Glass terrarium or large jar with dirt (covered with black paper)	Small food scraps or dead insects
Birds	Bird cage (ensure cage is large enough for bird to move freely)	Birdseed (nutritional mix from pet store—not wild bird seed)
Butterflies and Moths	Butterfly "tent" (sold in kits) or large jar with wire screen on top with small branches	Sugar water solution
Caterpillars	Medium-sized jar with holes in lid; includes a small branch	Leaves (preferably near to where they were found)
Chameleons and Lizards	Aquarium with screened top; dirt, stones, and branches on bottom	Mealworms or live insects
Fish	Aquarium with gravel and filter (dechlorinate water before use)	Fish food from pet store (do not overfeed); brine shrimp
Frogs and Toads	Aquarium with shallow water and rocks to climb out of the water	Mealworms, small caterpillars, or live insects
Fruit Flies	Small jars with fine mesh covering	A small amount of overly ripe fruit
Guinea Pigs and Rats	Large animal cage with secure openings and an exercise wheel	Guinea pig food; small amounts of fresh fruit and vegetables
Hamsters, Gerbils, and Mice	Medium or large animal cage with secure openings and an exercise wheel	Hamster or gerbil food; small amounts of fresh fruit and vegetables
Mealworms	Wide jar or plastic bucket with screen or mesh cover	Oatmeal and small slices of fresh apple
Newts and Salamanders	Aquarium with shallow water and rocks rising above water line	Mealworms and live insects
Rabbits	Large animal cage (rabbits will chew on cage, so avoid wood)	Rabbit pellets, fresh vegetables (avoid too much lettuce)
Snakes	Terrarium with secure openings; heating device (contact pet shop)	Live mice or insects (contact pet shop for specifics)
Spiders	Glass jar covered with screen	Live insects
Tadpoles	Aquarium 1/4 filled with water and rocks above the water line	Small insects or finely chopped meat
Turtles (land)	Terrarium with nonpoisonous plants and water pool	Mealworms, insects, earthworms; finely chopped vegetables
Turtles (aquatic)	Aquarium that is mostly water covered, but with small land area	Mealworms, insects, earthworms; finely chopped vegetables

[1]Contact the National Science Teachers Association (1840 Wilson Blvd., Arlington, VA 22201-3000 for the Guidelines for Responsible Use of Animals in the Classroom.
[2]All animals require plenty of fresh water. To remove the chlorine from water, leave it standing overnight.

APPENDIX E

SUMMARY OF CHILDREN'S THINKING

Thought Process	Intuitive Thought[1]	Concrete Operations	Formal Operations
Cause and Effect	Logic often contradictory, unpredictable. Events may occur by magic or for human convenience.	Contradictions avoided. Physical objects are linked to show cause and effect. Commonsense explanations may be wrong but logical.	Can separate logic from content. Systematic control of variables possible, as well as hypothetical "thought experiments," to test ideas.
Relative Thinking	Egocentric perceptions and language. Little grasp of how vertebrates interrelate. Physical properties viewed in absolute, not relative, ways.	Perceptions of position and objects more objective. Aware of others' views. Some understanding of interrelated variables, when connected to concrete objects and pictures.	Understand relative position and motion. Can define and explain abstract concepts with other concepts or analogies. May temporarily show some egocentricity in propositions.
Classifying and Ordering	Sort one property at a time. Little or no class inclusion. Trial-and-error ordering in early part of stage.	Understand class inclusion principle. More consistent seriation with diverse objects. Can follow successive steps, less discrete thinking.	Can recombine groups into fewer, more abstract categories. Can form hierarchical systems.
Conservative Thinking	Mostly do not conserve. Perceptions dominate thinking. Center attention on one variable and do not compensate. Little or no reverse thinking.	Can reverse thinking, consider several variables and compensate. Conserve most of the Piagetian test concepts.	Conserve all of the Piagetian test concepts, with displaced and solid volume usually last.

Table based on a format suggested by Robert Mele.
[1]Intuitive thought is the last period of the preoperational stage.

STATE EDUCATION AGENCIES

Alabama
Alabama State Dept. of Education
Gordon Persons Bldg.
Montgomery, AL 36130
(*http://www.alsde.edu/*)

Alaska
State of Alaska
Dept. of Education
801 W. 10th St., Ste. 200
Juneau, AK 99801-1894
(*http://www.educ.state.ak.us/*)

Arizona
Arizona Dept. of Education
1535 W. Jefferson St.,
Phoenix, AZ 85007
(*http://www.ade.state.az.us/*)

Arkansas
Arkansas Dept. of Education
4 State Capitol Mall
Little Rock, AR 72201
(*http://arkedu.state.ar.us/*)

Bureau of Indian Affairs
Dept. of Interior, BIA
1849 C St., NW
Mail Stop 3525, Code 521, MIB
Washington, DC 20240
(*http://www.doi.gov/bureau-indian-affairs.html*)

California
State Dept. of Education
1430 N. Street
Sacramento, CA 95814
(*http://www.cde.ca.gov/*)

Colorado
Colorado Dept. of Education
201 E. Colfax Ave.
Denver, CO, 80203
(*http://www.cde.state.co.us/index_home.htm*)

Connecticut
State Dept. of Education
165 Capitol Ave.
Hartford, CT 06145
(*http://www.state.ct.us/sde/*)

Delaware
State Dept. of Public Instruction
Townsend Bldg.
401 Federal St., Suite 2
Dover, DE 19901
(*http://www.doe.state.de.us/*)

District of Columbia
Education Program
D.C. Public Schools
415 12th St., NW, Rm. 1004
Washington, DC 20004
(*http://www.k12.dc.us/dcps/home.html*)

Department of Defense
4040 N. Fairfax Dr.
Arlington, VA 22203
(*http://www.dodea.edu/*)

Florida
Florida Dept. of Education
Florida Education Center, Ste. 522
Tallahassee, FL 32399
(*http://www.fldoe.org*)

Georgia
Georgia Dept. of Education
1862 Twin Towers East
Atlanta, GA 30334
(*http://www.doe.k12.ga.us/index.asp*)

Hawaii
Education Program
1390 Miller St.
Honolulu, HI 96804
(*http://doe.k12.hi.us/*)

Idaho
Idaho State Dept. of Education
650 W. State St.
P.O. Box 83720
Boise, ID 83720-0027
(*http://www.sde.state.id.us/Dept/*)

Illinois
Illinois State Board of Education
100 N. First St.
Springfield, IL 62777-0001
(*http://www.isbe.state.il.us/*)

Indiana
Indiana Dept. of Education
Rm. 229 State House
Indianapolis, IN 46204-2798
(*http://www.doe.state.in.us/*)

Iowa
State of Iowa
Department of Education
Grimes State Office Building
Des Moines, IA 50319-0146
(*http://www.state.ia.us/educate/index.html*)

Kansas
Kansas Dept. of Education
120 S.E. 10th St.
Topeka, KS 66612-1103
(*http://www.ksbe.state.ks.us/*)

Kentucky
Kentucky Dept. of Education
Capitol Plaza Tower
500 Mero St.
Frankfort, KY 40601
(*http://www.education.ky.gov*)

Louisiana
State Dept. of Education
P.O. Box 94064
Baton Rouge, LA 70804-9064
(*http://www.louisianaschools.net/lde/
index.html*)

Maine
Maine State Dept. of Education
State House Station #23
Augusta, ME 04333
(*http://www.state.me.us/education/
homepage.htm*)

Maryland
Maryland State Dept. of Education
200 W. Baltimore St.
Baltimore, MD 21201-2595
(*http://www.marylandpublicschools.
org/msde*)

Massachusetts
Massachusetts Dept. of Education
350 Main St.
Malden, MA 02148-5023
(*http://www.doe.mass.edu/*)

Michigan
Michigan Dept. of Education
P.O. Box 30008
Lansing, MI 48909
(*http://www.michigan.gov/mde*)

Minnesota
Minnesota Dept. of Education
1500 Highway 36 West
St. Paul, MN 55113
(*http://education.state.mn.us/html/mde_
home.htm*)

Mississippi
State Dept. of Education
Walter Sillers Bldg., Ste. 501
P.O. Box 771
Jackson, MS 39205-0771
(*http://www.mde.k12.ms.us/*)

Missouri
Missouri Dept. of Education
Dept. of Elementary & Secondary
Education
P.O. Box 480
Jefferson, MO 65102
(*http://www.dese.state.mo.us/*)

Montana
Office of Public Instruction
State Capitol Bldg.
Helena, MT 59620
(*http://www.opi.state.mt.us/*)

Nebraska
Nebraska Dept. of Education
301 Centennial Mall South
P.O. Box 94987
Lincoln, NE 68509-4987
(*http://www.nde.state.ne.us/*)

Nevada
Nevada Dept. of Education
Capitol Complex
Carson City, NV 89710
(*http://www.doe.nv.gov/*)

New Hampshire
New Hampshire Dept. of Education
1010 Pleasant St.
Concord, NH 03301
(*http://www.ed.state.nh.us/*)

New Jersey
New Jersey Dept. of Education
Division of Standards and Assessment
CN 500
Trenton, NJ 08625-0500
(*http://www.state.nj.us/education/*)

New Mexico
State of New Mexico
Dept. of Education
300 Don Gaspar
Santa Fe, NM 87501-2786
(*http://sde.state.nm.us/*)

New York
New York State Education Dept.
Bureau of Professional Career
Opportunity Programs
Empire State Plaza
Cultural Education Center, Rm. 5C64
Albany, NY 12230
(*http://www.nysed.gov/*)

North Carolina
Dept. of Public Instruction
116 W. Edenton St.
Raleigh, NC 27603-1712
(*http://www.dpi.state.nc.us/*)

North Dakota
Dept. of Public Instruction
600 E. Boulevard Ave., Department 201
Bismark, ND 58505
(*http://www.dpi.state.nd.us/*)

Ohio
Ohio Dept. of Education
65 S. Front St.
Columbus, OH 43266-0208
(*http://www.ode.state.oh.us/*)

Oklahoma
State Dept. of Education
2500 N. Lincoln Blvd.
Oklahoma City, OK 73105-4599
(*http://sde.state.ok.us/*)

Oregon
Oregon Dept. of Education
700 Pringle Pkwy., S.S.
Salem, OR 97310
(*http://www.ode.state.or.us/*)

Pennsylvania
Pennsylvania Dept. of Education
8th Floor, 333 Market Street
Harrisburg, PA 17126-0333
(*http://www.pde.state.pa.us*)

Puerto Rico
Office of Education
Office 809
Dept. of Education
Hato Rey, PR 00919
(*http://www.eduportal.de.gobierno.pr/
EDUportal/*)

Rhode Island
Rhode Island Dept. of Education
255 Westminster St.
Providence, RI 02903
(*http://www.ridoe.net/*)

South Carolina
South Carolina Dept. of Education
Curriculum Section
801 Rutledge Bldg.
Columbia, SC 29201
(*http://www.myscschools.com/*)

South Dakota
Dept. of Education and Cultural
   Affairs
700 Governors Dr.
Pierre, SD 57501-2291
(*http://www.state.sd.us/deca/*)

Tennessee
Tennessee Dept. of Education
4th Floor Northwing
Cordell Hull Bldg.
Nashville, TN 37243-0388
(*http://www.state.tn.us/education/*)

Texas
Texas Education Agency
1701 N. Congress
Austin, TX 78701
(*http://www.tea.state.tx.us/*)

Utah
Utah Dept. of Education
250 East 500 South
Salt Lake City, UT 84111
(*http://www.usoe.k12.ut.us/*)

Vermont
Vermont State Dept. of Education
120 State St.
Montpelier, VT 05602
(*http://www.state.vt.us/educ/*)

Virgin Islands
Dept. of Education
No. 44-46 Kongens Gade
Charlotte Amalie,
U.S. Virgin Islands 00802
(*http://www.usvi.org/education/*)

Virginia
Virginia Dept. of Education
P.O. Box 2120
Richmond, VA 23218-2120
(*http://www.pen.k12.va.us/*)

Washington
Office of Superintendent of Public
   Instruction
P.O. Box 47200
Olympia, WA 98504-7200
(*http://www.k12.wa.us/*)

West Virginia
West Virginia Dept. of Education
1900 Kanawha Blvd. East
Charleston, WV 25305
(*http://wvde.state.wv.us/*)

Wisconsin
Dept. of Public Education
125 S. Webster St.
P.O. Box 7841
Madison, WI 53707-7841
(*http://www.dpi.state.wi.us/*)

Wyoming
State Dept. of Education
241 Hathaway Bldg.
Cheyenne, WY 82002-0050
(*http://www.k12.wy.us/*)

INDEX

Page numbers for appendices are in italics.